Praise for *Good White People*

"...[Sullivan's] work is so far-reaching and thought-provoking that it is hard to imagine any reader finishing *Good White People* without having reexamined stale emotions and come to new realizations."

— *Bookslut*

"...Sullivan posits that it is white liberals' own 'anti-racism' that actually perpetuates racism by shutting down frank or nuanced discussions not only of race, but of white privilege, which created racial problems and still sustains them ... In advising white liberals how to honestly live their whiteness, rather than disown it or pretend it doesn't exist, Sullivan expertly deconstructs the familiar defenses ... Like W.E.B. DuBois and James Baldwin before her, Sullivan sees white domination as a spiritual problem that afflicts one group in particular but that touches us all."

— *Ms. Magazine*

GOOD WHITE PEOPLE

SUNY series, Philosophy and Race

Robert Bernasconi and T. Denean Sharpley-Whiting, editors

GOOD WHITE PEOPLE

*The Problem with Middle-Class
White Anti-Racism*

SHANNON SULLIVAN

Published by State University of New York Press, Albany

© 2014 State University of New York

All rights reserved

Printed in the United States of America

No part of this book may be used or reproduced in any manner whatsoever
without written permission. No part of this book may be stored in a retrieval system
or transmitted in any form or by any means including electronic, electrostatic,
magnetic tape, mechanical, photocopying, recording, or otherwise without the prior
permission in writing of the publisher.

For information, contact State University of New York Press, Albany, NY
www.sunypress.edu

Production by Jenn Bennett
Marketing by Fran Keneston

Library of Congress Cataloging-in-Publication Data

Sullivan, Shannon, 1967–
  Good white people : the problem with middle-class white anti-racism /
Shannon Sullivan.
       pages cm. — (SUNY series, Philosophy and race)
  Includes bibliographical references and index.
  ISBN 978-1-4384-5169-5 (hardcover : alkaline paper)
  ISBN 978-1-4384-5168-8 (paperback : alkaline paper)
  1. Whites—United States—Attitudes.   2. Middle class—United States.
3. Anti-racism—United States.   4. United States—Race relations.   5. United
States—Social conditions—1980–   I. Title.

E184.A1S954 2014
305.800973—dc23   2013025552

10 9 8 7 6 5 4 3 2 1

For Samantha, Sophia, and Phillip

Contents

Acknowledgments

I wish to thank a number of people who helped me with this book:

First and foremost, Phillip McReynolds. I couldn't begin to describe the ups and downs of writing, rewriting, and undergoing the review process of this book, and Phillip went through it all with me. He is my biggest supporter and best critic, and his positive feedback on an early draft of the introduction was especially important. He read all the versions of the book from beginning to end, providing crucial suggestions and comments. I know he is just as happy as I am to see it published.

I also am grateful to Lucius Outlaw, who provided some much needed moral support during the review process. He understood early on, better than I did, the spiritual side of the book, and that understanding was crucial to the final round of rewriting. I appreciate Melissa Wright's enthusiastic response to early versions of several chapters of the manuscript, which was important for keeping the project going. I happily thank Robert Bernasconi and T. Denean Sharpley-Whiting (series editors) and Andrew Kenyon (SUNY Press) for their interest in and support of this book. Andrew provided particularly helpful editorial guidance during the review process. I benefited from thoughtful feedback from members of the philosophy and the women's studies departments at Penn State University to whom I presented portions of chapter 4 as part of their colloquia series. I especially appreciate Vincent Colapietro's question about the place of religion in the overall project. I value the critical questions from audiences at the 2011 philoSOPHIA and especially the 2010 SPEP meetings at which I presented portions of chapter 4 and the conclusion. I also thank the anonymous reviewers for SUNY Press for their lively feedback. I hope that the improvements I made to the book as a result of their collective comments inspire additional vigorous debate in the field.

Many thanks to John Christman and Chris Long for serving as acting heads while I was on sabbatical, during which I finished final revisions of the book. I owe each of them a beer (or several). I am very grateful to Dean Susan Welch and Penn State University's College of the Liberal Arts for leave from my headship duties. Je tiens à remercier la bande de femmes à Paris qui m'a tenu compagnie pendant les derniers processus de critique et de révision: Caroline, Corinne, Rachel, Dominique, Elisabetta, Cécile, Nathalie, Fabienne, Irena, Aimée, Christelle, Laurence, Carole, Judith, Delphine, et surtout Sara. Et également les bons messieurs: Nicolas, André-Pierre, Benoît, Edward, et Serge. Nos rendez-vous du café Les Artistes et nos soirées de femmes me manquent déja! J'apprécie aussi l'amitié (et le prêt du mixeur) de Mariana. Un merci final aux propriétaires du café Le Parroquet, mon "bureau" pour l'année.

I gratefully acknowledge permission to use the following previously published material in this book. Chapter 2 includes a significantly modified and expanded version of "Whiteness as Family: Race, Class and Responsibility" (in *Difficulties of Ethical Life*, ed. Shannon Sullivan and Dennis Schmidt [Bronx: Fordham University Press, 2008], 162–78). A revised version of about half of "Transforming Whiteness with Roycean Loyalty: A Pragmatist Feminist Account" (in *Contemporary Feminist Pragmatism*, ed. Maurice Hamington and Celia Bardwell-Jones [New York: Routledge, 2012], 19–41) is sprinkled across the introduction, chapter 3, and chapter 4. The introduction, chapter 4, and conclusion also include a few modified paragraphs of "Whiteness as Wise Provincialism: Royce on Rehabilitating a Racial Category" (*Transactions of the C. S. Peirce Society* 44, no. 2 [2008]: 236–62). Earlier versions of small sections of "Sad Versus Joyful Passions: Spinoza, Nietzsche, and the Transformation of Whiteness" (*Philosophy Today* 55 [2011]: 238–46) are incorporated into chapter 4. Finally, chapter 4 and the conclusion include revised portions of "On the Need for a New *Ethos* of White Anti-Racism" (*philoSOPHIA: A Journal of Continental Feminism* 2, no. 2 [2012]: 21–38).

Given the controversy stirred up by some of the claims in those essays, it's not *pro forma* when I say that the book's flaws remain my responsibility alone. I dedicate this book with love to Phillip and our two daughters, Sophia and Samantha.

Introduction

Good White Liberals

The white liberal and the white supremacist share the same root postulates. They are different in degree, not kind.

—Lerone Bennett Jr., "Tea and Sympathy:
Liberals and Other White Hopes"

What can white people do to help end racial injustice? This is a question with a complicated history in the United States, in large part because most white people haven't wanted to ask, much less answer it. The question dates back at least until antebellum America when a small number of white people participated in the Underground Railroad, which enabled black slaves to escape their white masters, and helped work to end legalized slavery. It's a question that can be found in twentieth-century civil rights struggles when some—again, not many—white people engaged in lunch counter sit-ins alongside African Americans and traveled to the South to help register African Americans to vote.[1] More recently, it's a question that operated in the historic 2008 election of the first African American to the presidency of the United States, which was possible in part because approximately 43 percent of white voters supported Barack Obama.[2]

It's also a question that assumes that white people can do something positive with regard to racial justice. Not everyone would agree with this assumption. Perhaps most famously, Malcolm X recounts in his autobiography that when a white college girl heard him speak on white racism and agonizingly asked him "What can I *do?*" he dismissed her with the terse reply "Nothing."[3] Up until the last year of his life, Malcolm X argued that the white "man" was the devil, destroying black

1

lives, families, and communities, and thus there was nothing that white people could do to help the United States achieve racial justice for black people and other people of color. White people inevitably were the problem, according to Malcolm X, and the only positive thing they could do was stay out of black people's way.

White people *are* a big part of the problem. So too, of course, are white privileging institutions, tax codes, and other societal structures that help sustain white domination. But not all white domination operates on an impersonal level. A great deal of it functions through the practices and habits of individual white people and the predominantly white families and communities to which they belong. This does not mean that white people are atomistic individuals, sealed off from the world around them. On the contrary: like all human beings (and other living organisms), white people are constituted in and through transactional relationships with their environments.[4] Their experiences, beliefs, and behaviors both are shaped by and contribute to a white-dominated world. And so the personal question of what white people can do still needs to be asked and answered. To say that white people can do nothing is to let them off the hook too easily. It says that they do not have to respond to the racist damage that white people historically have and presently continue to cause, and it countenances their continued negligence and inaction with regard to white domination of people of color.

Racial justice movements are not dependent on white people for their success. The struggles, protests, and demands of people of color have been and most likely will continue to be the main motor driving racial justice movements. But white people can play a positive role in those movements as well. In fact, I think they have a small, but somewhat unique role to play given the persistence of de facto racial segregation in work places, neighborhoods, school systems, places of worship, and so on. Just as feminist movements need men who are willing to speak out against sexism and male privilege—especially in all-male settings such as locker rooms and fraternity houses—racial justice movements need white people who are willing to speak and act against white racism when they encounter it in their families, neighborhoods, workplaces, and elsewhere.[5] As important as women are to feminist change, eliminating sexism should not be reduced to "women's work." Likewise, white people who care about racial justice should not sit back and wait for people of color to clean up the mess that white people have made. White people need to make a positive contribution to racial justice even though their contributions will be secondary to those of people of color.

The question of what white people can do is important even though there are no such things as stable racial categories or universal racial essences. Racial categories, including whiteness, are historical and political products of human activity, and for that reason the human racial landscape has changed over time and likely will continue to change. Perhaps at some point in the future, racial categories no longer will exist. I don't think any of us today can know for sure. At this point in history, however, they do exist and cannot be quickly eliminated by pretending or simply declaring that they don't.[6] This means that, for better or worse, whiteness also is not going anywhere anytime soon even though its meaning and effects are not set in stone. The "beige supremacy" that the Latin Americanization of race in the United States is likely to produce, for example, would still be a racial hierarchy that privileges whites over mixed-race and light-skinned Asians and Latinos, the latter of which would share in beige people's domination over dark-skinned people, including most African Americans, who would count as black.[7] "The whiteness question," as Linda Martín Alcoff has called it, thus doggedly persists: what can white people do to promote racial justice?[8]

For all the urgency of the whiteness question, however, white people have done a miserable job of answering it. The few positive examples given above shouldn't mislead anyone: white people generally don't know how to live their racial identities in ways that promote racial justice. Even worse, their ignorance often poses as knowledge, making it all the more insidious. This is particularly true in the early twenty-first century, and it's true of the majority of white people, not just a small subset of them. I'm not merely speaking here of the avowed white supremacist who clearly has no interest in eliminating racial injustice. I am, primarily, addressing the bulk of white people in the post–Jim Crow United States and other similar white-dominated nations who consider themselves to be non- or anti-racist. These are the white liberals of which Lerone Bennett speaks, the "good" white people whose goodness is marked by their difference from the "bad" white people who are considered responsible for any lingering racism in a progressive, liberal society. ("White liberal" here thus does not designate a member of a particular political party. Both white Republicans and white Democrats in the United States often are white liberals.) What is particularly interesting and frightening about white liberals is that, unlike white supremacists, they usually think they know what white people can do to fight white racism. "Act like you know" has been the mantra of proper white identity after all, even as what good white people know or think they know has shifted over time.[9] Good white people today should, for example, refrain from making derogatory remarks about race, support multicultural celebrations in their communities, and so on. For white liberals, knowing and acting according to these answers ensures that a sharp, bright line is drawn between good anti-racist white people and bad white supremacists.

But white liberals and white supremacists are not as different as white liberals would like to believe and would like others to believe. They grow from the same tree of white domination, as Bennett suggests, and this means that many of the "anti-racist" habits, practices, and beliefs of the white liberal also are rooted in and help nourish white racism. White domination of people of color is alive and well in the twenty-first century, and most white people don't want to acknowledge their complicity with it. The oft-recited progressive narrative about improved racial justice in the United States from the days of slavery to the so-called Obama era is something of a convenient fiction that serves to reassure white people that significant problems of racial injustice no longer exist. Let me be clear: by no means am I advocating a retreat from the hard-won victories of civil rights and other racial justice movements. But white domination of people of color didn't end when the United States became more "enlightened" about race. It instead has tended to change its form to operate with and through liberal enlightenment. A great deal of change has taken place in the United States since the days of chattel slavery and Jim Crow; at the same time, a great deal of white domination has been maintained through those changes. White liberalism generally doesn't aim to end white domination. Quite the opposite: it aims to render it more tolerable, both to its beneficiaries and its victims, and so to perpetuate itself indefinitely—an aim it shares with its "enemy" white supremacy.

Having the same roots doesn't mean that white liberalism and white supremacy are identical, however. Understanding how white domination could continue after white supremacy became passé means understanding the particularities of white liberalism's style of white racism. (While some contemporary scholars have reappropriated the term *white supremacy* to refer to systematic racial oppression and privilege,[10] I will continue to use it, as Bennett does, to refer to overt white racism. I accordingly will use *white privilege* to refer to the seemingly invisible, often unconscious forms of white racism that pervade the United States' post–Jim Crow era, and *white domination* and *white racism* as general terms covering both white supremacy and white privilege.)[11] The most obvious difference between white liberalism and white supremacy is that the racial biases of white supremacists tend to be much more overt than those of white liberals, an observation that is not necessarily to the credit of white liberals. The racial biases of white liberals often are more difficult to detect (at least by white people), especially as they tend to operate in the name of non- or anti-racism, and thus they can be much more difficult to challenge than the racial biases of white supremacists.

Perhaps less acknowledged about white liberal anti-racism is its use of white class hierarchies to perpetuate white domination of people of color. The pernicious tangle of race and class oppression will be the primary focus of this book. Intra-white class biases might seem to have nothing to do with people of color, but as I will argue, they are one of the central ways by which middle-class white people avoid taking responsibility for and fighting against white privilege. White liberals' answers to the whiteness question tend to be covert attempts to maintain and secure their race-class status. These attempts might not always be consciously designed; in fact, many of them probably operate unconsciously. But they nonetheless exist and are effective in maintaining white domination of people of color.

One of the main ways that white class hierarchies operate is through the production and display of white middle-class moral goodness. This is achieved by establishing the moral badness of poor and lower-class white people. Lower-class white people supposedly are the retrograde white people who still believe and act in racist ways; they are the real problem when it comes to lingering racism in our enlightened times. Knowing this, white middle-class liberals know and/or take steps to ensure that they are different in kind than the white lower class, and this process of othering secures white liberals' status as good. *Those* white people (the lower class) are racist; we middle-class whites are not like them; therefore we are not racist. At the heart of this anti-racism, however, is not necessarily an attempt to eliminate racial injustice—which, to be successful, might involve strategies or tactics that don't make white people look or feel morally good—but a desire to be recognized as Not Racist, perhaps especially by people of color. As Steve Biko has argued in the context of racial struggles in South Africa, "instead of involving themselves in an all-out attempt to stamp out racism from their white society, liberals waste lots of time trying to prove to as many blacks as they can find that they are liberal."[12] A similar situation holds in the United States and many other white-dominated liberal nations. George Yancy provides an excellent example of this sad fact when he recounts being on an academic job interview and having to endure a white philosopher's hour-long speech about *his* anti-racism. The white person spent so much time explaining and illustrating his own racial goodness that there was virtually no time in the interview to talk about Yancy's accomplishments and achievements.[13] Class hierarchies, racial oppression, and moral sanctimoniousness are intertwined in much of white liberal anti-racism, and for that reason critical philosophy of race needs different answers to the whiteness question than the ones liberalism tends to offer. Liberal political projects may be well intended, but as Wendy Brown has argued, they often "inadvertently redraw the very configurations and effects of power that they seek to vanquish."[14]

The quest of middle-class white people for their moral redemption tends to be especially, though not uniquely attractive to white middle-class women. As feminist sociologist Sarita Srivastava has documented in her research on white feminists in anti-racist organizations, white women in particular tend to "become mired in self-examination and stuck in deliberations on morality and salvation. Not surprisingly, this ethical self-transformation is still framed by the poles of good versus evil, newly interpreted as the fraudulent nonracist versus the authentic antiracist."[15] I'll return in chapter 4 to the issue of ethical framing of good versus evil in the context of white participation in racial justice movements. Here I wish to highlight what Srivastava calls the "desire for innocence" in the face of racist "sin," which characterizes a great deal of white people's, and perhaps especially white women's involvement in anti-racist activities.[16] Srivastava's research supports María Lugones's observation that white women often want to see themselves as innocently ignorant of, or at least confused about the nasty operations of racism.[17] Whether gender-inflected or not, the white desire for innocence is implicated in the middle-class dumping of responsibility for racism on lower- and working-class white people, who are posited as the true source of ongoing racial injustice. Lower-class white people allegedly are the bad white people who are too unintelligent or unenlightened to know that people of color aren't inferior to white people. With their disdain, scorn, and even hatred of lower-class white people, good white liberals often use their guilt and shame to exploit class differences among whites, which allows them to efface their own complicity in white racism and white domination.

My focus on white middle-class goodness might seem odd since it doesn't concentrate on economics, and following Karl Marx, economics has been the dominant focus of scholarly analyses of class hierarchy. I don't deny that the chasm between the white middle class and lower class involves wealth and other economic factors. I also acknowledge that economic concerns are at the heart of a great deal of white frustration, working-class and otherwise, with current political systems and leaders. But the causes of white lower-class frustration are not identical to the ways by which the middle-class others them. These are two different topics, and economics is not the only, or perhaps even primary factor at work in the othering of poor whites. An orthodox Marxist revolution that eliminated bourgeois ownership of property likely would leave many classed habits in place—working-class and middle-class alike—even as such a huge economic transformation surely would impact those habits. As sociologist Steph Lawlor has argued, "[T]he inequalities of a class society do not end with economic inequality: indeed, economics may not necessarily be the most meaningful way to talk about class."[18] My approach is something closer to a Bourdieuian than a Marxist under-standing of class as trading on various forms of capital: social, cultural, and educational, as well as economic.[19] On this account, the white mid-dle-class quest for goodness is as much a feature of white class inequality as is economics. In fact, given the rhetoric of the Protestant work ethic that pervades middle-class whiteness in the United States, economics could be considered a subcategory of moral goodness rather than the other way around: the lower class's lack of money supposedly is a result of laziness, intemperance, and other moral failings.

I will use the term *middle-class* very broadly to include wealthy peo-ple that might be considered upper-class. In this sense, my use of "mid-dle-class" could be understood as "middle and middle-to-upper class." I will stick with the shorter term, not just for simplicity's sake but because of the ideological hegemony of the middle class in the United States. While some people in the United States clearly make enough money to be considered something other than middle-class—think here of the top 1 percent who are estimated to control 35 percent of the United States' total wealth[20]—across the income/wealth spectrum in the United States, the rhetoric of the middle class holds sway. It's inseparable from the American Dream and the Protestant work ethic: everyone who works hard can succeed. There supposedly are no social barriers or caste systems that would block a person's ability to change her status in life. This is assumed to be different from Great Britain, for example, where royalty still exists and class analyses often operate with more explicit consider-ations of a ruling class, in addition to the working and middle class.[21] In an odd way, then, the middle class represents the supposed lack of a class system in the United States. Whatever the reality, the perception in America is that virtually everyone in the country is middle-class. The exception might be a small minority of very poor people and an even smaller number of very rich people, but even the rich are said to have made it the way that anyone could if they tried hard enough. Likewise, the poor are assumed to be at fault for their poverty, getting (or not) what they deserved. The middle class in the United States thus is less a precise economic category than a broad rhetorical designation for the vast majority of Americans who see themselves as the moral norm: hard workers who deserve their success and who have endless possibilities for improving their lives even further.

The four main chapters of this book will focus on four central strands of white liberal anti-racism, demonstrating how intra-white class biases operate within white anti-racism to shore up the racial goodness of white liberals. I'll call the first strand dumping on "white trash." Through a process of abjection, white middle-class anxieties about the failures of poor whites are managed by expelling white trash from the realm of proper whiteness. Conflating white lower-class status with white supremacy, middle-class white people use class etiquette to posit poor whites and the white working class as irremediably racist. Middle-class white people thus are able to deflect their responsibility for and complicity with white domination onto white trash, thereby ensuring their own racial innocence and goodness.

The second strand of white liberal anti-racism also involves a process of othering, this time with respect to white people's history and ancestry. We could call this strand demonizing the past, making white slaveholders in particular seem incomprehensible to white people today. How could white people in the eighteenth and nineteenth centuries have owned, whipped, starved, raped, and abused other people the way they did? It's inconceivable, so the response goes, and thus the only answer is that white slaveholders were so evil as to be inhuman. As I will argue, slaveholders surely did these horrific things, but demonizing them takes their actions and lives out of the realm of the human, reassuring good white people today that they would never be capable of doing anything similar. Functioning hand in hand with a progressive narrative of whiteness, demonizing slaveholders allows contemporary white liberals to congratulate themselves on their racial enlightenment and moral superiority, relieving them of the need to examine the different ways in which they too might be participating in racist evil.

Both of these strands of white anti-racism serve to distance good white people from racism. Whoever the real racists are—white slaveholders, white supremacists, poor white people—they are over there, not here where the middle-class white people are. The third strand of middle-class whiteness also distances good white people from complicity with white racism, in this case by distancing them from race altogether. This strand is white color blindness, which chapter 3 examines in the specific context of white childrearing. Color blindness entails not seeing race and seeing "just people" instead. Racism requires the existence of racial categories; therefore, racists are the people who use those categories, not non- or anti-racist people. On this logic, good white parents and teachers should not use or recognize racial categories on pain of being or appearing as one of the bad racists. As good white children are taught, color blindness supposedly is a marker of a white person's evolution beyond racism, demonstrating that she is so racially advanced that she isn't even aware of the racial categories on which racism depends.

The fourth strand of middle-class whiteness on which I will focus is cultivating the emotions of white guilt, shame, and betrayal, the latter in the figure of the white "race traitor." These tend to be the recommended attitudes toward whiteness that contemporary white people should embody. The best way for a good white person to ensure that she isn't mistaken for one of the bad white people is to display guilt and shame about her racial identity and history and to distance herself from whiteness by traitorously calling for its abolition. These affects are not equally available or deployable by all white people, however. They tend to function as forms of cultural capital for middle-class white people in particular. Wielding forms of emotional class privilege, middle-class white liberals help ensure that they are (seen as) different from lower-class white people, who don't feel properly guilty about white racism.

What are some alternatives to these four strands of middle-class whiteness? The one that I will explore in the book's final two chapters is a white person's self-love. Love can be thought of as an affect that binds a person to that which she loves, and in that way love can counter the distancing tendencies that many good white people have toward their whiteness. I will argue that rather than try to create distance between themselves and their racial identity, white people need a closer, more intimate relationship with it if they are going to be effective in racial justice movements. Rather than try to flee their whiteness, white people need to embrace it more tightly. Rather than despise their whiteness, white people need to learn to love it.

I have in mind here the kind of white love well described by James Baldwin nearly fifty years ago. As he claimed about the United States, "White people in this country will have quite enough to do in learning how to accept and love themselves and each other, and when they have achieved this—which will not be tomorrow and may very well be never—the Negro problem will no longer exist, for it will no longer be needed."[22] Baldwin brilliantly captures the relationship between the lack of white self-love—white self-loathing—and white oppression of people of color. The so-called Negro problem is really a problem of white domination, and that problem is connected to white people's inability to acknowledge, accept, and even affirm themselves as white.

This affirmation is not a way to let white people off the racist hook that they've hung themselves on. Love is consistent with and even requires a willingness to be severely, yet constructively critical of what one loves, and white people are in need of a great deal of criticism.[23] As I understand it, the loving acceptance called for by Baldwin isn't necessarily an enjoyable experience. Love is an emotion, but not always in the sense of being a pleasant sentiment. It can be and often is discontent, especially with situations, actions, and passions that separate people from one another, for example, through oppression and domination. A white person's loving herself as a white person means her critically caring enough about the effects whiteness has in the world to work to make it something different and better than what it is today. Although likely a difficult experience to undergo, this loving transformation of white identity would be to the benefit of both people of color and white people.

As I explore both white middle-class goodness and alternatives to it based in self-love, I often will take up relationships between white family members, such as white children, white parents, and white grandparents. I do so because one of my primary motivations for writing this book is to grapple with the down-to-earth, real life question of how to live as a white person. That real life question means for me, as it does for many other white people, how to live day to day with white family members for and to which one is responsible. For example, how can I honor and respect my elders if many of them were or are openly racist? How can I rear my children in ways that effectively challenge rather than unconsciously replicate white domination? As feminists demonstrated when they argued that the personal is political, family is where a number of important social and political issues hit home. The problem of ongoing white domination is no exception. In the words of one cultural anthropologist, family "is perhaps the most critical site for the generation and reproduction of racial formations," and "the meaning of race depends to a large degree on whether particular families reproduce homogenous or heterogeneous racial categories."[24] The whiteness question thus isn't merely a theoretical issue. It's also a down-to-earth practical matter enacted in daily experiences, conversations, and interactions that often involve close family members.

Of course, some white people have family members that aren't white. Many white people in the United States and Great Britain, for example, are not considered mixed race but have black ancestry (often without knowing or acknowledging it).[25] Some white people also have contemporary family members who are not white, and in particular the legalization of interracial marriage in the United States in 1967 resulted in an increase in mixed-race children.[26] All people can have family members from more than one race, but the facts of mixed-race identities and multiracial families do not erase the simple truth that a large number of white people also have family members who count as white. Those personal relationships should not be ceded to white domination. They are too socially valuable and personally meaningful to too many people to discard them as trivial. "The revolution of the American family," as Ronald Sundstrom argues, "is an important condition of social justice," and so white people need to critically and creatively wrestle with how to live family in ways that don't reproduce white racism.[27]

Because of my concerns about the harmfulness of so-called white anti-racism, I will describe a white person whose racial identity and habits challenge white domination as a "white ally," rather than the more obvious "anti-racist white person." I also will use phrases such as "racial justice struggles" and "racial justice movements" rather than "anti-racism" to describe the activities that white allies pursue. It's important to note that the figure of the white ally is more ideal than real. I'm not sure if many white allies yet exist, and perhaps they never will. The white ally nonetheless can serve as an ideal for which white people might strive even if they never achieve it. In fact, the white ally might need always to be considered an unachieved ideal and never a fait accompli. Given the monumental history of white domination, which will never disappear even if white domination someday does, a white person's relationship to her whiteness must always be a critical one. This means that the process of creating a white allied identity necessarily will be ongoing and capable of improvement.

I also choose "white ally" because I see white people who fight for racial justice as allied with people of color who are doing the same. A relationship of alliance is not necessarily the same thing as friendship. As I will elaborate in the book's conclusion, I'm somewhat suspicious of some efforts of white people to befriend or develop close personal relationships with people of color. Too often white efforts to make non-white friends can have more to do with making guilty white people feel better about themselves or with white people's accumulation of cultural credit, than with promoting racial justice. A white ally may or may not have close, affectionate relationships with people of color, but she can be aligned with them and their interests in that she struggles for racial justice.

The term *white ally* also is appealing because it resonates with *straight ally*. In the 1980s, groups such as the Gay and Lesbian Alliance Against Defamation (GLAAD) and Parents, Families, and Friends of Lesbians and Gays (PFLAG) developed the term *straight ally* to describe heterosexual people who fight homophobia, heterosexism, and oppression based on sexual orientation and gender identity. Just as a straight person's heterosexuality can but doesn't have to conflict with struggles against gender and sexual oppression, I think that a white person's race can—and often does—interfere with the pursuit of racial justice, but it doesn't have to.

"Ally" also is useful for my purposes because its etymological root is the Latin *alligāre*, which means "to bind." Rather than attempt to flee their whiteness, white people need to consider themselves bound by it, and they need to acknowledge the particular constraints that their whiteness places on them to best serve as white allies of people of color. Whiteness is not a club in which a white person can just decide to drop her membership. Whether a white person likes it or not, at this moment in history she is white and she is implicated in the effects of whiteness. How she takes up and lives her complicity in white domination will help determine the quality of her contributions to racial justice movements.

Finally, *ligāre* also is the etymological root of the word *religion*, which literally means to re-bind or re-tie. While I do not think that a person has to belong to a formal religion or believe in a supernatural being to be a white ally, my interest in the whiteness question could be described as a spiritual concern. The term *psychological* might be considered a synonym for *spiritual* here except that *psychological* can imply a narrow focus on the psyche or mind considered apart from the body. For that reason, *psychosomatic* would be more accurate, understood as a dynamic, co-constitutive relationship of body and mind always transactionally formed in and through a person's activity in her environments. ("Psychosomatic" thus does not mean imagined or unreal.)[28] My concern is *spiritual* in that it examines what psychosomatically animates white people in their pursuit of racial justice. And it's a *concern* because I believe that white people's animation qua whiteness generally is malignant. Can what animates white people be spiritually healthy instead? How might white people's animation constitute them by binding them to, rather than allowing them to flee from their whiteness? With her or his critical self-love, the figure of the white ally attempts to offer a psychosomatic alternative both to white supremacy, on the one hand, and to white liberals' relentless attempts to distance themselves from their racial identities and histories, on the other.

It has been argued that white racism has cost white people their capability for intimacy, their affective lives, their authenticity, and their sense of connection to other people.[29] These are some of effects of white racism that I would characterize as spiritual. In different ways, of course, many people of color also have experienced devastating spiritual (and other) effects of white racism. The harm done to white people by white racism does not compete with or outweigh the brutal impact of hundreds of years of white supremacy and white privilege on people of color. Neither is it a reason to feel sorry for white people or to view them as "victims" of white domination, as if white domination harmed and/or benefited everyone equally. To recognize the spiritual damage done to white people by white racism is instead to acknowledge that one of the messes of white racism for which white people need to take responsibility is white people themselves.

W. E. B. Du Bois's discussion of the souls of white folk illuminates both the spiritual concerns of this book and my claims about the malignancy of white people. In his scathing analysis of white efforts to dominate the world, Du Bois lays bare the ugly thoughts, emotions and motivations—many of them unconscious—that constitute white people. The picture that emerges is of a people who overwhelmingly are composed of hatred, jealousy, and greed but who loftily and deliberately (mis) understand themselves as noble, civilized, and kind. These are the souls of white folks, and they have little to do with the question of whether white people will survive bodily death in a heavenly or hellish afterlife. Indeed, peering into white people's souls already is a "descent to Hell" here on earth because in their souls one sees "the great billows . . . of human hatred" that reveal "dark and awful depths and not the shining and ineffable heights of which [white people] boasted."[30] Du Bois's essay suggests that a great deal of "soul work" on the part of white people is needed if white domination truly is to be uprooted.[31] Of course, as Du Bois makes clear, a lot of global and economic change is needed too, and all of these changes are dependent on "that fight for freedom which black and brown and yellow men must and will make [until] their oppression and humiliation and insult at the hands of the White World cease."[32] That fight is likely to proceed more quickly and successfully, however, if white people's souls also are changed.

Contemporary efforts to live whiteness responsibly often are based on the excavation of the past to find examples of white people who supported racial justice, but I don't think that successful white soul work can be fully accomplished in this way. I say this not because white allies can't find anything in their white past of which to be proud. I agree with Linda Martín Alcoff's argument that white people should "retriev[e] from obscurity the history of white antiracism [sic] even while providing a detailed account of colonialism and its many cultural effects."[33] As chapter 2 will elaborate, I am keenly interested in how the past, especially in the form of white slaveholding ancestors, is connected to the present. But I think that just as, if not more important than a white person's finding something in her white past of which to be proud is her acting in the present, understood as deeply constituted by the past, to build a future worthy of celebration and joy that might include race. As I will develop it, white people's self-love is not at all dismissive or neglectful of the past, but it does not rely on discovering historical instances of white people's struggling against racism. This means that my arguments concerning the transformation of whiteness do not depend on being able to uncover enough (how many?) past examples of white "race traitors." It may turn out that there are very few of these, at least in comparison with instances of white brutality and violence. But whiteness can still potentially function as an identity grounded in racial justice even if white people have relatively little in their racial past of which to be proud.

Some readers might object to my use of the general terms *whiteness* and *white identity* since whiteness never exists apart from gender, class, nationality, sexuality, and other significant axes of identity and power. Ontologically speaking, there's no such thing as whiteness all by itself. In addition, identity categories often have been used to oppress people, justifying unjust treatment toward "others" who are not like "us" and requiring brutal policing of boundaries that keep the two groups rigidly separate.[34] Attempting to transform whiteness into an identity grounded in racial or any other kind of social justice thus might seem naive at best and harmful at worst, but counterproductive either way.

I disagree that identity and so-called identity politics (if I could be said to be engaged in that here) necessarily are oppressive. Rather than a rigid, ready-made category whose boundaries must be violently secured, identity can be a lived, existential position from which to fight for social justice. As Alcoff has argued, "Identities are best understood as ways in which we and others around us represent our material ties to historical events and social structures. . . . To say that we have identities . . . is simply to say that we exist."[35] It is to acknowledge the transactional ways that culture, history, and power have shaped the person that one is and to recognize the social, other-oriented roots of one's individual habits, values, beliefs, and experiences. Feminists, critical philosophers of race, and other white-allied scholars need not be politically afraid of identity as such, and this includes white identity. The key issue for avoiding oppressive (mis)uses of identity is "how to transform our current interpretations and understandings of [our identities]. How might we imagine them differently within a less violent and stratified social context?"[36]

I fully agree with the claim that whiteness never exists by itself. Yet I still find the category of white identity to be both useful and necessary. To take myself as an example, it is important to identify me as white and, in some situations, to identify me as white while omitting the other significant aspects of my identity: middle-class, Texan, American, female, and so on. While I acknowledge the importance of intersectional approaches to race, gender, and class (to focus on just three salient axes of contemporary lived experience), I also think that intersectionality must be used in historically and contextually sensitive ways. In some contexts, instead of illuminating the ways in which race operates in interlocking ways with gender and class, insisting on intersectionality can cover over the significance of race.[37] In those situations, insisting on intersectionality, ironically, can serve to promote rather than undermine racial injustice. In my case, sometimes it is my racially dominant position of whiteness that is most relevant to the situation at hand, and thus distinctions between my race, my gender, and my class (and my nationality and my sexuality and so on) can and should be made in the interests of racial justice. These are not substantive distinctions, of course. A person's race is never ontologically sealed off from her gender, class, sexuality, nationality, and other major axes of lived experience. But functional distinctions between them can be important for critical philosophers of race and other white-allied scholars to make because they enable a focus on race as it inflects or shapes a particular situation.

Consider white terror, which has been a common thread tying white people together and ensuring their racial solidarity.[38] Not surprisingly, terror also has been a primary representation of whiteness in the black imagination.[39] White female slaveholders and white male slaveholders admittedly terrorized their female slaves in different ways, as the nineteenth-century slave narrative of Harriet Jacobs demonstrates.[40] And perhaps white women were more likely than white men occasionally to take the side of their slaves in a dispute.[41] But what Jacobs also shows is that both white women and white men tormented their slaves. Across their gendered differences, it was the race of white male and female slaveholders that allowed them to harass, threaten, and assault black people with impunity. We must retain the general concept of whiteness to name and grapple with this terror.

Especially in a post–Jim Crow era—and, as we often hear in the United States, an Obama era in which race supposedly has been transcended—it can be very important to tease whiteness out from its co-constitutive relationships. Our allegedly postracial era makes it easy for white privilege to hum along invisibly, undetected, and the categorical insistence that race should never be singled out only adds to this problem. Above all, I am concerned that in the case of white ethnicities, insisting that whiteness always be considered in connection with other axes of identity tends to erase race and deflect attention away from white domination. Whiteness means different things for Irish Americans and Italian Americans, for example, and these two groups of white people have different racial histories and therefore at least somewhat different racial presents. But the full meaning of whiteness is not contained in those different ethnicities. There is something to being white that being Irish or Italian alone does not capture, and that something is a pattern of domination, exploitation, and oppression based on race. For this reason, I am opposed to universally or automatically replacing the term *whiteness* with references to ethnicity.[42]

I'm also opposed to this replacement because it does not fit with the lived experience of many white people. Here I disagree somewhat with Terrence Macmullan, who has proposed ethnic habits of remembrance as a strategy for remaking whiteness. Arguing that white people need to find a way "to be proud of their cultural past without simultaneously fanning the flames of racism,"[43] Macmullan turns to ethnic differences within whiteness as an appropriate site for white memory:

> [W]hat we need to remember is that every person who is now white has, somewhere in the stretch of history, a history or set of histories that either predate the invention of whiteness or offer the sort of life-sustaining value that whiteness lacks. If we go back far enough or look carefully enough, we can find a culture and a history that is predicated on *particular memories and particular experiences*, not on the exclusion of others.[44]

Every white person allegedly can find a piece of their ethnic past that predates the moment when their ethnicity was whitewashed into a dominant race. Remembering the past will allow white people to construct an identity that is not based on the racial exclusion of others.

This strategy is effective for some white people, such as Macmullan who movingly writes of his Italian, German, and Irish roots, including the life of his Irish immigrant great-grandmother who suffered mistreatment at the hands of white Bostonians in the nineteenth century. And this strategy probably works for other white people as well. I have no quarrel with white people's excavating meaningful memories of their ethnic histories. What I want to point out is that this strategy is not available to all white people. (I also think that it doesn't really remake whiteness, but instead sidesteps race in favor of ethnicity.) Some white people in the United States don't have thick family stories of what happened when their ancestors immigrated to this country. I am one of those people, for example. I suppose I could be accused of not going back far enough or looking carefully enough, especially to my presumed Scots Irish roots. (Names don't get much more Irish-sounding than "Shannon Sullivan," and my mother's maiden name clearly is Scottish.) But I don't have any stories about those roots handed down from generation to generation. My family is not pedigreed in that way. Trying to take up stories about nineteenth-century Scots Irish people as intimately related to me feels about as meaningful as trying to take up stories about nineteenth-century black slaves. In both cases, there are valuable and life-sustaining histories to be embraced by people today, and I agree with Macmullan on their importance. But it would be false to both those histories and to my experience to pretend that I have a lived personal or familial connection to them. My family is more like a mutt: it lacks meaningful traceable ancestry, as do many of the Scots Irish white people who primarily settled the South and quickly became the nation's white trash. I can't help but feel that a whiff of class privilege surrounds white ethnic histories when they are used as the sole or primary challenge to white privilege. White ethnic histories can be an importance source of countermemory to white domination, but they also can be a piece of cultural capital unavailable to lower classes of white people.[45] One reason that white allies need to *transform* whiteness—not evade it through white ethnicity—is that whiteness is all that some of us have got. If we are going to find a source of life-sustaining value in our racial-ethnic identities, it must be a viable option to find it in our whiteness.

I know some readers will be concerned about this book's tight focus on whiteness, and not merely because of ethnic and class differences between white people. If part of the problem of white privilege is that white people always see themselves as the rightful center of attention, then focusing on white people would seem only to perpetuate, rather than challenge white privilege. I won't pretend that this book is immune to this problem, but I don't think the problem is fatal since a critical focus on whiteness and white people can play an important role in racial justice struggles. Feminists have learned that sexism and male privilege depend not merely on a particular construction of femininity, but also on a form of masculinity that needs to be understood, criticized, and transformed. Likewise, in the past decade or so, theorists concerned about racial justice have come to realize that challenging white racism requires critically examining how race operates not only in the lives of people of color, but also in the lives of white people. Critically focusing on whiteness need not perpetuate white privilege and domination of people of color.

A more cutting version of this concern might be that this book focuses too much on the agency of white people, as if their personal efforts are fundamental to the possibility of transforming whiteness. As Alcoff has argued, whiteness is going to change at least somewhat no matter what white people do, thanks to changing demographics in the United States.[46] In 2008, the U.S. Census Bureau projected that by 2042 white people no longer will be in the majority in the United States.[47] And white people have already turned into the minority race in most major U.S. cities, as Alcoff points out. This demographic shift will lead to a change in whiteness regardless of white people's agency or actions. The question thus is not whether white people will bring it about, but how they will undergo it.

Sonia Kruks sounds a similar alarm in her criticism of the politics of self-transformation. Kruks is concerned that when white feminists in particular have come to reflect on their racial privilege, they tend to stop thinking of privilege as structural and instead conceive of it as "the personal possession of an autonomous self."[48] Intensely individualistic, the politics of self-transformation assumes that personal will power is what is needed to end privilege. It tells feminists and others: address your ignorance of other racial groups and learn to be more sensitive to them, and white privilege will be eliminated. Frequently moralistic, the politics of self-transformation tends to encourage a focus on one's self that can be self-indulgent but also hypercritical if a person does not seem to be working on herself diligently enough. The reality, however, is that a great deal of privilege operates on an impersonal, institutional level that individual efforts do not impact. As Kruks explains, this means that a politics of self-transformation might not be very effective in bringing about positive change. The result of that failure, which is experienced as a personal failure, is feelings of guilt for evidently not working hard enough, and these feelings tend to lead to despair, self-hatred, and—ironically—immobilization in the face of persistent privilege.[49]

I agree with Kruks's criticism of autonomous individualism, especially as she links reliance on a concept of individualistic agency to the production of white guilt. In contrast to the politics of self-transformation she describes, my project assumes a transactional self (as I have developed elsewhere),[50] and it explicitly articulates an approach to white identity that does not rely on white guilt or shame. Thus, even though I am interested in the question of white transformation, this book is not accurately thought of as a politics of self-transformation in Kruks's sense. It fits more closely the "the politics of personal transformation" described by Lisa Tessman, "in which transformation of one's self or character is meant to go hand in hand with working to bring about other sorts of liberatory changes."[51] I also agree with Alcoff that many factors outside of white people's control, such as changing demographics, will play a large, perhaps even the main role in the transformation of whiteness. Her question about how white people will undergo, rather than engineer this transformation is important, and it helps situate my account of white transformation. A white person's individual actions may not be a primary motor in the transformation of whiteness, but she still has to figure out how to live as a white person. The individual, personal question of how a white person might respond to demographic and other structural changes in whiteness remains.

To be successful, critical philosophy of race needs to examine the personal side of whiteness and white privilege, that is, how whiteness and white privilege are experienced and impact the lives of flesh and blood people, white and nonwhite alike. This examination is just one piece of the puzzle and must be complemented by work that focuses on the structural, institutional face of white privilege, including strategies for change that could be effective on an impersonal level. This book is a small piece of that larger puzzle. It does not purport to be a solution to the entire puzzle itself. The personal and the institutional are not divorced from one another. Institutional commitments and effects operate through personal actions and choices all the time, and certainly this is true in the case of white privilege. Thus, how individual people experience—resist? embrace? ignore?—those effects is an important question if they want to try to change them. Devising actions for individuals to take in the face of structural inequalities and injustices, such as white privilege, need not assume an atomistic individual with autonomous agency.

So what might a white person who is concerned about racial injustice do? Is there anything that she can do, especially given that there is no guarantee that her efforts won't be undercut by her unconscious racial habits? I think that it is important to answer "yes" to this question because the alternative implicitly tells white people that racism really is people of color's problem, not also their own. And furthermore, it tells white people that even if they are concerned about racism, all they can or need do about it is wait for people of color to show up—in their schools, their neighborhoods, their towns—to do something about it. This too easily relieves white people of their racial responsibilities and becomes a way for white privilege to perpetuate itself through the nonchalance of supposedly well-intentioned white people. I am not sanguine about white people's ability to challenge, or even recognize white privilege in their lives. Nowadays, habits of white privilege tend to operate too unconsciously, too covertly and sneakily, for white people to easily detect and transform them. But this doesn't mean that they are not responsible for them and cannot try to change them.

Another reason that I am in favor of focusing on white people is because of their tendency toward ontological expansiveness.[52] Ontological expansiveness is the habit, often unconscious, of assuming and acting as if any and all spaces—geographical, psychological, cultural, linguistic, or whatever—are rightfully available to and open for white people to enter whenever they like. (The title of one recent book neatly captures this phenomenon: *Everything but the Burden: What White People Are Taking from Black Culture*.)[53] If a space is blocked or closed off to a white person—for example, when a white person is uncomfortable entering a predominantly black neighborhood—then that situation is perceived as unfair or unjust. The habit of ontological expansiveness has allowed and continues to allow white people to destructively invade the spaces of nonwhite people, and it tends to do so in the well-intentioned name of promoting diversity and learning about other cultures in hopes of eliminating white domination. Ontological expansiveness usually disguises itself as a challenge to white privilege, in other words, and as a result it is able to operate relatively undetected (at least by white people) and thus inflict more damage than if it openly declared its aims.

The opposite of what one might initially think about white people's attempts to immerse themselves in the cultures and lives of people of color frequently turns out to be true. Those attempts often are part of the problem, not the solution to white domination of people of color. Ontological expansiveness is a white privileged habit that white people need to try to learn to resist, and one way to do so is for them to stay home, so to speak, rather than travel to other racial locations. Rather than setting aside one's whiteness in an attempt to learn about other races, white people can begin to do effective racial justice work by cleaning up their own house. This does not mean intentionally avoiding people of color so that a white person can maintain an all-white environment. Nor is my claim an objection to the kind of world traveling described by María Lugones, in which a white person comes to see herself and others from the perspective of people of color, a perspective that challenges white domination and supremacy.[54] But the practical fact of ongoing, de facto segregation in the United States means that many white people already live and work in persistently white environments. The question is whether racism can be challenged by white people from such a location, whether a white person can world travel right in her own white backyard.

Again, I think the answer is yes: whiteness can be a legitimate social location or identity from which to challenge white racism. I agree with Lisa Heldke, who makes a similar claim in the specific context of persistently white colleges. Complementing W. E. B. Du Bois's account of how segregated all-black colleges could work toward black liberation, Heldke argues that white universities lacking in racial diversity can help combat racism by "plac[ing] the problem of white identity at the center of [their] educational mission."[55] Rather than sit back on their heels and assume that diversity is a panacea for white privilege, predominantly white universities could place themselves in solidarity with black universities by foregrounding and critically analyzing white racism. Even though a white university might not be a racially diverse place—and even though it can and should work to end the de jure or de facto segregation that produced it—a white university can still be an effective site to challenge racism. This is because "the 'problem' of white society to which a historically white college ought to attend is the role of white people in the preservation of white racism, *not* 'the absence of people of color.' "[56] While this proposal might sound paradoxical or counterintuitive, Heldke argues we should "consider that predominantly white places are just the sorts of places to which white supremacists are attracted. Would they not also, then, by important places from which to launch white antiracist [sic] work?"[57]

Heldke's impulse is right on target even though it flies in the face of most conventional wisdom about how to combat white racism. Rather than avoid the white places and identities that white supremacists are attracted to, white allies can work for racial justice from within them. This is not "to play [the] dangerous game" that concerns Noel Ignatiev when he argues against "promot[ing] whiteness as a legitimate identity."[58] The danger, as he sees it, is that legitimating white identity necessarily legitimates racist white power advocates and thus leaves white allies with no way to distinguish themselves from those advocates. Ignatiev gives the example of a conference in Boston sponsored by the Center for the Study of White American Culture, which a white power advocate wanted to attend because he wanted to foster white identity and pride. The conference sponsors did not want him to attend but, according to Ignatiev, they were stuck because they "had no principled basis on which to exclude him."[59] Ignatiev might be right that the goals of this center and conference were wrongheaded, especially if the center didn't explicitly take a critical approach in its examination of whiteness.[60] But he is wrong that the promotion of whiteness as a legitimate identity necessarily is uncritical. He also is wrong that white allies should shun all contact with white power advocates, a claim that I'll elaborate in following chapters. Rather than cede the meaning and effects of whiteness to white supremacists, whiteness can be developed into an identity grounded in racial justice that is in solidarity with people of color working against white racism.

Lucius Outlaw recently asked the question, "Rehabilitate racial whiteness?" and he replies in the affirmative, adding that the question needs "definitive answers that must be taken up and lived by folks who identify as 'white.'"[61] Put bluntly, Outlaw calls for white people to stop waiting for black and other nonwhite people to do all the work. White people need to get off their duffs and begin figuring out what whiteness might mean other than the ongoing domination of people of color. This book is inspired by Outlaw's call. I hope to provide a critique of the class-based structures of white racism and an account of white self-love that can be used to transform the meaning and effects of white identity.

Dumping on White Trash

Etiquette, Abjection, and Radical Inclusion

> The trailer park has become . . . the only acceptable place to dump one's racist inclinations.
>
> —Jim Goad, *The Redneck Manifesto*

One February weekend in 2002, critical whiteness scholar and English professor Mike Hill infiltrated the fifth American Renaissance conference. The theme for that year's meeting was "In Defense of Western Man," and the three hundred conference attendees—all apparently white men—were gathered in the name of "white genetic solidarity."[1] In past years, the conference had focused on non-European immigrants and citizens of color in the United States. In 2002, its emphasis shifted to "the vicissitudes of white identity as it seemed to disappear before our eyes," with the goal of bringing about "the racial awakening of an Anglocentric nation in crisis."[2] Hill, a white man who edited *Whiteness: A Critical Reader* in 1997, attended the meeting with permission; he was given an invitation when he truthfully lied that he wrote on whiteness.[3] Unbeknownst to the American Renaissance organizers and attendees, Hill was at the conference as a spy on behalf of *The Journal of Blacks in Higher Education*. His task was to write "a sort of antiracist exposé" for the journal, which he did for their Spring 2002 issue.[4] The American Renaissance Web site labels its approach to race as one of "race realism," and in noninflammatory ways explains that "race is an important aspect of individual and group identity. . . . Race and racial conflict are at the heart of the most serious challenges the Western World faces in the 21st century. The problems of race cannot be solved without adequate understanding . . . of all aspects of race, whether historical, cultural, or biological."[5] But as Hill reports, the seemingly respectable title "American Renaissance" is in fact "the name of the most vicious collection of . . . racists who assemble every two years to discuss among themselves how blacks and other racial minorities are destroying Western civilization."[6] In the name of racial justice and in solidarity with black and other people of color, Hill felt that the American Renaissance's true mission should be exposed. For that reason, Hill was willing "to hold [his] nose and mix it up with people looking more or less like [him]," spending "three agonizingly isolated days among his own kind, mulling over a fantasy of whiteness now storied to be gone."[7]

The image of an academic playing the role of a spy is striking, and I can't help but wonder about the anxiety Hill must have experienced in situations when he was in danger of being found out. But what I find most significant about Hill's story is his description of moments of connection with American Renaissance members that made him profoundly uncomfortable. Hill writes of his irritation that the conference attendees kept bewailing what they called the death of the white race, and then he admits that what was even more irritating was that the weekend "turned out to produce certain moments of intimacy that I would have liked to let go unnoticed."[8] As the attendees generated excitement over the topic of whiteness, Hill "could not help making some unseemly comparisons closer to home" between their excitement and the exuberant academic "rush to whiteness" that Hill's edited volume helped create.[9] Another significant moment of closeness that Hill wished he hadn't experienced revolved around class. Many of the conference attendees were "remarkably well attuned to the plight of white working-class men," and Hill found himself identifying with the American Renaissance's "white guy next door" who is concerned about declining wages, corporate manipulations of the workforce, and the domestic crisis of the state more broadly.[10] Disturbed by repeated moments of sympathizing and identifying with American Renaissance (AR) attendees, Hill laments "while covering the AR story, I noticed how the same kinds of hopes and fears garnering whiteness its share (and then some) of academic attention were meshing too easily with the tortured hearts and twisted minds I mixed with at the AR conference."[11] Hill makes clear that his commitment to racial justice was never in question at the conference, but this is precisely why his experience was so unsettling. As he asks, "Who would really want to admit to the confusing prospect that opposing evaluations on the white majority's so-called death could mimic one another on class" and other issues?"[12]

"Tortured" and "twisted," American Renaissance members also are Hill's "own kind" whose views on class mirror his own. How could Hill, a white person committed to racial justice, find himself identifying with white supremacists? It seems that, by definition, this situation could not happen, and yet it did—hence Hill's painful cognitive dissonance and existential confusion. I bet that Hill's experience would not be unique, however. Many middle-class white people, me included, probably would have felt just as unsettled and disturbed as he did. My point in recounting this story is not to single out Hill, but to show how his experience reveals the commonplace assumption that there should be no points of contact, similarities, or shared interests between white supremacists and white allies. If there are shared interests between them, so the assumption goes, then this fact calls into question a white person's commitment to racial justice. This assumption is problematic because its denial of connections between white allies and white supremacists posits white supremacists as irremediably other, and as I will argue, this othering supports the very thing—white racism—that white allies are trying to combat.

Hill's story also helps expose problematic assumptions about who white racists are. They often are thought to be members of an uneducated white lower class: their alleged stupidity is why they continue to think that white people are superior to nonwhite people. This assumption operates in the opposite direction as well: poor white people—so-called white trash, rednecks, and hillbillies—often are automatically assumed to be white racists, and if they aren't (yet) members of a white supremacist organization, then they are thought to be the best recruiting pool from which white supremacists can draw. As Jim Goad argues, "rednecks are fingered as the primary source of [racial] prejudice," so much so that "white supremacist" (or "overt white racist") and "white lower class" often are treated as synonyms.[13] This claim is confirmed by studies in cultural anthropology that demonstrate how "a comfortable conviction holds sway among middle-class whites that racism is concentrated in the lower classes—that it is certainly present in working-class whites, but bubbles up most vigorously from the hearts of poor whites, as allegorized in the cultural figure of 'white trash.'"[14]

In contrast to this stereotype of white racists, the men at the American Renaissance conference were not lower-class, poor, or white trash. They were members of a relatively upscale white middle class. This meant that they were Hill's own kind not just because they were white and male, but also because they were professionally dressed, well educated, and well spoken. "We white racialists must put away our boots and put on our suits," as American Renaissance speaker Nick Griffin claimed, reflecting an unspoken dress code clearly in force at the conference.[15] With their coats, ties, and glasses of chardonnay, the American Renaissance conference was not a stereotypical gathering of big-booted white supremacists shouting near a burning cross in a muddy field. "Gathered in a gentlemanly way," many of the conference attendees possessed postgraduate degrees from leading universities such as Yale, Cambridge, University of North Carolina, Cal State Northridge, and University of London.[16] Hill's identification with them is unseemly, as he confesses, which is to say indecent, coarse, in poor taste—all the things that an educated middle-class person is not supposed to be and all things that are identified with white racism in a post–Jim Crow world. If the American Renaissance men can be simultaneously unseemly (because racist) and middle-class, then other middle-class white people, such as Hill, cannot be confident that their middle-class status prevents them from being racist.

In this chapter, I examine corrosive divides between classes of white people on which white racism depends, exploring how white trash are othered by good white liberals particularly through race-class etiquette and the resulting abjection of poor whites. If white people are going to figure out how to live their whiteness in ways that challenge racial injustice, then white middle-class othering of white lower classes must be confronted because it serves the interests of white domination. As I will argue, those interests can best be countered by a type of radical inclusion that involves white people of all classes—the "bad" white people as well as the "good" ones—in racial justice movements.

∾

Etiquette concerns conventional requirements or expectations for social behavior. The word originated in eighteenth-century France, meaning "ticket" or "label." Small cards—*les étiquettes*—were printed with instructions for how a person was to behave in court or how a soldier was to behave in his lodgings.[17] *Les étiquettes* ensured that a visitor to the king wouldn't offend him and that a soldier obtaining lodging wouldn't harm the property or disturb its owners or other lodgers. Today, of course, we use the word more broadly to refer to a variety of social situations and groups of people. But in all cases, etiquette means the regulation of relationships between individuals by prescribing and proscribing particular forms of their conduct with one another.

Bertram Wilbur Doyle's classic study of the etiquette of race rela-tions in the U.S. South is useful not only for examining the role that etiquette played between white and black people in antebellum and Jim Crow America, but also for analyzing some of the general features of etiquette.[18] Etiquette is concerned primarily with personal relations, but its meaning and impact stretch far beyond the personal. At its heart, etiquette is a form of social control that defines and maintains social distances between people.[19] If a black person routinely steps off the side-walk to let a white person pass, this act is more than merely a private matter between the two people. It embodies, repeats, and supports social expectations of black deference and subordination to white people. Even in a case involving two social equals, etiquette tends to regulate their behavior, including the degree of social distance that is supposed to exist between them. Thus, two academics at a conference might shake hands or kiss cheeks when greeting each other, depending on what country they are in (or what kind of philosophy they study). If one person refuses to do so, the breach of etiquette requires an explanation, such as having a bad cold and not wanting to spread germs, which has spawned new forms of etiquette such as the elbow bump. Absent an explanation, the breach of etiquette produces a rupture in social order—in this case, the person refusing the greeting asserts herself as superior to someone who was presumed to be an equal. This rupture in the social fabric leaves the offended party and those who witnessed the snub unsure of how to behave toward the person who violated a social code.

The emphasis on *social* distance here is important. Etiquette sometimes regulated physical distances between people, as the sidewalk example above illustrates. But the physical distances prescribed by eti-quette were and are always in the service of the more crucial matter of social distance. Etiquette is what makes possible physical proximity and intimacy between social superiors and inferiors without collapsing their social status.[20] For example, racial etiquette allowed white masters and black slaves to work together side by side on the plantation and black slaves to tend to the most intimate matters of their white master's hygiene, all without any threat to the white person's status as superior. As long as both white master and black slave observed the appropriate rules of address and gestural codes of behavior—etiquette is a code that binds both the dominant and subordinate, after all—then significant social distances could be maintained in the midst of intimate physi-cal proximities.[21] What the example of racial etiquette from antebellum America shows is that "far more than physical separation, white south-erners wanted social distance."[22]

For Doyle, etiquette is a form of government, and we can understand this term in a Foucauldian sense.[23] Michel Foucault understood government not as a top-down form of state power, but as a horizontal form of social control embodied in institutions such as schools, medical facilities, and prisons. Governmentality combines strategies and technologies for influencing others with those of caring for or regulating the self.[24] In a similar fashion, Doyle argues that the government provided by etiquette is much more basic and extensive than that of legislation or political bodies. Etiquette operates throughout virtually all of our social relationships, and its "jurisdiction" often precedes and operates alongside official legislation and then continues after laws and other formal regulations have been abolished.[25] (This was the case after the Civil War, when slavery-era etiquette between white people and newly freed slaves continued even though slavery legally had been abolished.) Etiquette governs informally, and this is precisely why its form of social control is effective.

Another way of approaching etiquette's informality—and thus also its effectiveness—is to understand etiquette as a form of habit. Habit is a predisposition for transacting with the world in a particular way. Habits operate on subconscious and sometimes even unconscious levels: they are what we do "without thinking." This doesn't mean, however, that habits necessarily are trivial or minor, as when, for example, a person absentmindedly twirls a lock of her hair while reading. Just the opposite: some of the most complex skills that human beings acquire—such as playing the violin or driving a manual transmission automobile—are only fully acquired when they have become habit. But even these examples do not make the point about habit's ontological significance strongly enough, for habit is constitutive of the self. The gendered, raced, classed, and other patterns of transacting with the world that a person develops help constitute who that person is.

Etiquette does not always take the form of habit. This is because it sometimes is an act that a person consciously decides to engage in. But when etiquette is at its most effective, it operates subconsciously or unconsciously. Quoting William Graham Sumner and using Sumner's "social ritual" as a synonym for "etiquette," Doyle explains that "ritual, as Sumner points out, 'is not something to be thought or felt. It is something to be done.' In fact, 'ritual is strongest when it is perfunctory and excites no thought.' "[26] As in the case of all habits, etiquette can become so engrained in the self that it can seem instinctual, as if it were not learned behavior. This explains how black slaves sometimes appeared "naturally" or "natively" deferential toward white people.[27] When it takes the form of habit, etiquette allows people to engage each other with the least expenditure of energy required by conscious thought. In this way, it facilitates smooth and easy transactions with one's environment.

As it does so, however, the social order preserved by etiquette also exerts its most effective—and thus potentially most harmful—control.[28] While some contemporary white philosophers have argued that etiquette must be part of attempts to defeat racism and thus that etiquette has a transformative role to play in an oppressive society, the forms of etiquette they describe tend to be mere pleasantries between people that eliminate social tension but for that reason don't bring about any substantial change.[29] (I'm reminded of Martin Luther King's criticism of "the white moderate, who is more devoted to 'order' than to justice; who prefers a negative peace which is the absence of tension to a positive peace which is the presence of justice.")[30] The primary function of etiquette remains the conservative one of protecting an existing social order by keeping people in different social groups in their "proper" place.[31] In the case of Jim Crow America, racial etiquette helped support white supremacy by securing racial hierarchy in situations of propinquity between white and black people; by regulating affect and emotional expression on the part of white and black people; and by reducing feelings of guilt on the part of white people about their domination of nonwhite people.[32]

During Jim Crow, racial etiquette was (and perhaps still is) a key method for training each new generation of white people into whiteness. With regard to white children, racial etiquette was "the closest thing to a 'core curriculum' that white southerners had," the main ticket to whiteness that white children needed to possess.[33] Learning habits of behavior with nonwhite children and adults that would last them a lifetime, white children were less likely to question legal, institutional, and other forms of discrimination against black and other nonwhite people. Racial etiquette's governance of interpersonal relationships thus had structural implications and effects. The central role that racial etiquette played in the education of white children also meant that racial etiquette had a special connection with white mothers, who were the primary source of their children's ticket to whiteness. Because of their key role in childrearing, white mothers were the main adults who taught white children how to use bodily gestures and forms of address to maintain social distance between themselves and nonwhite people. Teaching racial etiquette to white children thus amounted to "one of white women's chief forms of collusion in the maintenance of white supremacy."[34]

Racial etiquette doesn't just operate interracially, however. It also governs intraracial behavior across class lines. This probably is true for most racial groups, but here I focus on intraracial white etiquette because it is one of the primary ways that white people experience race and shore up white racism.[35] As cultural anthropologist John Hartigan claims, "It is forms of etiquette—and importantly, their transgression—that maintain and reproduce the unmarked status of white identity."[36] White social etiquette crystallizes around the figure of white trash. White trash are the poor white people who fail to live up to middle-class expectations of white behavior, and their "failure" is at least threefold. First, white trash allegedly are uneducated and stupid. Epithets such as idiot, imbecile, and moron regularly are used to describe white trash, reflecting the influence of the eugenics movement on middle-class white people's views of race and class.[37] Second, the bodies of the white trash are problematic. They yell and shout, talking too loudly and coarsely. They are unkempt and unclean, often barefoot and always dirty. And they are sluggish and lazy, which is why they are poor (and perhaps also why they are unclean). Across the board, their "actions, smells, and sounds . . . disrupt the social decorums that support the hegemonic, unmarked status of whiteness as a normative identity in [the United States]."[38] Finally—and intimately related to the first two "failures"—white trash share too many similarities of speech, behavior, diet, and lifestyle with black people.[39] White trash are uncomfortably close to those whom they are supposed to be radically different from. Whether willfully or ignorantly, white trash fail to speak, eat, dress, and otherwise behave as proper (middle-class) white people are supposed to do, and their breach of white social etiquette threatens the boundary between white and nonwhite (especially black) people.

This consideration of white etiquette brings out the bodily dimensions of class distinctions. While race often is examined in terms of bodily habits and behavior, class typically is not. Some critical philosophers of race even have claimed that "class is not inscribed on the body the way that race is."[40] But when etiquette has become sedimented into habit and operates without a person's thinking about its demands, then class has become part of the bodily self that one is. As Pierre Bourdieu's work in particular shows, "the body is the most indisputable materialization of class tastes. Bodies are the physical sites where the relations of class, gender, race, sexuality and age come together and are em-bodied and practiced."[41] In that case, class is not "just about the way you talk or dress, or furnish your home, it is not just about the job you do or how much money you make doing it; nor is it merely about whether or not you went to university, nor which university you went to. Class is something beneath your clothes, under your skin, in your psyche, at the very core of your being."[42] Incorporated into the self via its habits, white etiquette is constitutive of the self, in a complex dynamic relationship with raced, gendered, and other salient habits.

White social etiquette circulates within several race-class slurs for the white lower class, including "hillbilly," "redneck," and "cracker," but "white trash" carries a special significance. Unlike these other terms, which sometimes have been used to establish an antibourgeois identity, "white trash" generally has not been rehabilitated or reclaimed by the white lower class.[43] (Think here of the rehabilitation of "redneck" performed by Jeff Foxworthy's stand-up comedy and books, which focus on the one-liner "You might be a redneck if . . ."[44]) In contrast, white trash "carries an irreducible debasing connotation," and the few "attempts to regard 'white trash' positively, to redeem it as a cultural identity, reveal an active remainder of social contempt and loathing that cannot be fully expelled."[45] The word *trash* helps explain why the term has remained irredeemable. "More than all these other labels, [white trash] articulates exactly what is at stake in intraracial efforts to maintain white racial identity—it encapsulates the self-conscious anxiety among whites over threats of pollution that threaten the basis for belonging within whiteness."[46] White trash is whiteness's dirty garbage, its refuse, its waste product. It is that which threatens whiteness with pollution and contamination from within.

Of course, whiteness also experiences itself as threatened from without—witness so-called yellow peril, black peril, and all other sorts of "menacing" forces that other nonwhite races represent. Historically, miscegenation and immigration—the mixing of white and nonwhite "blood"—probably have served as the two greatest "threats" to the purity of whiteness. But especially with the rise of eugenics at the turn of the twentieth century, the white middle class became increasingly concerned about the threat to whiteness posed by (some) white people themselves. These were and are the people who count as white but do not uphold "proper" standards of whiteness. The danger posed by white trash is particularly alarming because "the source of the threat is depicted as arising from the allegedly purest of Anglo-Saxon strains, rather than through transgression of the color line."[47] Policing the color line between whites and nonwhites thus wouldn't be sufficient to uphold white domination of nonwhite people, even when carried out by stronger means than racial etiquette, such as lynching. White social etiquette also was needed to internally discipline whiteness. White bodies and behavior had to be governed so that white superiority wouldn't destroy itself, and this meant "instilling [classed and raced] habits that are policed by concepts of disgust and embellished through ideas about pollution and dirt."[48]

Here we can see how white trash operate as the abject. As Julia Kristeva argues, the abject is crucial to societies and cultures that are based on rigid subject/object distinctions, but the abject itself is not an object completely other to the subject. The abject instead is what troubles sharp, clear boundaries between subject and object, self and other. The abject does have one, but "only one quality of the object—that of being opposed to I."[49] The abject's opposition to the subject functions in a different way than that of the object. Put another way, the differences between abjection and objectification demonstrate how othering can take place in related, but different ways. Like the object, the abject is jettisoned from the subject, but "[the abject] lies there, quite close," threatening the dissolution of the bounded subject through its proximity.[50] In that sense, the abject is a different kind of threat to the subject than the definable object is. Even though the excluded object menaces the subject in its otherness, the sharp distinctions posited between subject and object provide a kind of safety and security for the subject. A gulf appears to exist between the subject and object that reassures the subject of its identity. Not so with the abject. The abject is uncanny, familiar in its strangeness. While the abject also safeguards the subject from its dissolution, the protection it offers is murkier, slipperier, and less firm than that which the object provides.

The division between white trash and proper white people also is slippery, revealing how white trash operate as whiteness's abject. White trash are opposed to the proper, white subject, but their opposition is troublesome because it isn't clear, sharp, or absolute. Like people of color and black people in particular, white trash are excluded from whiteness proper. But the othering of people of color and of white trash tends to happen in different ways. White trash lie uncomfortably closer to proper white people, threatening the dissolution of hegemonic forms of whiteness from within. Because of their whiteness, white trash threaten the coherence and identity of the proper, white subject in a related, but different way than people of color generally do. The presumed gulf between proper white people and people of color cannot be confidently assumed between proper white people and white trash. White trash are uncannily familiar to proper white people because of their shared race, and this murky point of contact is why white trash have to be forcefully expelled from whiteness. White trash thus become a "means of boundary maintenance through white identity operates, containing or expelling certain whites from the social and political body of whiteness."[51]

The need to expel white trash demonstrates how white trash are considered to be repulsive, even as they, like the corpse, simultaneously can be considered horrifyingly fascinating. As Jim Goad argues, middle-class white people tend to have a "steaming liberal revulsion for white trash."[52] But this revulsion reveals more about middle-class white people than it does about any so-called objective features of white trash. Since white trash are not absolutely other to proper white people, the proper white person who attempts to jettison white trash from whiteness can never do so completely. As the proper white person expels white trash, she also expels herself. As Kristeva explains about abjection more generally, "I expel *myself*, I spit *myself* out, I abject *myself* within the same motion through which 'I' claim to establish 'myself.' . . . 'I' am in the process of becoming an other at the expense of my own death."[53] For Goad, images of disease, as well as death, implicitly help illuminate white middle-class revulsion for white trash: "To the white elite white trash must seem like a disease in remission inside *all* whites, one that might flare up again given the right circumstances. When white blue bloods are repulsed by white trash, they are uncomfortably reminded both of what they used to be and what they may yet become."[54] White trash is not me—the proper white subject—and yet it is not safely not-me either. Like death and disease, white trash is what threatens proper whiteness with nonexistence. Ashes to ashes, dust to dust: what I used to be and what I might yet become is the dirty white trash that I am and the dirty white trash to which I shall return.[55]

The biblical reference to dust, or dirt, is particularly fitting for abjection since the abject often manifests itself as the unclean. Filth, waste, and excrement are common instances of the abject: "the repugnance, the retching that thrusts me to the side and turns me away from defilement, sewage, and muck."[56] As Kristeva documents, the Judeo-Christian Bible is permeated with strategies for managing the unclean and impure: certain foods, dead bodies (both human and nonhuman), diseases such as leprosy, and even speech.[57] But it is not the case that there is something "naturally" unclean or menacing to human health that then is repelled because of its "natural" threat. It may be that dead bodies can spread disease, for example, but this is not why they are considered abject. It is the ability of dead bodies, and other abject beings, to erase borders and boundaries that makes them repulsive. In Kristeva's words, "It is thus not lack of cleanliness or health that causes abjection but what disturbs identity, system, order. What does not respect borders, positions, rules."[58]

Above all—more than corpses, rotting food, or disease—what greatly disturbs identity, system, and order is the maternal body.[59] This is why the incest taboo is central to societies who found the subject on sharp subject/object dichotomies. "Abjection preserves what existed in the archaism of pre-objectal relationship, in the immemorial violence with which a body becomes separated from another body in order to be."[60] The other body from which I separated in order to be is the maternal body, which is a space (*chora*) where "I" did not yet exist as a distinct subject but was ambiguously merged with a being who was both me and not-me. The maternal body—and women more generally, along with menstrual blood and pregnant bodies—is what the (male) subject used to be a part of and what he may yet again become enmeshed with if he tries to return to it. Thus, incest, especially between mother and son, is prohibited. Sexual relations between mother and son are repulsive and improper not because of a genetic health risk to any offspring they might produce, as we might try to explain the scientific reasons for prohibitions against incest. Rather, they are repulsive and improper because human existence inside the womb is a time of nonsubjectivity that should never be returned to, on pain of dissolution of human subjectivity as we know it.

We don't have to follow psychoanalysis all the way to the oedipal complex to appreciate the way that the incest taboo functions in the abjection of white trash. Perhaps more than anything, white trash are considered repulsive and are objects of ridicule because they allegedly have sex with all sorts of improper beings. Pointing out how rednecks and their hillbilly and white trash kin are seen as intrinsically rapist, murderous, and otherwise violent, Goad sarcastically jokes, "The hillbilly . . . serves all the function of a modern American scapegoat. And in the hillbilly, we receive an extra added bonus—a scapegoat who also *fucks* goats."[61] Even more often than nonhuman animals, however, the improper beings that white trash allegedly have sex with are their own nuclear family members. The alleged stupidity of white trash is due to the fact that they breed with each other; white trash is "inbred, degenerated, momma-impregnating vermin and scum." As two of Jeff Foxworthy's jokes go, "You know you're a redneck if your state's got a new law that says when a couple get divorced, they are still legally brother and sister," and "You might be a redneck if your family tree doesn't fork."[62] Goad claims that "the topic of inbreeding occurs with such frequency among white-trash stereotypes that its symbolic function begs analysis,"[63] and while I agree with him about the frequency of the stereotype, I think it benefits from, rather than begs the (psycho)analysis of abjection.[64] It's not merely that proper white people "*need* to see hillbillies as stupid" in order to distinguish themselves as smart, as Goad rightly claims.[65] It's also that the alleged incest on the part of white trash threatens fundamental structures of binary divisions out of which white subjectivity is formed. Inbred white trash don't just assure proper white people of their intelligence. They also threaten the identity of proper white people because they show proper white people that whiteness is no guarantee of subjectivity clearly distinguished from stupidity.

White trash also reveal that whiteness is no guarantee of subjectivity clearly separated from people of color, and black people in particular. As mentioned earlier, white trash do not speak, eat, dress, and otherwise behave as proper white people are supposed to do, and their breach of white social etiquette threatens the boundary between white and nonwhite (especially black) people. The geographical origins of white trash, and other related figures such as the redneck and the hillbilly, help explain the powerful ability of white trash to efface boundaries between white and black. First circulating in popular discourse in the North of the United States in the 1850s and 1860s, the term *white trash* was used to bolster antislavery sentiment.[66] "White trash" captured the effects of slavery on poor whites living in the South. Because black slaves were used as laborers on Southern plantations and farms, the poor white Southerner was denied the opportunity to develop the ability and willingness to work. The result, as one nineteenth-century Northern scholar wrote, was a class of white people who were "degraded, half-fed, half-clothed, without mental or moral instruction, and destitute of self-respect and of any just appreciation of character."[67] An outgrowth of the enslavement of black Americans, white trash was "a uniquely southern phenomenon."[68]

The distinction between white trash and hard-working, "respectable" poor whites was and is difficult to maintain. This is because of "the lack of fixed, distinguishing criteria" between the two groups and "the intense concerns generated by the need to keep whiteness and blackness distinct."[69] No matter how hard one works, a poor white person is at risk of being viewed as lazy, ignorant, and morally deficient. Unlike the black person who likely experiences racial discrimination in education and the labor market, a poor white person has no way to account for her poverty and related moral "failures." As one middle-class white person dismissively remarked to cultural anthropologist Kirby Moss, "For White people there is really no excuse [for poverty] because they are not treated differently because of their race."[70] Whether mental, moral, or financial, a poor white person's impoverished situation must be the result of her own failure: her refusal to work, her lack of intelligence, and her failure to adopt a proper work ethic. As Moss explains, to many middle-class white people in his study, "poverty was [merely] a ploy, an individual's excuse to not contribute to the progress of society."[71]

Occasionally, the liminal position of white trash has been used to support, rather than condemn a white person for his or her perceived proximity to blackness. Writing about then-president Bill Clinton's 1998 impeachment due to the Monica Lewinsky sex scandal, Toni Morrison infamously claimed that Clinton was being attacked because of his blackness. As Morrison argued, "White skin notwithstanding, this is our first black President. Blacker than any actual black person who could ever be elected in our children's lifetime. After all, Clinton displays almost every trope of blackness: single-parent household, born poor, working-class, saxophone-playing, McDonald's-and-junk-food-loving boy from Arkansas."[72] I'll set aside the question of whether Clinton is blacker than Barack Obama, who was elected to the U.S. presidency in Morrison's lifetime. What's important here is that Morrison is not trying to slander Clinton by emphasizing his trashiness. Reversing the usual valence given to blackness, Morrison's comment is sympathetic to the president. Even more germane is that it's not the case that Morrison sees Clinton's blackness as resulting from his particular views on race or white racism. As Morrison explained in the wake of Obama's 2008 election, her 1998 claim "was deploring the way in which President Clinton was being treated . . . I said he was being treated like a black on the street, already guilty, already a perp. I have no idea what his real instincts are, in terms of race."[73] What Morrison's remark underscores is the blurring of boundaries between black and white that white trash represents. Clinton's perceived blackness comes from being white trash: white-skinned and poor, with crude culinary tastes, and raised in a defective family in the South.

The seemingly small detail concerning Clinton's Southern roots is significant. Just as white trash and poor whites often are conflated, the distinction between white trash and Southern whites also tends to be blurry and difficult to maintain. The geographic origins of "white trash" continue to impact the connotations of the term: simply to be a white person from the South of the United States is to risk being considered white trash. As the old joke goes, "You can tell a Southern virgin . . . when you see a girl who's running faster than her father and brothers."[74] The joke doesn't have to specify that the Southern virgin is a white woman; the trope of inbred white trash conveys that message by itself. The joke also says nothing about the Southern virgin's economic status. Regardless of whether one is poor, to be a white person from the South is to be in an at least somewhat abject relationship to proper whiteness.

This too is the product of a distinctively Northern perspective on the legacy of black slavery. White Southerners generally were seen as being too close to black people. Whether poor or not, white Southerners were in closer physical proximity to black slaves than white Northerners were, and they shared (too) many regional characteristics with them: similar accents and styles of speech, similar tastes in food, and similar sensibilities and lifestyles.[75] We can see this perspective at work in 1940s and 1950s Detroit, where the label "hillbilly" was applied by Northern whites in an unrehabilitated way to white people who transgressed white middle-class mores. "Hillbillies" began arriving in Detroit from the South in large numbers in the 1920s, and they soon were blamed for the decline in living conditions for working-class whites in the city.[76] In Detroit, the term *hillbilly* was used to "shor[e] up an imperiled sense of white identity that was challenged by the way shared traits of white and black southerners undermined northern convictions of a qualitative difference between the races."[77] In a similar fashion, Chicago complained of being invaded by Southern hillbillies, as the national publication *Harper's* documented in 1958: "The city's toughest integration problem has nothing to do with the Negroes. . . . It involves a small army of white Protestant, Early American migrants from the South—who are usually proud, poor, primitive, and fast with a knife."[78] Like white trash, hillbillies were seen by white Northerners as embodying characteristics that had been exclusively associated with blacks. Admittedly, Southern heritage did not ensure that one would be called a hillbilly, and the term sometimes was used for non-Southern whites who transgressed standards of proper whiteness.[79] Transgression of whiteness is what is central to the figures of the hillbilly and white trash, in other words. But Northern anxiety over that transgression was intensely focused on white Southerners, making white transgression and white Southernness difficult to untangle. It was white Southerners' cultural and physical proximities to black people that tended to trouble Northerners' understanding of the color line between white and black people.

These proximities weren't problematic in the same ways for white Southerners, but this is not because Southerners were less racist than their white Northern counterparts were. An African American folk saying, still repeated today, captures the difference: "In the North, they don't care how high you get, as long as you don't get too close. In the South, they don't care how close you get, as long as you don't get too high."[80] The particular role of racial etiquette in the South is crucial to these regional differences. Southern racial etiquette maintained both white domination and white Southerners' sense of racial superiority as blacks and whites mingled together in the South. Admittedly, sometimes etiquette was not enough to manage physical proximities between whites and blacks, and then legislation was needed to keep the color line in place. Mississippi's 1865 vagrancy law, for example, declared, "All white persons assembling themselves with freemen, free Negroes, or mulattoes, or usually associating with freedmen, shall be deemed vagrants, and on conviction thereof shall be fined."[81] In this case, merely gathering with free or light-skinned black people legally transformed a white person into a shiftless vagrant—into white trash, in other words. But generally Southern racial etiquette worked to ensure that physical proximities and cultural similarities did not collapse racial hierarchies in Southern society. When proper etiquette was observed on all sides, black slaves could serve white masters their food, for example, and it could be the same type of food from the very same pot, without blurring the boundary between master and slave. (Eating that food together was a different story. Racial etiquette made that act taboo during the days of slavery and Jim Crow.)[82]

Likewise today, as long as the proper forms of address are used and appropriate gestures are embodied, the black "help" can work in the kitchen side by side with her white employer, preparing the Southern foods that they both love, without any serious threat to white racism. The taboo against interracial eating also has dissolved. But social rather than proximal distance between white and nonwhite people continues to be important in the postbellum South. Keeping black people "in their place" is and has always been "more behavioral than spatial in nature. . . . Valuing hierarchy more than they feared propinquity, whites casually rubbed elbows with blacks in contexts that sometimes startled northerners. Yet the requirements of caste . . . were zealously enforced" in the South nonetheless.[83] As a legacy of their proximity to black slaves, white Southerners generally have available to them more nuanced—which is *not* to say less racist—forms of interacting with black people than white Northerners do. Those nuances tend to allow for more intimate encounters between black and white people without troubling white Southerners' sense of the color line between them.

There exists "a nebulous but enduring sense of cultural difference between northern and southern whites," and that difference expresses itself in Southern and Northern perspectives on white trash.[84] White Southerners use somewhat different characteristics than white Northerners to distinguish who counts as white trash. First and foremost—and somewhat obviously—for Southerners, the sheer fact of being a Southerner isn't relevant to distinguishing proper white people from white trash. Nor is sharing certain cultural traits with black Southerners, such as having a Southern accent, embodying a relatively slow pace of speech and movement, and enjoying Southern food. For Southerners, these traits do not indicate stupidity, laziness, or a boorish sense of taste.[85]

But this doesn't mean that Southerners don't worry intensely about hierarchical divisions between white and black or the blurring of racial lines that white trash perform. For Southern, as for Northern middle-class whites, white trash are those white people who "embod[y] a degraded form of whiteness—that is, whiteness without key forms of individual supports (striving for upward mobility) or institutional ones (from homeownership to political activity)."[86] For example, proper whiteness includes an appreciation of the aesthetics of restoring historical homes, including and perhaps especially ones from the antebellum era. In contrast, black people often are perceived as uninterested in or even hostile to the activity of historical restoration—and perhaps for good reason since this activity often involves an inchoate desire to restore an era of slavery or Jim Crow.[87] Thus, for a poor white person to be unable or unwilling to restore a historic home is for her to embody a degraded form of whiteness that shares problematic characteristics with blackness. White trash represent the threatening possibility that a white person could slide into blackness, which would mean for her to lose her racial status by means of losing her class status. Whether a white Southerner's regional identity increases the likelihood of this threat depends a great deal on whether one takes a Southern or Northern perspective on the question.

The tendency of middle-class white people to distance themselves from white trash to maintain their whiteness might seem to make class reducible to race. We might think that protecting their whiteness ultimately is what matters to middle-class white people and thus that their class status merely is an interchangeable means toward that end. On the other hand, the tendency for middle-class white people to distance themselves less from middle-class black people than from poor white people might seem to make race reducible to class.[88] From that perspective, race might seem incidental to the ultimate white middle-class goal of protecting class status. In my view, however, both of these perspectives are misleading because of their reductive character. Class differences within the group of white people make a meaningful difference to their race, and this is a constitutive, not an additive difference. Class differences aren't lumped on top of a homogenous whiteness; they instead help constitute whiteness differently for poor and middle-class white people. But the constitutive difference that class makes to race doesn't mean that race has been collapsed into class. While different from people of color in different ways, white trash and middle-class white people still are raced as white. And it tends to matter to white middle-class people that they are white, not just that they are middle-class. For example, while the amount of money varies, white people consistently respond in scientific studies that they would require a significant amount of money to agree to be switched to or born as a black person.[89] For many white people, becoming black would be a loss of something valuable that deserves compensation.

Another way to appreciate the complex, irreducible "threat" that white trash pose to middle-class white people is to compare white trash to middle-class black people. With respect to middle-class white people, the black middle class could be considered the inverse of white trash: while white trash are similar to middle-class white people in terms of race but different in terms of class, the black middle class is similar to middle-class white people in terms of class but different in terms of race. White trash and the black middle class thus would seem to be equally like and unlike white middle-class people, albeit in reverse ways. Why then do white middle-class people often prefer to socialize, work with, and otherwise commingle with middle-class black people more than with poor white people?[90] Why don't middle-class black people threaten the white middle class as white trash do?

The answer might seem to be that class status, not race, ultimately is what really matters to middle-class white people, but I think comparing white trash and the black middle class demonstrates instead the different ways that class and race function in relation to each other. In the case of white trash, class makes race (whiteness in particular) unstable and slippery. Class differences within the group of white people fracture whiteness at the same time that they are used by the middle class to protect their whiteness. The fracturing of whiteness makes the supposedly firm differences between white and black people potentially unstable as well, resulting in the possible loss of whiteness. This fracturing and instability is the slipperiness of abjection, which establishes boundaries between self and other that always leak, bleed, and threaten to collapse. In contrast, the relationship of the white and black middle class is more like one of objectification. The division between subject and object that it creates tends to reassure the (white) subject of its identity, rather than trouble it. In this case, race (whiteness in particular) is not destabilized by class, which means both that whiteness is not fractured by class similarities between blacks and whites and that perceived racial differences between blacks and whites are not eliminated by their class similarities. With regard to the black middle class, we could say that class similarities with the white middle class rely on or assume firm racial differences in order to operate. The assumed firmness of racial differ-ence is why class similarities with the black middle class generally are not threatening to middle-class white people. Class similarities generally allow middle-class white people to be comfortable interacting with black middle-class people without risking a loss of their whiteness.[91]

Beyond not threatening whiteness, the black middle class some-times is even perceived by good white people as moral validation of the (white privileged) liberal world in which they live. White trash do not and cannot provide such validation. This is illustrated by the experience of Kirby Moss, who is African American. Moss recounts a conversation with a white middle-class woman in his anthropological study in which the woman was criticizing white people on the other side of town for being "kind of trashy." When Moss followed up on her comment, the woman replied that she never really thought much about class differenc-es, but instead she hung out with "people who are doing things and are pretty successful. People like *you!*"[92] As Moss explains, at that moment he realized that he had become "the pivotal go-between representation" for this woman and many other white middle-class participants, revealing "the way [his class/education] privilege coupled with his Blackness served the unintended purpose of empowering the very middle-class Whites [he] met." As Moss continued to reflect on the interview, he saw that

> in their contact with me, [the white middle-class participants] in a way expanded their own representation of themselves (in particular, self-described liberals or radicals like Carol [another white woman in the study]) as being open and accepting. They (the dominant culture) were the ideal and I was the product of their ideals, a product, in their eyes, of the meta-ideology of productivity and success in the rhetori-cal land of opportunity. . . . In this situation, my Blackness made privileged Whites more complete, and privilege was not really a commodity for me because they already possessed it.[93]

Good white liberals tend to use the fact of a black middle class (some-times unconsciously, but other times explicitly and consciously) to affirm their belief that the basic structure of liberal society is just and fair. In contrast to the black middle class, however, the existence of white trash threatens both white liberal ideals of opportunity and white liberal assumptions of openness to and acceptance of people who are different than oneself. White trash are not able to perform the same reassuring roles for white liberals as the black middle class, and so white liberals can tend to be more comfortable around black middle-class people than they are around white trash.

⌒

The public sphere in the United States and other white-dominated countries would look much different than it does today if hierarchical class divisions between white people were dismantled or even just reduced. It would look different both in terms of who is included as a rightful member of that sphere and in terms of what topics and issues are seen as important problems for the public to consider. In particular, if abjected white people could participate meaningfully in public conversations and other creative activities that shape the public sphere with regard to race, racism, and white domination, those conversations and activities likely would unfold in different ways than they tend to do today. I think the participation and inclusion of abjected white people is important to racial justice movements, and so I want to explore here some of the implications of that inclusion. I will call it a form of radical inclusion since it aims to include white trash, white racists, white supremacists, and other white people who typically have been cast as unwanted in conversations about racial justice and as incapable of shaping a society's views on race and white racism in helpful ways. It's also a radical form of inclusion in that it does not restrict control of the terms of participation to the white middle class.[94] Such tightly controlled "inclusion" turns out to be another form of exclusion in disguise. In my view, racial justice can be achieved only if every group that is party to racial oppression is allowed to be involved in its elimination, and thus inclusion in the name of racial progress should not rely on other forms of exclusion, such as those based on class (and other exclusionary divisions, such as gender, sexuality, (dis)ability, and religious affiliation). This means that even the white people with whom good white liberals often don't wish to talk must not only have a seat at the table, but also help decide if sitting, standing, stomping, or spitting is the best way to proceed. They cannot be written off in advance as too stupid, racist, or violent to participate meaningfully in the public sphere. As Goad colorfully puts the point, "If you're going to argue that rednecks simply don't have the " 'right stuff'—that they breed violence, stupidity, and other undesirable character traits—you're wandering into a eugenical argument and undermining any pretense toward liberalism or egalitarianism. If you embrace equality, sooner or later you'll be forced to hug white trash, and don't blame me if you can't handle the smell."[95]

I find it helpful to think of white trash, white racists, and white supremacists as part of a white-dominated society's political unconscious. Following Noëlle McAfee's development of the concept, the political unconscious is not a thing or a location. It instead is the effect of a social process involving power relations in which people are disenfranchised and the harm of this disenfranchisement is not dealt with. The disenfranchised become speechless in that very few people will listen respectfully to what they have to say. The political unconscious is what results when elements unwanted by a society—ideas, movements, even people . . . perhaps especially people—are driven out of the center of the public sphere into the margins. Like an individual's unconscious, the political unconscious lies on the edge of consciousness, but it is not a lack or absence. Excluded from the consciously, publicly endorsed aspects of a society, the political unconscious is "a realm teeming with discontent."[96] Like an individual's unconscious, the political unconscious may be marginalized and it may be speechless through legitimate channels, but it nonetheless has significant and real effects on the "center" of the individual or society, as the case may be. The language of center and margin has to be used carefully here, of course. While a functional distinction between those who are at a society's center and those who lie at its margins can help clarify power relations in a society, that distinction is never absolute. As McAfee claims of the political unconscious, "This other, this foreign territory, is never entirely other."[97] It is abject, and the abject who lie at society's margins in its teeming political unconscious often have very real and significant effects on that society's center. Those effects tend to be destructively violent since legitimate channels for sublimated communication and creativity have been denied to the marginalized.

One of the main ways in which the political unconscious is created is by making the strict use of reason a necessary criterion for admission into the public sphere. This criterion comes from a liberal conception of the political realm, which assumes that political and other differences are, or should be, decided by the better force of rational arguments. Liberal theory is pluralistic in that it seeks to find common ground between people who do not agree with each other. But its pluralism only goes so far: it only includes those who agree with liberal procedures of using appeals to reason—and not, say, religious faith—to solve disagreements. Those who do not consent to these ground rules for deliberation tend to be considered irrational and often are excluded from the public sphere. But what liberal theory fails to reckon with is that the ground rules themselves often are what are most heatedly contested in political debates.

As McAfee explains, "It is counterproductive to say that the differences between liberals and nonliberals—about whether God belongs in politics; whether people of various ethnicities or genders have any dignity; whether violence should be used to solve problems; whether 'the other' should be tolerated or annihilated—are outside the realm of politics or that politics has no means to deal with them."[98] To say that these types of questions are off the deliberative table is to beg the hard questions and reserve political deliberation for the easy ones, effectively leaving force as the only way to handle the difficult ones. In the name of giving public voice to all people, understood as autonomous individuals subject only to their own rational will, liberalism relegates many of them to the mute, "irrational" realm of the political unconscious.

Liberal analysis of this problem leads to a dead end—and we should hear "dead" fairly literally here since "even the best liberalism has force pick up where reason leaves off."[99] We need another approach. As McAfee asks while grappling with the false inclusiveness of liberalism, "How [can] a political theory . . . make sense of the growing global schism between those of radically different worldviews[?] Is it possible for people with few, if any areas of agreement on fundamental questions to find a way to live together peacefully? Can political solutions be found when what counts as properly political is itself in question?"[100] McAfee's answer is to develop a broader notion of political theory that allows for the "unreasonable" processes that are at work in the formation of a public and its problems. This is a radical form of inclusion that aims at including the entire public in political deliberation—that is, *all* people who are affected by the same problem, even if they have radically different ideas about how to solve it, or indeed, radically different views of what the problem itself is. This also is genuine democracy: it takes the hard road of attempting to include everyone, even the "irrational." As McAfee explains, "A true democracy begins early and deep, in the ability of *all* members of the polity to feel themselves members of a common public space who have a hand in shaping the contours of that space. . . . Where oppressive societies alienate members from membership in a common world with others, a democratic society should be able to create pathways for citizens to talk with each other, coordinate their aspirations, and help fashion and shape the public world."[101]

I want to pursue this hard road by means of the specific example of white supremacists, who tend to be pushed to the margins and thus into the political unconscious of today's post–Jim Crow society in the United States. This may sound like a strange way of describing white supremacists, who themselves marginalize people of color—more point-edly, they ridicule, exclude, threaten, violently attack, and even some-times kill them. In that sense, white supremacists seem like part of America's racist center that is creating a racist political unconscious by silencing nonwhite people, not part of the marginalized political unconscious itself. It would appear that, regarding race, a true democ-racy should be focused only on the full political inclusion of people of color and not concern itself with white supremacists. As James Baldwin has claimed, it is completely unacceptable that black Americans should have no meaningful voice in the political affairs of the United States.[102] They must be included in a democratic America, and this means it is completely unacceptable that that white supremacists should attempt to silence them and other nonwhite people.

Baldwin is absolutely right, and I want to be entirely clear on this point given my argument concerning radical inclusion. The description of America as having a racist center also is entirely correct. But it's not completely accurate nowadays to say that white supremacists are positioned at that center. They used to be, one hundred, sixty, perhaps even forty years ago. But today white domination in the United States and many other Western countries operates by means of covert white privilege, rather than overt white supremacy.[103] While white supremacy has not disappeared, white racism generally is no longer a political or personal position that white people can openly endorse in a liberal democratic society. Most white people, and certainly most middle-class good white people, consciously and publicly condemn racism and pres-ent themselves as accepting people of all different races—albeit often by means of color blindness, or supposedly not seeing a person's race at all. This frequently includes condemning other white people, such as white supremacists and white trash, for their racist actions and beliefs. In the name of expanding democracy to include people of color—as it well should—American society often attempts to render white supremacists and white trash speechless and minimize their participation in the pub-lic, shared sculpting of the world based on their particular desires and concerns. Even if enacted with good intentions, however, this exclusion is problematic. White supremacists generally do not agree with nonracist ground rules for democratic deliberation and so they tend to be barred from it. They have Web sites and occasionally appear on daytime talk shows that seek to exploit their extremism, but when they speak, they rarely are greeted with respectful listening (which, I note, is not neces-sarily the same thing as agreement). "One suffers as much from not being heard as from not being able to speak," as McAfee explains, and white supremacists can be said to suffer in that their desires and worldviews tend not to be taken seriously by contemporary mainstream society.[104]

I find it very difficult to write the word *suffer* as I describe white supremacists, especially given the suffering that people of color have endured at white supremacists' hands. But here is the hard road that I think white allies need to walk: it is counterproductive to racial justice movements to say that differences between white allies and white supremacists, such as disagreements over whether white people are superior to nonwhite people or whether people of color should be respected as full persons, are outside the realm of political deliberation. This doesn't mean that white supremacists should have a prominent place in mainstream politics. But anti-racist liberals cannot decide by fiat that they are excluded—at least not if we are going to live in a true democracy that tries not to dehumanize some of its members by driving them underground into speechless and violent discontent. For people concerned about racial justice to unilaterally exclude white supremacists—and I'm thinking here of middle-class white people in particular—is for them to reenact the dehumanizing and destructive marginalization that white supremacists inflict upon people of color. It is to engage in a repetition compulsion that suggests our society has only scarcely begun to deal with its traumatic history of racism and white domination. That history is not past, and one of its current manifestations is white middle-class abjection of white supremacists and other white people. While people of color also sometimes treat white supremacists as abject, white middle-class liberals tend to be the primary agents of white abjection because it allows them to deflect their responsibility for white racism.

How might we, white and nonwhite people alike, cope better with a racist history that is still very much present? One answer is that we need to work through our collective past/present through a form of public dialogue that can "serve a psychoanalytic function for the public sphere."[105] Nations and other social entities cannot be simply equated with the individual, of course, since each has a different kind of unconscious. But there is a connection between how the individual unconscious and a national/cultural unconscious emerges, which psychoanalysis can help explain. "The connection is that traumas that beset individuals—and their affective consequences—show up in the public sphere . . . and circulate there, creating a ripple effect upon others."[106] Psychoanalysis can provide a model for how to deal with debilitating public symptoms produced by the ripple effect of trauma. Freud's talking cure is not only effective for individuals suffering from repetition compulsion, repression, projection, and other neuroses. It also can be effective for a public that suffers in similar ways because it has alienated significant portions of itself.

But is psychoanalysis's emphasis on talking just another manifestation of liberal class privilege? If the bourgeoisie is, as Donoso Cortés has called it, "a discussing class" who uses conversation to defuse social conflict and avoid political action, then even a radically inclusive form of public talk would seem merely to reinforce class distinctions and privileges rather than challenge them.[107] The answer to this question is that while literal conversation, deliberation, and negotiation are an important part of what is needed to address the harmful effects of a society's political unconscious, participation in the creative "dialogue" of the public sphere can and does take many other forms. It involves music, art, dance, theater, architecture, and many other ways (including "street" forms) of fashioning through creative sublimation what a society thinks, believes, and hopes when it comes to racial (and other) matters. The radical inclusion of those who have been cast into the political unconscious involves the movement from speechless to participation, not merely to speech or conversation.[108] Moreover, history has shown that conversation should not be reductively dismissed as a bourgeois phenomenon. In the form of negotiation, meaningful conversation between white and black people about humiliating racial storefront signs in 1960s Birmingham, for example, was the goal of Martin Luther King's nonviolent direct action.[109] Forcing white people to the table to talk with people of color used social tension to bring about political changes in Birmingham that would better enable its black citizens to help shape and fashion the city.

The role of affect and emotion is important in the conversations and creations of the public sphere. This is a point that is misunderstood by both emotivist and rational proceduralist understandings of what takes place when deliberating, especially when people have conflicting moral or political views. Emotivists hold that moral values are personal and arbitrary and thus that no reasons can be given to persuade another to change her mind—hence, the loudest shouter or emoter is the one who wins an argument. In contrast, rational proceduralists believe that reasons can be given and be effective and thus that the force of the better argument will settle who wins it. For all their differences, however, emotivists and rational proceduralists are alike in misunderstanding or too narrowly construing the role that affect plays in interpersonal interaction. As McAfee explains, people are "*affectively* capable of and interested in finding ways to understand each other."[110] Emotions don't necessarily seal us off from other people, nor are they out of place in rational deliberation.

Public deliberation only sometimes or partially is about argumenta-tion and the give-and-take of reasons, as Democratic strategist Donna Brazile's account of "green room conversions" illustrates.[111] Green room conversions sometimes occur when people on the talk show circuit, who typically would never talk to each other because of their political, reli-gious, or other differences, are thrown together and begin to chat in television studio waiting ("green") rooms. When those conversations become conversions, they lead people to change their minds about the other people they're talking with, rather than change their mind about the issue at hand. That might seem like a failure of deliberation, but in fact it's a remarkable success. This is because the goal of public delibera-tion isn't necessarily for everyone to come out of the process holding the same views. It is to provide ways "for people with few, if any areas of agreement on fundamental questions to find a way to live together peace-fully."[112] And living together peacefully with people who don't agree with you about fundamental questions means learning to relate to and respect them as full persons, not sub-persons.[113] Hearing—really hearing—how other people "came to have the views they have and what their experi-ences are that shaped their sense of the world" can be extremely powerful because it can help participants in deliberation "change their views of others' views."[114] Not necessarily their own views, which might still con-flict with the views of others. But as a result of conversation/conversion, other people and their different views no longer can be easily written off as crazy or evil, the two most common rhetorical strategies for dis-missing someone as beyond the democratic pale.[115] By "enlarg[ing] their understanding of problems and begin[ning] to appreciate the complexity of how issues affect other members of the community," participants in deliberation can begin to see the implications of their own views in a different light.[116] Seeing others not as incomprehensible enemies, but as full persons also impacted by the problem at hand makes it possible for people to "work through, in the Freudian sense, what they might be willing to give up in order to make progress in light of the broader public knowledge they have gained."[117]

A transformed public sphere that didn't abject certain classes of white people would be a sphere in which white trash, white racists, and white supremacists were included—really included—in public delibera-tions about the direction of the country and the role that race plays in it. This inclusion would mean talking *with* and listening to white supremacists, for example, to learn how they came to view white people as superior to people of other races and how their experiences have shaped the their sense of the world. It would mean eschewing one-way discussions in which well-intentioned anti-racists talk *to* poor whites and white supremacists in order to educate them about people of color and racial justice.[118] It would mean, in other words, respecting white trash and white supremacists as full persons, and not dismissing them as evil or crazy, even though one might strongly disagree with many of their views. Because this process of conversation/conversion would reckon with, rather than repress competing values, it would make room for openly acknowledging, accepting, and even mourning what was lost or sacrificed. This would mean that what was given up in the deliberative process—which could not be safely determined in advance of the process itself—would not be pushed aside to become part of a political unconscious that teems, seethes, and later violently erupts.

Respecting white trash and especially white supremacists as full persons, particularly in political conversations that include race, might sound like an outlandish proposal, but African American musician Daryl Davis has done this very thing. He provides a powerful example of the kind of interaction with white supremacists that white allies can and need to pursue. In the 1990s, Davis set out to discover why people who do not know him hate him because of the color of his skin. He arranged and conducted conversations with numerous Ku Klux Klan leaders in their own homes, taking on all the difficult points of disagreement between them: Black pride, white pride, Martin Luther King, the Holocaust, Klan violence, interracial marriage and procreation, and more. With some of the Klan leaders, Davis found occasional common ground, concerning, for example, safe schools and the protection of children. With others, the conversations were much more tense and oppositional, with few, if any points of agreement. Often Davis had to work hard to stay emotionally strong and not lash out verbally at his interlocutor. Once or twice, he did lose his temper and had to re-steer an overly inflamed conversation. But throughout his many meetings, Davis respected the Klansmen by listening to their views and trying to understand why they held them, while also offering his own views in cases where some trust had emerged through their conversations. As Davis explains, "I remained honest with each and every Klanmember I met, and, most importantly, I remained honest with myself. I did not pretend to be anything other than what I am, and though I allowed each Klanmember to know where I stood, I never forced my beliefs on anyone. Over a period of time, this, I believe, became the basis for their trust and respect for me."[119] Not all of the Klanmembers whom Davis talked with came to trust and respect him, but some, such as Grand

Wizard Roger Kelly, developed a close enough relationship with Davis to make him the godfather of Kelly's baby daughter.

The response to Davis's book recounting his experiences with the Klan is interesting and relevant here. The official reviews were terrible. As Kirkus Reviews scathingly charged, "Davis gets taken for a ride by the KKK in this futile and pointless volume."[120] The reviewer goes on to complain that Davis is oblivious to the possibility that he is being used by the Klan and that his book might be the perfect vehicle for Klan recruitment since it makes the Klan look "not all that bad" if its members are willing to talk to a black man. The informal reviews provided by amazon.com contributors were remarkably different, however. All of them (twelve at last count in 2012) praised Davis, for example, for allowing "'the enemy'" to maintain his dignity and for treating Klan members as human beings and shedding light on their concerns. The informal reviewers lauded Davis for his courage and saw his conversations with the Klan as providing "hope for a better world."[121]

While the concerns of the Kirkus reviewer are understandable, I think the informal contributors better comprehend Davis's project. As one of the informal contributors put it, "the Kirkus reviewer seems to have overlooked the book's most endearing quality: bringing to light that a true and lasting solution to the race problem in the United States is neither political nor legislative, but spiritual. Mr. Davis is intuitively aware of this truth, and it shows in his approach to tackling the problem head on."[122] Since Davis's book does not focus on religion, I take "spiritual" here to mean a concern for the psychosomatic and (inter)personal, similar to my own use of the term. Davis understood that deliberative conversation with someone involves the whole person, including her fears, desires, anger, joy, and other emotions. Being affectively present with and open to another person can allow for moments of understanding that standard politics and legislation do not, and this spiritual phenomenon can occur even between people that disagree about the basic ground rules of deliberation. As Davis attests, "Though the idea of being friends with a person whose belief system you despise sounds like an impossibility, I believe I have demonstrated that it is indeed, very possible for two diametrically opposed human beings to learn and accept enough about each other to co-exist without strife."[123] Davis refers to friendship rather than citizenship, but I think his conversations/conversions with the Klan are exactly the sort of public talk that white allies need to pursue. While it might sound paradoxical, experiences with white supremacists like Davis's have the potential to shrink the United States' racist political unconscious by reducing the alienating silencing of white supremacist groups. By including Klan members as people whose voices count in the makeup of the world—which, again, is not the same thing as saying that white supremacy should carry the day—white allies can help reduce the destructive force of the United States' political unconscious and, indeed, the destructive force of the Klan itself.

The feedback from informal reviewers of Davis's book points to another important aspect of Davis's work, which is the positive effect that his book had on many of its readers. While Davis's friendship with Grand Wizard Roger Kelly certainly is striking, it is not the only, and perhaps not even the most important result of his efforts to talk with Klan members. After all, it's nothing new for white racists, even white supremacists, to talk civilly and be friends with individual black people. Interracial friendship is not a panacea for white racism, nor should it be the goal of racial justice movements. White racists will always admit that there are a few acceptable black individuals, but those black people are considered the exception to the rule. But even if Davis were merely an exceptional black person to Kelly, the publication and circulation of Davis's book offers a valuable working-through of a political unconscious composed of white supremacists. The book itself is a product of creative sublimation in which white supremacists participated in the public sphere through Davis's respectful listening to and talking with them. The outcome was not just a friendship between Davis and Kelly (problematic or not), but a group of readers who saw that the seemingly impossible was indeed possible. If a black person fighting for racial justice and a white supremacist Klan member can have a meaningful conversation/conversion in which each maintains his dignity, then there is hope for a better world.[124]

Radical inclusion does not mean, however, that everyone has to talk to everyone else or, more to the point, that people of color have to attempt to have transformative conversations with white supremacists as Davis did. For many people of color, it could be too personally and spiritually toxic to engage with someone who openly disparages and endorses violence against nonwhite people. But if racial justice movements aren't going to reenact the very types of exclusion against which they struggle, *someone* needs to talk with white supremacists. In many and perhaps even most cases, that "someone" can and should be another white person. Here is an important role for white allies in particular to play in struggles against racism. As activist Sheila Wilmot argues, "Part of taking responsibility [for white supremacy and racism] is for whites to talk with other whites so people of colour don't have to do all that work."[125] White allies generally don't risk being harmed as severely as people of color by attempting to engage in respectful conversations with white supremacists. I say "generally" since the particulars of each situation must be taken into account. Gender, for example, surely can make a difference in terms of how and whether respectful conversations can take place between white people, and given white supremacist views of gender roles, it might be much more effective for a (feminist) white man than a white woman to talk with a male white supremacist. But the broader point still stands: it's crucial that white allies undertake this task as part of their support for racial justice.

What I have in mind here mirrors what bell hooks has claimed about the importance of men as "comrades" or allies in feminist movements.[126] Sometimes there are social situations or occasions where a man can have a more positive effect exposing and transforming men's sexism than a woman can. All-male or male-dominated spaces, such as the fraternity house or the philosophy classroom, are ready examples. Likewise, the many all-white spaces that still exist—in classrooms, neighborhoods, cocktail parties, and elsewhere—are examples of where white allies are needed to respond to the racist joke, the subtle (or sometimes not so subtle) slur made against people of color, and so on. Mike Hill's experience at the American Renaissance conference would be another example except that he couldn't respond to the racist remarks he heard without revealing himself as a spy. Nonetheless, *The Journal of Blacks in Higher Education* needed a white person in particular to successfully infiltrate the conference and produce its exposé.

hooks does not elaborate on how men should respond to sexism when they see or hear it, but I would argue that to be effective, the response probably won't take the form of a direct challenge to the person who made the sexist comment. Direct confrontations all too often make the other person defense and thus are ineffective in bringing about feminist change. They tend instead to serve the purpose of self-righteously establishing oneself as one of the "good guys" who is opposed to sexist oppression.

Likewise, a response to a racist remark or situation that truly seeks personal transformation probably needs to involve a genuine conversation, rather than a direct or public attack. As I have seen in the college classroom when observing new white instructors, for them to publicly chastise white students when the students inadvertently make racist comments often closes down conversation and creates hostility and resentment on the part of many students who feel as if only "politically correct" comments are permissible. In a similar fashion, some white people who feel that they "get it" unfortunately want to preach to others about how to end white domination. As one white graduate student in an educational theory class zealously expressed the view, "Many of us may feel we have the answers [to white racism]; now it is our turn as disciples to go spread the word."[127] In contrast, responses to racism tend to be more effective when they include judgment about when it's "time to share information [about race and racism] and a way to share it so that it doesn't come off as preaching or blaming."[128] Chip Berlet, a white ally working to deal with Klan and neo-Nazi gangs in his working-class neighborhood, sums up the point well: "If I'm going to start with my [white conservative] neighbors on the block, I can't just tell everybody who disagrees with me [about race] to go get fucked. It ain't a strategy, folks; it's not going to work."[129]

In the neighborhood block meetings that Berlet helped set up, the goal was not to shame white neighbors for their racism. Rather it was to

> have these meetings with our neighbors, listen to what they have to say, and then tell them what we thought. We didn't tell them how much we disliked what they said, and we didn't say that we're here to discuss racist segregation. They would have just gone out the door. . . . How are you gonna move them if that happens? Suddenly the whole vocabulary that you used to use to deal with white racism changes.[130]

Progressives sometimes called Berlet called a "sellout" because he didn't confront his neighbors' racism in seemingly forceful enough ways. But after ten years of hard work, he and his partners successfully ended the firebombing, riots, and other forms of violence that were intended to discourage black people from moving into the neighborhood. They succeeded by generating an alternate discourse that opposed violence without overtly mentioning race but that also targeted young white men since they were the ones carrying out the violence.[131]

Berlet's case offers an example of a white ally's doing something similar to what Daryl Davis did: talking respectfully with people who harbor racist views. Berlet's situation admittedly is not as striking as Davis's since he did not sit down face-to-face with Klan and neo-Nazi gang members. And in the spirit of radical inclusion, we might ask: Why not? Perhaps he attempted to do so but for some reason failed; he does not say. Maybe Berlet's efforts would have paid off more quickly if the gang members had been included in the neighborhood's public talk. In any case, Berlet's white neighbors were adamant that did not want black people moving into their neighborhood. Rather than condescendingly lecture them on the error of their racist assumptions about the effects of integration, however, Berlet found a way to respectfully engage them in coalition-building conversation. Did those conversations end all racism in the neighborhood? No, but they did end the racial violence, "and that has made other things possible."[132]

I've focused on radical inclusion in the public sphere, but let me close this chapter with a few words about radical inclusion in the academic fields of critical philosophy of race and critical race theory as well. Just as in the public sphere, academic discussions of race would look different than they do today if hierarchical class divisions between white people were dismantled. They would look different both in terms of who is included in the discussion: not just middle-class people, but also working-class white people, white trash, and even white supremacists. (If you doubt that an academic can be a white supremacist, recall Mike Hill's experience at the American Renaissance conference.) Critical philosophy of race and critical race theory also would look different in terms of what topics and issues were seen as important problems for critical race scholars to consider. As education scholar John Preston has claimed, "The contribution of working class whites to a critical theory of race . . . [would be] substantively different from that of middle class whites," and surely that of white supremacists would be substantively different as well.[133]

Preston offers as a provocation to critical race theory a form of whiteness critique that he calls "trash crit."[134] Trash crit would challenge the centering of middle-class experiences in whiteness critique by paying more attention to the specific and different contexts in which whiteness functions. This would allow a more effective criticism of whiteness and white domination from its boundaries while simultaneously challenging sharp divisions between "majoritarian" and "counter" stories. Trash crit would challenge essentialized racial identities insisting that intersections between race, class, gender, and other salient axes of identity be examined. Above all, trash crit would downplay the importance of guilt in white people's contributions to racial justice movements since white guilt is a form of cultural capital not readily available to lower-class white people. Trash crit would demonstrate that white guilt serves more to subordinate poor white people than it to eliminate the oppression of people of color. (I'll say more about guilt, class, and race in chapter 4.) Trash crit isn't guaranteed to produce criticisms of whiteness that would further racial justice movements, of course, but neither is "regular" critical race theory or critical philosophy of race. At minimum, trash crit would provide a needed alternative to the academic status quo, in which "the voices of the white working class are not heard, are assumed to be racist, or are patronized and appropriated by the academic middle classes."[135]

Another helpful example of how working-class or "redneck" contributions to critical philosophy of race and critical race theory would improve them is provided by Ladelle McWhorter's insightful analysis of line dancing.[136] More specifically, McWhorter's example concerns Southern rednecks and the need that racial justice movements have for white people's self-love. A self-identified redneck living in Virginia, McWhorter describes the psychosomatic discipline demanded by line dancing that produced for her an experience of power, freedom, and pleasure unlike any other. This was a freedom made possible by intense discipline and thus it is poorly understood in terms of traditional oppositions between free will and determinism. As McWhorter felt the dance flow through her, she experienced "sheer joy" that comes from "the expanse of possibility."[137] Her dancing was an experience of self-affirmation that came through an embrace of her redneck heritage.

Despite her joy, however, McWhorter was troubled about the whiteness of line dancing—not so much the history of country music or country dancing, which isn't exclusively white, but the embodied experience of being a white redneck when pulling on her boots to go dance. After noting the associations of redneck with stupidity, degeneracy, and a love of cruelty including racist violence, McWhorter explains, "When I put on those boots, I put on that history and those social significations as well. And when the boots felt good and sexy and right around my feet, I was scared by the possibility that those characterizations were somehow fitting too."[138] McWhorter realizes that she cannot just distance herself from the ugly side of redneck culture, even if much of that ugliness is a fabrication of middle-class abjection. And so she wrestles with how to participate in one aspect of redneck culture without seeming to condone all of it. She realizes that she could stop dancing and "act as if [she] didn't *come from there*," the rural South that doesn't "fit the mold of the well-educated, sophisticated, enlightened and unprejudiced college professor."[139] But in the end, she chooses "to keep dancing, keep working on the discipline and expanding myself into the freeing spaces that dancing gives to me."[140]

In my view, when McWhorter chose to keep dancing, she chose to love herself. In that context, it's not quite right to say that she could stop dancing. McWhorter couldn't stop dancing without damaging herself through a form of self-denial or self-loathing. We could say that her choice to keep dancing, to embrace her boot-wearing Southern self, was important for her spiritual well-being. But it was not only beneficial to her. I think it also positively affected the impact she could make in critical philosophy of race by participating in the field as a Southern redneck ally. Line dancing and academia are not unrelated, as McWhorter's delightfully ambiguous use of "discipline" above suggests. Working on one discipline— the one required to learn more complicated dance moves—increases the spiritual, psychosomatic capacity she needs to work effectively on the other—the white-dominated discipline of philosophy. Dancing helps McWhorter to create freeing spaces within academia (and elsewhere) for her to think critically about white domination and to challenge the way that "rednecks bear the stigma of whiteness, the ugly part of white-ness, so that middle class people with college degrees don't have to."[141]

What then, finally, about the role of white supremacists in criti-cal philosophy of race and critical race theory? Genuine inclusion of rednecks and white working-class people is one thing, but the inclusion of white supremacists might seem to be a very different and much more dangerous matter. What should be done with them?[142] I think a multifac-eted response to this question is needed. To begin, I would challenge an assumption that can lurk in the question that a sharp line exists between "them" (the dangerous whites) and "us" (the safe, trustworthy ones). As I have argued, white supremacists and well-intentioned white people are not as dissimilar as this question might presume. The question can smack of a paternalistic confidence that "we" good white people fully understand what next steps are needed in critical philosophy of race and racial justice movements more generally.

Challenging the question need not be the same thing as sidestep-ping it, however, especially if the "with" in the question is appropriately emphasized. In its most valid form, the question would not be the uni-lateral "What should 'we' do *about* 'them?'" but the reciprocal "What are we—all of us—going to do together, *with* each other, as we con-front issues of race and racism?" And here the really hard work begins. There might need to be clear and strong conditions for public dialogue and debate, and/but those conditions would need to be developed by everyone, not just the good people who aren't white supremacists. In other words, issues of inclusion and exclusion don't emerge merely in the context of debating issues of race and racism. They emerge at the earlier stage of establishing ground rules for the conversation itself. This admittedly will slow down the process, seemingly making it difficult to get to the "real" conversation. But in fact, the real conversation already begins at the point of establishing rules for debate because doing so requires listening and dialogue across salient differences.

Given that requirement, perhaps we could say that something like mutual willingness to engage one another is a necessary condition for participating in public dialogue.[143] In that case, someone who came to the table wanting only to lecture or berate the other "side" wouldn't satisfy the conditions for inclusion. This ground rule seems very reasonable, and I'm hard-pressed to come up with a better or more basic criterion for productive dialogue. And yet—or perhaps precisely because it's so sensible?—I remain somewhat wary about mandating this or any other kind of fundamental condition for inclusion. I suspect that such conditions tend to operate as a cover for liberal rationality, so "reasonable" and seemingly "neutral" that no sane person could disagree with them. Merely questioning the condition of willingness to engage in this case would mark a person as unreasonable and disqualify him or her from the conversation.

White supremacists who only wanted to rail against black people or Jews or whomever would fail to satisfy the necessary condition of willingness to engage. That's easy to recognize, and I think it's the typical situation in which conditions for inclusion tend to be invoked: to justify exclusion of a particular group of people already deemed inappropriate and unwanted (by whom?) in the conversation. What often is overlooked is that white liberals who only wanted to castigate white supremacists similarly would fail to satisfy the condition. What is most problematic, however, is that in some contexts insisting on the willingness to engage can discriminate against historically oppressed groups. For example, this insistence can camouflage imperialist demands that subordinate groups always be cooperative and available to educate well-intended dominant groups about their subordination.[144] As María Lugones and Elizabeth Spelman have argued, white people who wish to join forces with people of color to fight white racism will need to get used to *not* being engaged much of the time: to being ignored and sitting on the sidelines as the focus shifts to the interests, lives, and ideas of people of color.[145] People of color sometimes might not be willing to engage white people, and their refusal should not disqualify them from participation in public conversations about race and racism.

Necessary conditions for public dialogue tend to be too abstract and high-level to handle well the messy complexities of real life situations. They bring a blunt hammer to a task that needs delicate tools instead. They tend not to be sufficiently context-sensitive to respond adequately, in this case, to people of color who resist engaging good white liberals (as well as bad white supremacists) out of a need to challenge the insatiable white desire for mastery and knowledge.[146] In addition to this problem, I worry that a necessary condition of inclusion based on mutual willingness to engage smuggles in liberal, middle-class assumptions of what counts as proper engagement. Could shouting, stomping, or spitting be considered legitimate ways of engaging others, for example, or would such actions be judged as unreasonable and as disrespectfully shutting down communication? Taken together, these concerns strongly suggest that insisting on a willingness to engage could interfere with, rather than support genuinely inclusionary public dialogue about race and white racism.

The messy challenge of how to radically include all members of a society in conversations about white domination remains pressing. I do not wish to be Pollyannaish about the difficulty of this challenge, nor am I terribly sanguine about the prospects of meeting it. What is clear, however, is that white-dominated societies should not try to evade it by unilaterally and universally excluding white supremacists from their public spaces. By trying to simplify the problem in this way, the problem ultimately is only exacerbated. It's true that white supremacists, as well as white trash, sometimes and perhaps often think, say, and do viciously racist things. But so do good middle-class white people, and that is the point. There are no saints to be found here. White liberals are just better at pretending that there are. This means that critical philosophy of race and critical race theory should not be about making overt white racists or poor white people confront themselves with a truth about white domination that only good white people allegedly possess. This would be another lesson that trash crit would teach us. Middle-class white people are not the exclusive site of the truth about racial justice, and often they aren't much of a source of race-based truth at all. To assume that they possess the answers to questions about race and white domination and that they know in advance who can make helpful contributions to racial justice movements is to replicate problematic structures of exclusion central to white domination. Effective transformations to those exclusionary structures, both within academia and without, will require a radical inclusion that cuts across invidious class lines within whiteness.

Demonizing White Ancestors

Unconscious Histories and Racial Responsibilities

> To accept one's past—one's history—is not the same thing as drowning in it; it is learning how to use it.
>
> —James Baldwin, *The Fire Next Time*

> In the end, [white slaveholding] Southerners were asking, "What is history about? What is it for?" In what measure are human beings the children, grandchildren, and great-grandchildren of those who have gone before?
>
> —Elizabeth Fox-Genovese and Eugene Genovese,
> *The Mind of the Master Class*

History is replete with horrific accounts of things that white people have done to people of color. The most difficult for me to read are the stories in slave narratives of children being forever separated from their mothers as the children were sold as slaves. Harriet A. Jacobs's *Incidents in the Life of a Slave Girl* is full of such stories, and one of the most wrenching occurs when a mother's youngest child is sold to a slave trader. As Jacobs recounts,

> Could you have seen that mother clinging to her child, when they fastened the irons upon his wrists; could you have heard her heart-rending groans, and seen her bloodshot eyes wander wildly from face to face, vainly pleading for mercy; could you have witnessed that scene as I saw it, you would exclaim, *Slavery is damnable!*[1]

In another agonizing account, a white church leader approached a mother whose children recently had been sold. Weeping and groaning on the church floor, the woman begged that God would take her soon. As she sat down "quivering in every limb," Jacobs saw the white man "become crimson in the face with suppressed laughter, while he held up his handkerchief, that those who were weeping for the poor woman's calamity might not see his merriment."[2] Jacobs reveals that white people didn't just rip black families apart by buying and selling African Americans like livestock. They sometimes also took intense pleasure in it, finding the agony of black people to be a source of amusement.

Confronted with stories such as these, one cannot help but think: it's not just slavery that's damnable, but slaveholders too. How could anyone do such a thing? How could a person not only torture another person in the most excruciating way possible—physical torture and even death for enslaved mothers arguably would have been easier on them than losing their children to slave traders—but also thoroughly enjoy it? It seems incomprehensible and monstrous, even literally inhuman. It becomes difficult to understand slaveholders as regular human beings. Given the inhumanity of white history, white people today thus can find it difficult, and even refuse to relate themselves to white racists of the past. Distancing themselves from their white forebears can seem to be the only responsible way for contemporary white people to (not) deal with their racist history. It can seem to be the best way to demonstrate that they disapprove of slavery and that they are not racist like previous white generations.

The horrors of white history are painfully real, but I think that white people need a different way of reckoning with them than trying to pretend the past isn't relevant to the present. This is because, in William Faulkner's famous words, "the past is never dead. It's not even past."[3] Contemporary white people cannot separate themselves from their racial history, because that history is now. The racism and white domination found in the days of chattel slavery has changed, but it nonetheless lives in transformed ways in the practices, habits, and lives of white people today. While conspicuous and deliberate displays of white domination in the United States and other Western nations generally have disappeared in the last forty or so years, white racism against people of color continues to operate, and it does so in increasingly hidden, seemingly nonexistent ways.[4] Unconscious connections with earlier generations of white people are one important means by which those earlier generations are not dead. Even though they may be in the grave, the parents, grandparents, and great-grandparents of white people today can live on through their descendants.

We need to grapple with the ways in which the racial habits of white people today are the offshoot of those of white people from centuries ago. In particular, I want to reckon with racial habits associated with white slaveholding. To do this, I turn to some of the transgenerational unconscious connections between white people, focusing on white Southern slaveholders of the nineteenth century. I argue that in the best interests of racial justice movements, white slaveholders should not be dismissed as monstrously evil and thus of no relation to white people today. Contemporary white people only replicate the racist process of othering people who are different from them when they shun their white ancestors in this way. Affirming a relationship with white slaveholders, I show how objectionable messages from them concerning white supremacy can be retranslated into a valid concern about caring for white people across class lines. This care is important to racial justice movements because it helps disrupt the process of othering that supports white domination of people of color. Learning to reckon with and critically accept rather than quickly dismiss white people whom one finds objectionable is a way to live one's whiteness in a way that supports racial justice struggles.

∾

How might we make sense of Faulkner's point about the past specifically in the context of race, such that the habits, beliefs, and values of contemporary white people might be recognized as related to those of previous white slaveholding generations? How can we best understand the unconscious ways in which racial and racist messages are passed down from generation to generation? Jean Laplanche's psychoanalytic theory is a helpful starting point for answering these questions because it explicitly accounts for the development of the unconscious in a sociopolitical world. For Laplanche, human beings are not born with an unconscious; it is created through a process of seduction of children by the adult world.[5] "Seduction" here is intended in its original etymological sense of alteration, especially by leading someone away (or astray). Seduction occurs when adult caregivers send messages to children at least a portion of which the children cannot understand. Most of the time, adults don't realize they are sending these messages, and their messages tend to be sent via bodily gestures, actions, and comportment rather than verbal comments or lectures. The remnants of messages that are not understood become parts of a child's unconscious. For example, even if an adult remains measured and calm, her facial expression might become subtly tense when explaining to a two-year-old child that the child should not reach into the toilet to touch feces. (As any parent knows, babies and young children don't initially experience feces as disgusting. This reaction is something learned.) The child might understand the explicit verbal explanation that feces can carry germs that make people sick and so they shouldn't be touched, but the tension on her parent's face conveys an additional message about the repulsiveness of bodily waste (according to many, but not all cultures) that the child probably does not understand. The adult's discomfort suggests that there is something more interesting or troubling about feces to know, but this "something else" isn't explicitly addressed and thus remains consciously unknown, becoming part of the child's budding unconscious. In their everyday communication with children, adults thus transform their psyches, leading children away from the relatively straightforward experience of consciousness to the complicated development of unconscious desire, fantasy, and belief.

The example of feces resonates with Sigmund Freud's developmental account of sexuality (the anal stage in particular).[6] Laplanche instead gravitates toward breastfeeding to explain seduction: an infant developmentally cannot understand what the mother communicates to and wants from her child in the act of nursing, nor can the mother due to past repressions involving her own sexuality. (Given the eroticization of breasts in many cultures, breastfeeding is not necessarily or always a simple act of nourishment. Some women's sexual pleasure when breastfeeding a baby speaks to this point, as does many Western societies' discomfort with public breastfeeding.) But seduction is not limited to or isolated within the nuclear family. The example of breastfeeding could even be considered metaphorically. Its point is not that an infant must encounter a literal breast to develop an unconscious, but that the "outside" world is the source of (sexually charged) material for the beginnings of the unconscious.[7] The entire adult world, with all of its social, political, global, and other complexities, sends enigmatic messages to young children. These messages may be channeled through a mother and father in many cases, but seduction is not primarily an oedipal process. In fact, on Laplanche's own terms, the theory of seduction "take[s] psychoanalytic account of a plurality of cultural scripts from the very beginning of an infant's life . . . opening up a space for the mediation of psychoanalytical and socio-historical categories."[8] Those categories can and often do involve more than sexuality. While Laplanche never discusses race, he allows that "certain psychoanalytic parameters—all psychoanalytic parameters—may vary as a result of cultural differences."[9] In a white privileged world, those differences include race and racism, which regularly contribute to the enigmatic messages sent to children from the adult world.[10]

The degree and ways in which messages are enigmatic can change over time. Messages about white superiority, for example, probably always had an enigmatic aspect to them for very young children who developmentally did not understand racial hierarchies. The example of white men cutting off the genitals and other body parts of lynched black men to keep as souvenirs suggests that something more than the straightforward infliction of pain, punishment, and even death was at work in those situations.[11] But in the days of U.S. slavery and Jim Crow, most messages sent by white people about alleged white supremacy were hardly subtle and therefore fairly easy to translate. Compared with the twenty-first century, white Americans in the eighteenth, nineteenth, and first half of the twentieth century experienced relatively few anxieties when dominating nonwhite people. White slaveholders, for example, often comfortably discussed the sale and purchase of black slaves as if it were no different than the sale and purchase of farm equipment.[12] The relatively transparent message of white supremacy became more opaque after World War II, when shock at the Nazis' attempted genocide of Jews, Roma, and others was followed by the civil rights movement in the United States. Messages about white supremacy were and are still sent in today's post–civil right era, but they are increasingly enigmatic given most contemporary white people's reluctance to openly espouse or affirm racist beliefs.[13]

One of the central messages concerning race and white supremacy that has been transmitted from white slaveholders to white people today is the claim that those who were different from them were absolutely other. In this Manichean worldview, the other usually is cast as monstrous—as difficult to see as or relate to as a human being—and as such is absolutely evil. Black people were the other to white slaveholders: more like a thing than a person, and evil in their tendency to rape, steal, and flee their white owners. As Charles Mills explains, "The terms of the [slavery] contract require of the slave an ongoing self-negation of personhood, an acceptance of chattel status."[14] The othering of black people is part of the message of white supremacy, fairly transparent hundreds of years ago although contributing to the enigmatic white desire for black others that had to be repressed. Today this message operates in much more opaque, unconscious ways. Racist beliefs about black and other nonwhite people tend to function without using racial terms, almost as if they are nonexistent. They operate, for example, through immigration policies, housing segregation, judicial systems, and other "color blind" policies and institutions.[15] The ultimate message communicated, however, is still that black (and the category of nonwhite more generally) is bad, white is good, and the two are irremediably opposed.

While white slaveholders' relationship to their black slaves offers a striking example of othering, the process is not restricted to a black-white binary. Othering also has operated, for example, between Latinos and blacks in post–civil rights Texas, between blacks and Koreans in post–Rodney King California, and between whites and Arabs/Muslims in a post-9/11 world. And it occurs between groups of white people themselves, as chapter 1 demonstrated.[16] Without slighting the effects of othering on people of color, I want to focus here on white people's othering of white Southern slaveholders as incomprehensibly alien. This is because white Southern slaveholders might have something useful to teach white allies today, but only if we can approach them as human beings instead of as inhuman monsters.

Let me underscore that what we have to learn from white slaveholders is *not*, for example, that one race is superior to the other. Nor is it that some of the slaveholders' means (for example, of feeding and housing their slaves) were commendable even if their ultimate end of slavery was morally objectionable. These two claims defend white slaveholders, and the project of retranslation is not one of defense, even as it also refuses to demonize. If we are going to learn something useful from white slaveholders, we must reject the false dichotomy of either defending or demonizing them. Too often, these appear to be the only options for good white people to take: if one isn't castigating white slaveholders as inhuman monsters, then one must be minimizing and even excusing their horrific deeds—and so one had better castigate quickly and harshly. But this dichotomy does nothing to retranslate the messages sent by white slaveholders. It leaves their messages intact, either by uncritically accepting them, as in the two claims above, or by refusing to engage with white slaveholders, on the assumption that no retranslation of their messages is possible and thus that any engagement with them is tantamount to approval of white domination. Retranslation offers a third alternative that disrupts this dichotomy, a different way of relating to white slaveholders that can allow us to comprehend them as flawed human beings whose situations and experiences can teach contemporary people something important. As we will see, what that important thing ultimately turns out to be is that good white people also are flawed human beings, complicit with rather than hovering apart from white domination.

The othering of white Southern slaveholders began as early as the first half of the nineteenth century, when Northerners often addressed them as inferior idiots. As Virginian Albert Bledsoe complained on behalf of Southerners in 1860, Northern abolitionists

> have seldom condescended to argue the great question of Liberty and Slavery with us as with equals. On the contrary, they habitually address us as if nothing but purblind ignorance of the very first elements of moral science could shield our minds against the force of their irresistible arguments. In the overflowing exuberance of their philanthropy, they take pity of our most lamentable moral darkness, and graciously condescend to teach us the very A B C of ethical philosophy![17]

Not much has changed in this regard in the last 150-plus years, except that the attitude of Northern abolitionists toward the South has spread across the nation. To most contemporary white people—including many white Southerners—white slaveholders from the nineteenth century often seem like a class of people very different from themselves, not just historically separated from white people today but also morally and psychologically divorced from them.

But isn't it an objective fact that white Southern slaveholders were different than contemporary white people in at least one crucial way: they enslaved people, and we do not? Given this fact, any similarities between the two groups of white people would seem to be trivial in comparison. I will call this objection "playing the slaveholding card." In some respects, of course, the answer to the question is yes. Chattel slavery of the type practiced in the United States in the eighteenth and nineteenth centuries does not exist in twenty-first century America. In other respects, however, the answer is no since modern slavery still exists across the globe, including in the United States. Millions of people are still forced to work by physical and/or mental threats, owned or controlled by other people, physically constrained in their movements, and dehumanized by being bought and sold as property.[18] But let me stick primarily with the first answer, in part because it probably is true that most contemporary white people in the United States are not (directly) modern slaveholders. I also want to focus on that answer because it will allow me to better make my point about the problem of playing the slaveholding card. Even if, counterfactually, no forms of slavery existed today, the so-called objective fact of our differences from eighteenth and nineteenth-century Americans doesn't settle the question of contemporary white people's relationship to white slaveholders. The truth of those differences can operate in different ways, and in this context it is somewhat tautological. By definition, it is true that antebellum slavery doesn't exist in the United States today since we now live after the Civil War. What, then, does playing the slaveholding card achieve? Operating as a red herring, the slaveholding card not only ensures that we don't detect modern forms of slavery. It also tries to throw us off the trail of the relationship between contemporary white people and white slaveholders by establishing an insurmountable moral gap between "us" and "them." One of the effects of insisting on the relatively uncontroversial fact that eighteenth- and nineteenth-century white slaveholders participated in chattel slavery and white people today do not is the othering of white slaveholders. This in turn serves to reassure white people today that they are racially innocent in contrast.

There can be something very comforting to a contemporary white person concerned about racial justice in the characterization of white slaveholders as other. As in the case of white trash, if an unbridgeable gulf exists between white slaveholders and white people today, then as a white person I can be sure that I am not like them. If they are inexplicably evil, then I can understand myself as good. If they are quintessentially racist, then I can be confident that I am not. The irony here, however, is that when they demonize white slaveholders in this way, contemporary white people engage in an act of othering that is very similar to the one white slaveholders engaged in with black slaves. Viewing white slaveholders as incomprehensibly evil and therefore Not Like Us replicates the very patterns of white racism that the repudiation of white slaveholders is meant to challenge.

It also attempts to absolve contemporary white people of any connection or complicity with white domination. Regarding white slaveholders as racist monsters is intimately connected with the positing of good white liberals as racially innocent angels. In one sense, of course, monsters and angels are polar opposites, but in another sense they are eerily identical: both are inhumanly fantastic in that each figure attempts to place people outside of the realm of the human. We could say that the white angels of today and the white monsters of yesteryear are each other's mirror image. The two figures crucially depend on each other, and thus to challenge one is to undercut the other. This dependent relationship means that if and when slaveholders are allowed to regain their humanity, good white liberals might too. Recognizing white slaveholders as regular human beings—with all their flaws, even atrocious ones—goes hand in hand with acknowledging good white liberals as regular human beings too—with all their flaws, and perhaps some of those also are atrocious. The return of white slaveholders to the domain of humanity need not and should result in white liberals' taking their place as the new evil monsters. But it can and hopefully will help free white liberals of their fantasy of angelic innocence. Both the white slaveholder and the good white liberal need to regain their humanity, and this transformation can't take place for one without also taking place for the other.

If white people no longer distance themselves from white slaveholders by treating them as monsters and themselves as angels, they will be better able to see how their ancestors' damnable acts live on in their own lives. This is a form of accountability for white ancestors that white allies need to strive for. Even if a particular white person's "blood" ancestors never owned slaves or lynched black people, she still can and needs to take responsibility for the racism of earlier generations of white slaveholders. I realize that this expectation might seem unreasonable. As Jean-Paul Sartre once charged in the wake of World War II, "If one is going to reproach little children for the sins of their grandfathers, one must first of all have a very primitive conception of what constitutes responsibility. . . . One must believe that what their elders did the young are capable of doing."[19] But thinking of contemporary white people as responsible for white slaveholders does not necessarily entail a crude notion of responsibility. It does not mean reproaching a person today for the racism of her ancestors years ago, as if she personally chose their racist beliefs and actions for them. It does, however, mean acknowledging that white people today *are* capable of doing awful things similar to what white slaveholders did. Compared to chattel slavery, white violence toward people of color today might be more difficult to detect, but it can destroy nonwhite lives, families, and communities nonetheless. Of course, white people are not the only ones capable of harming people of color, and thus they are not the only people to be held responsible for this harm.[20] But the fact that white people's accountability might not be unique does not erase the need for it.

The kind of accountability I have in mind involves giving history its due by appreciating how contemporary white people are bound to generations of white people that preceded them and that will follow them. An individual white person could not personally know all of her white ancestors, nor is she directly related to all white slaveholders. But she can be accountable for past generations of white people nonetheless by recognizing that white people's habits today can echo racist habits of past generations. Given the constitutive relationship between the past and the present, we might say that accountability backward is related to accountability forward, and vice versa. How a white person lives her whiteness is not just an issue of how she responds to racial justice issues today, such as housing discrimination, affirmative action, and so on. It's also an issue of how a white person seeks to remedy the injustices of the past. Or more accurately: because the past is not divorced from the present, we cannot fully understand and adequately respond to the racial injustices of the present without understanding racial injustices of the past. Many times, the racial discrimination or exploitation of the present is not a new creation, but rather a redesigned extension of oppressive structures and beliefs of the past.

"The new Jim Crow" of the criminal justice system in the United States provides a fitting example of this point.[21] The legal structures of Jim Crow might have been dismantled in the 1950s and '60s, but white domination found a color-blind way to continue the legal disenfranchisement of black people and the ripping apart of black families and communities through the war on drugs and the subsequent felony imprisonment of millions of black men. We cannot adequately comprehend the criminal justice system in the United States today if we do not reckon with Jim Crow, and we cannot understand Jim Crow if we do not confront the way it preserved the core of chattel slavery after legal emancipation. The daily racial privileges that white people generally enjoy with respect to the police force, the prison system, and their educational, housing, and political rights as nonfelons are different only in degree, not kind, from the daily racial privileges that slaveholders enjoyed two hundred years ago. Attempting to distance oneself from white slaveholders, as if they were completely different from white people today, is to attempt to cover over the ways that the lives and habits of contemporary white people and white slaveholders are similar.

But who are the white ancestors, the white slaveholders, for which a particular white person today is accountable? When I began writing this chapter, I assumed that to answer this question in my own life, I would need to undertake genealogical research to discover whether any of my distant ancestors owned slaves. This was a daunting prospect, however, not so much because I feared I would find slaveholders, Klan members, and other white supremacists filling my family tree, but because I don't have much knowledge of who my family is beyond my grandparents' generation. The task seemed impossible. Not only do I not know any of my distant relatives' names, I don't have a stock of family stories—even vague, sketchy ones—about where they lived, how and when they came to the part of the United States that they did, and so on. I found myself strangely jealous of white allies such as Kim Hall, who knows that she has male ancestors who fought in the American Revolution and for the South in the U.S. Civil War.[22] Like the Confederate flag that Hall's father wants her to cherish, this knowledge can be a source of anger, fear, and pain for Hall, and she wrestles with feelings of betrayal when she refuses to take pride in her Southern heritage, as a "good" Southern white daughter should do. While not wanting to minimize the complexity of Hall's relationship to her family or the reality of her pain, I admit I was envious of her situation: she knows who her ancestors are. (And if I were honest, I would admit that I also was envious that she knows she has bona fide Confederate ancestry, which likely includes slaveholders. More on this shortly.) In contrast, all I know is that the past couple of generations of my family all count as white and lived in rural West Texas: undereducated, poor, and fairly itinerant on at least one side of the family until my parents' teenage years. I have no significant family stories—racist or otherwise—explicitly handed down from generation to generation to reflect on. This was a problem because it seemed to mean that I wouldn't be able to figure out what I should be responsible for in terms of my white ancestry.

I also found myself jealous of Warren Read, who offers one of the most striking examples of a contemporary white person's taking responsibility for his racist white ancestors. In *The Lyncher in Me: A Search for Redemption in the Face of History*, Read recounts how he discovered that his white great-grandfather incited a riot in 1920 in Duluth, Minnesota, that resulted in the lynching of three black men who were falsely accused of raping a white teenage girl.[23] Horrified by this discovery, Read comes to understand how his great-grandfather's life fed into the angry and violent upbringing that Read experienced at the hands of his father, as well as how Read's angry outbursts toward his own son are "toxic hand-me-downs" inherited from his male ancestors.[24] Struggling with what to do in the wake of his discovery, Read realizes that he cannot merely bury his father and grandfather even though they both are literally dead. He has to figure out how to be responsible for their living legacy. "It's horrifying to own," Read confesses, "but the spores of my forefathers are in the soil that feeds me, like a dormant fungus lying in wait, and they keep appearing, breaking through in spite of what my heart and my memory are telling me. . . . I can't select from the things I own. . . . The best I can do is work to understand those poisons that are there."[25] Read accepted responsibility for his great-grandfather's life by participating in a memorial service for the three lynched men, at which a monument in their honor was dedicated. Speaking at the service, Read told the story of his discovery of his great-grandfather's actions and apologized for his family's role in the lynchings.

Read's situation helps explain why I felt envious of those, such as Hall, who know something specific about their racist past. Read's knowledge of his ancestry gave him something specific for which to be responsible, something specific to do in the face of his racist ancestry, and having something specific to do seems to make it easier to redeem oneself as a white person. With his apology and participation in the memorial service, Read seemed to absolve himself of the responsibility and guilt produced by his knowledge of the lynchings. I don't wish to be dismissive of Read's struggles with his discovery of his great-grandfather's crime or the difficulty of directly apologizing to the lynched men's families. And to be fair, Read never claims that his search for redemption (as his book is subtitled) ended once he apologized at the memorial service. But because he had something specific in his family's history to own up to and a concrete way to do so, his search for redemption achieved a kind of success that white people without much knowledge of their ancestral past cannot hope for.

Read's story helps illustrate why my jealousy is problematic from a perspective of racial justice. Whether or not Read was successful, his goal was to redeem himself in the face of his family's history, and I felt jealous that he had such a clear-cut and public—even dramatic—opportunity for redemption. But white redemption is a troubling goal for racial justice struggles; it has very little connection with ending white domination of people of color. A related reason for my concern about jealous quests for white redemption is that it tends to result in washing one's hands of white history. Any debt owed to lynching victims, slaves, or other targets of racist injustice has been paid—redeemed—and thus a white person need not think any further about her white past. These reflections show the problematic character of my jealousy of another white person's opportunity for redemption. They reveal a desire to pay off and thus sever my connections with white history.

As I wrestled with the question of how to be accountable for my racist past, I realized that my ignorance of my distant ancestry wasn't necessarily an obstacle to my taking responsibility. In fact, in this case such ignorance could be something of an advantage if knowledge of specific ancestry leads white people to think they can limit their responsibility to a few particular white ancestors in order to more easily free themselves of guilt. This isn't to say that it's pointless to do genealogical research to find out who one's "blood" kin are. But contemporary white people do not have to be related via physical reproduction to slaveholders from the eighteenth and nineteenth centuries to have a kinship with them. (And a similar point could be made about Ku Klux Klan members and other white supremacist ancestors.) A person doesn't have to have explicit, conscious knowledge of her distant ancestors to have received enigmatic messages from them about race. My "blood" ancestors might never have owned slaves, and yet growing up white in the United States means that white slaveholders can and should be thought of as my forebears. White slaveholders have sent me and other contemporary white people messages about white supremacy, just as surely as my known relatives have done. The present world of white people is impacted by enigmatically racist messages from the past. That is to say, the enigmatic messages concerning race transmitted by white slaveholders to contemporary white people are real: they have real effects in the lives of white and nonwhite people today. Acknowledging this reality can help white people more effectively struggle against white domination.

Given that the unconscious of adults was formed through failed attempts to translate enigmatic messages sent to them as children by their adult world—and so on and so on—the budding unconscious of any particular child is impacted by the unconscious life of an adult world much larger than the one immediately surrounding her. Seduction, in other words, should be thought of as "a multiply transgenerational project."[26] Enigmatic messages passed from one generation to the next are not identical. They are altered, sometimes slightly and sometimes greatly, in the attempt to translate them, and it is the remnants of those attempts, not the entire message, that compose one's unconscious. But a powerful link exists between the unconscious of a contemporary person and that of the adult world existing hundreds of years ago, helping explain how a culture reproduces itself even as it is transformed. Across time and space, seduction connects generations of people through the formation of their unconscious lives.

This means that contemporary white people are linked in significant psychosomatic, spiritual ways to generations of white people who preceded them. Of course, it was not just white people who made up the adult world hundreds of years ago in, for example, the United States. African Americans and Native Americans in particular were part of that world, even as they were treated by white culture as non-adults in the form of irrational children or wards of the state. Both white and nonwhite adults sent enigmatic messages to the white children in their care, influencing their unconscious development. A full account of racial seduction would need to address the various relationships that adults of color had with white children, especially black women's frequent roles of nursemaid and nanny. I focus here on the constitutive relationship between contemporary white people and earlier generations of white adults because of contemporary white people's tendency to other their white forebears. Seduction theory has significant implications for nonracist white people who think of themselves as very different from white slaveholders, white supremacists, and other white racists. Acknowledging the seductive link between earlier generations of white slaveholders and white people today means acknowledging that a contemporary white person's unconscious has been formed out of enigmatic messages sent by white racists. It means that the racism of years ago lives on in the unconscious desires, fears, and beliefs of well-intentioned white people today.

This does not mean that contemporary white people are doomed to repeat the racism of the past. But to avoid repetition of the past, the link with earlier generations of white people must be recognized rather than denied. In this historical moment, whiteness is compulsory for white people; it is not a club that they can simply leave. What, then, should a person do if she is born into a race that she does not like? Rather than try to quit it as if she were not a member of it, a white person instead should acknowledge the network of relations with white people in which she is bound and for which she is responsible. And being responsible for them means confronting how you are implicated in their behavior as white people, as well as how you are responsible to them for your own behavior as a white person.

These last two points help explain why some white people might object to thinking of themselves as bound to other white people through their whiteness. White people, especially those in the middle class, generally are not accustomed to thinking of themselves as defined by group membership—and especially not their racial group membership. They tend to see themselves as individuals and believe that they should be treated as such. On this line of thinking, white people might belong to various social groups, but that membership does not and should not determine what they are expected to do or how they are viewed by others. By contrast and according to the same racial logic, it is black, Latino, and other nonwhite people who are constituted by their racial identities and thus who are accountable for the actions of other members of their racial groups. While it might not always be conscious, this way of thinking of white and nonwhite people is evident in many everyday occurrences. It reveals itself whenever a white person repeatedly confuses her two Asian students because she can't tell them apart, but she has no such problem correctly naming the many similar-looking white students in her class. It also is apparent when the actions of, say, a black burglar are taken as a reflection of the criminal tendencies of all black people and thus as a justified reason for white fear of blackness. The actions of a white burglar, in contrast, generally are taken a reason to condemn that one white person. The ability to be seen as an individual is an ontological privilege that has been carefully reserved for white people. It is a manifestation of their racial domination.

When this type of white privilege has been challenged, the challenge has tended to take the form of extending individuality to nonwhite people. The criminal actions of one black person should be seen as reflecting poorly on that one person, for example, and not on any other black person or black people in general. In many respects, this is a positive development. It makes it less likely, to continue the example, that police will arrest the first black man they see near the site of a burglary because he fits a generic description of the burglar: a black male. But it does not challenge white ontological privilege as radically as questioning white individuality does. It is one thing to insist that black people are individuals; this is a relatively easy concession for white domination to make since it does not necessarily impact white identity. While it would seem that treating black people as individuals would affect white identity by eliminating individuality as a marker of difference between white and nonwhite, the expansion of individuality instead can operate as a form of assimilation of nonwhite people to white ontological standards. White people might have to allow that some nonwhite people are "like us," but that is precisely the point: "we" white individuals still serve as the standard by which all other people are judged. Even more importantly, extending individuality to nonwhite people does not threaten a white individual's control over her identity. The behavior of other people, white or otherwise, does not reflect on her or say anything about what sort of person she is.

The white privilege of individuality often operates differently across gender and class lines. The behavior of children often is seen as a reflection of their parents, for example, and since parenting is still seen as the proper domain of women, children's behavior often is seen as a reflection of a woman's worth, which has been collapsed into her worth as a mother. Individuality, as many feminists have pointed out, tends to be a very male-privileged and masculinist ideal. It also tends to be classed. It is middle and upper-class white people in particular who are seen as quintessential individuals, while lower-class white people sometimes are lumped together into an indistinguishable white trash. When a member of the white trash does something stupid, crass, or criminal, it is seen as an indication of the inferiority of all white people who couldn't manage to separate themselves enough from black people to become full-fledged white people (individuals). Some white people's status as individuals is precarious, in other words: white mothers of all classes and white lower-class men and women often do not count as individuals in the same way that middle to upper-class white men do. But I would venture to say that all white people, regardless of their gender, class, or other salient aspects of their identities, generally are unaccustomed to thinking of themselves as responsible for one another simply because they are white. White people don't get this sort of training in racial identity. Habits of group accountability are relatively foreign to them, and they do not have many habits of racial group accountability in particular.

Those habits need to be developed, and their development must include taking responsibility for some of the worst behavior of white people. This returns me to the question of what might it mean for a white person today to take responsibility for the actions of white slaveholders hundreds of years ago, even if none of them are known to be one's "blood" kin. Taking a cue from Laplanche, we can say that assuming responsibility for racist white ancestors means de- and then re-translating the increasingly enigmatic messages they sent about the otherness of people different from themselves. De-translation is at the heart of analysis, which helps clear the way for a new, richer translation.[27] This is especially true for "extramural psychoanalysis," which addresses cultural messages, such as those concerning race, outside the walls of an analyst's office.[28] To take responsibility for messages about racist othering sent by white slaveholders means not to create a situation of transference that repeats, with a difference, an original traumatic scene in which the messages were communicated. In the case of contemporary white people's relationships with white slaveholders, there is no original scene to which to return. The specific authors of the message are absent, not only dead but also distanced by hundreds of years of history, and the cultural message received from them "is received by [people today] without having been explicitly addressed to [them]."[29] Instead of transference, what often is needed in the case of racist messages about othering is their loosening: "For what is new in analysis, in relation to culture, is not transference, it is . . . analysis—that is, *Lösung* . . . analysis, solution and resolution, dissolution."[30] Loosening makes possible the creation of a "better" translation in that it is "more complete, more comprehensive, and less repressive."[31] Beginning with a present translation, analysis returns to the past to loosen that translation, which can enable a different future based on a new translation.[32]

To begin loosening and then retranslating enigmatic messages, we need to realize that the people sending them were not entirely the people we think they were.[33] This is true in general, and also in the particular case of white slaveholders' racist message of othering. White slaveholders' worldviews were not completely abhorrent, and they had valid concerns that can and should be affirmed by white people allied with racial justice struggles. This is true for white slaveholders *as slaveholders*. Here is where the hard work of retranslation is needed so that one does not replicate the false dichotomy of defense versus demonization when hearing this claim. It does not work to separate off the slavery-related aspects of a slaveholder's person or life as evil and then affirm the remainder, for example, his or her gentleness with animals, patience with children, or generous giving to civic and religious causes. In part, this is because, to varying degrees, slavery was woven into every aspect of slaveholders' lives, and thus their lives cannot be neatly compartmentalized. But more importantly, it is because this seeming affirmation of white slaveholders is a covert form of disavowal. It continues to view the slavery-related aspects of white ancestors' lives as beyond the pale, admitting of no points of meaningful contact with the lives and concerns of reasonable white people today. This "affirmation" still regards white slaveholders as irremediably other.

White slaveholders were persons, not inhuman monsters. But this is precisely the problem: How can one respect as a person, which is different from approving, an ancestor who knowingly and willingly engaged in horrific acts of wrongdoing? As Cheshire Calhoun explains, to be considered a person by others is to be someone with whom others could have an interpersonal relationship, which means entering sympathetically into the lives of each other.[34] How can we today enter sympathetically into the lives of white slaveholders? And why would we want to do this given the complicity with slavery that such an act would seem to involve? To avoid this complicity, we usually relegate white slaveholders (and other infamous racists, such as Germany's Adolf Hitler and South Africa's Eugene de Kock)[35] to the realm of the inhuman. One variant of this banishment is to attribute a psychological defect to white slaveholders. As Calhoun explains, we tell ourselves that evil others have the bizarre worldview that they do "because their ways of thinking and feeling have gone terribly wrong or are dramatically undeveloped."[36] Slaveholders' actions and beliefs are incomprehensible, and so we aren't obligated to respect them as persons. In fact, even if we wanted to, it would be impossible to sympathetically understand their lives and decisions because slaveholders are "malignant vitalities or psychologically stunted individuals" too radically different from us to participate in an interpersonal relationship.[37]

Underlying the denial of personhood to slaveholders is the need to make moral sense of their choices and actions, as well as the need to protect one's own sense of moral righteousness. But there are other ways of making sense of wrongdoing that are consistent with treating the wrongdoer as a person and forgiving the wrongdoer for his or her actions. We often think of forgiveness as requiring the wrongdoer to repent of her sins. Either she must have a genuine change of heart so that she no longer wishes to do wrong or—ideally—she was unaware that her actions were wrong and now has the requisite knowledge to eliminate her harmful ignorance. In either case, forgiveness is possible because the acts and choices of the wrongdoer now make moral sense. In contrast to this minimalist account of forgiveness, aspirational forgiveness, as Calhoun calls it, operates with a different *ethos* based on making biographical sense of an individual's wrongdoing. Aspirational forgiveness recognizes that "in living through time, normal persons need to make the sorts of choices that will add up to and sustain and integrated, rather than fragmented, biography. They need their actions to make sense with, or to make sense of, their past and projected future lives."[38] Acts of wrongdoing—even horrific acts such as torturing and enslaving another person—can make sense in this way, and for that reason we can comprehend the lives and choices of white slaveholders. Comprehend, not condone: making biographical sense of white slaveholders' actions does not transform slaveholders into people of whom one approves. It is not a way to defend them. But it does treat them as people we can relate to and perhaps even forgive.

What does this kind of forgiveness entail? It means "that one stops demanding that the [wrongdoer] be different from what she is" and that one accepts that "an indecent flaw . . . is the person's way of holding her life together."[39] Morally speaking, the wrongdoer is still culpable and can be found lacking, of course, but in that case genuine forgiveness is not possible. Genuine or aspirational forgiveness occurs when we are able to focus sympathetically on something other than moral culpability. It occurs, as Calhoun explains, when we choose "to place respecting another's way of making sense of her life before resentfully enforcing moral standards."[40]

But wait: respecting the sense that white slaveholders made of their lives? Really? Applying the concept of aspirational forgiveness to white slaveholders might sound preposterous, like the suggestion of a blatant white supremacist. How is this not exactly the wrong road that white-dominated countries have been on for hundreds of years? The answer is that it can be; that's for sure. But it doesn't have to be if it is part of a project of retranslation. The rhetorical effect of this objection is to refuse retranslation, to revert to the false dichotomy of defense versus demonization of white slaveholders, and we need to resist that move. Refusing to jump automatically to the resentful enforcement of moral standards is important if and when those moral standards are merely ways to defensively shore up one's own moral goodness. Compulsively made and loudly shouted moral condemnations of white slaveholders can be more of a knee-jerk attempt to prove to others that one is not racist than an effective blow struck against white racism. I realize that it is difficult to use words such as *respect* and *forgiveness* when speaking of one's relationship with white slaveholders (as well as notorious racists of the twentieth century, such as German Nazis, South African apartheid supporters, and Ku Klux Klan members in the United States). Like other good white people, I struggle to use those words in their retranslation and not to hear them as an uncritical acceptance or defense of white racism.[41] But that struggle is important because it is part of good white people's resisting the temptation to absolve themselves by othering white slaveholders. If white slaveholders are regular human beings, then it's possible to make some kind of sense of their lives.

So how might we do that without condoning slavery? What might we learn from slaveholders if we approach them also with aspirational forgiveness rather than only moral condemnation? In my view, the answers to these questions revolve around the issue of the relationship of individual to society. As nineteenth-century slavery apologist James Henley Thornwell argued, "It is not the narrow question of Abolitionism of Slavery—not simply whether we shall emancipate our Negroes or not; the real question is the relations of man [sic] to society . . . a question as broad as the interests of the human race."[42] The answer to that particular question, according to white Southerners, was that organic social relations are the proper basis for human life.[43] Southern writers on the subject closely followed Aristotle in claiming the social basis for individuality.[44] Humans are not individual atoms sealed off from one another. They are interconnected, communal beings who can live and thrive only in networks of supportive relationships with one another. Love, loyalty, and family were some of the important ways that people were tied together. The social, political, economic, and other structures of a nation-state should support the human need for those ties. This was the only way to establish a stable society in which individual human beings can flourish.

According to apologists for slavery, slavery was the best way to do just that. White slaveholders viewed slavery as a network of mutual responsibilities that established reciprocity between themselves and their slaves.[45] On their view, it was a network, moreover, that successfully dealt with the allegedly different capabilities of the parties involved. Many slaveholders saw the revolutionary ideals of liberty and equality as misguided and thought they should be openly recognized as such.[46] Even though masters and slaves were considered unequal, each party had a duty to the other: the duty to serve well, in the case of the slave, and the duty to be a good master, in the case of the slaveholder. The result, allegedly, was the development of meaningful ties between the two parties based on loyalty and love. Black slaves were a part of the household that, along with his wife and children, the male head firmly but lovingly cared for. "My family, white and black"—this was at the heart of white Southern social philosophy.[47] Defending slavery concerned more than defending human bondage. Above all, it concerned a Southern way of life that placed close-knit social and family relationships at its center.

This helps explain why Southerners refused the North's offers of compensated emancipation, including Lincoln's offer of $400 million shortly before Northern victory in the Civil War. Such offers misunderstood the larger Southern worldview into which slavery fit, reducing it to merely an economic issue.[48] The call for abolition was particularly alarming to Southerners, moreover, precisely because it came from Northerners. In Southern eyes, the free-labor industrialism of the North was built on a radical notion of individualism whose effects were "egotism, greed, and 'unmanly homage to Mammon.' "[49] Southerners claimed that without an organic basis to Northern society, the greedy pursuit of wealth was the only thing that tied Yankees together. And a feeble tie it was, producing the oppression and exploitation of the poor by the rich. Closely connecting capitalism and individualism, Southern apologists for slavery charged that capitalism destroyed the social bonds that produced caring human relations.[50] As George Fitzhugh, the nineteenth century's most radical defender of slavery, insisted, "We deny that there is a society in free countries. They who act each for himself, who are hostile, antagonistic and competitive, are not social and do not constitute a society."[51] Free labor resulted in all social relations being reduced to their monetary value. The "callous and brutal relations of the cash nexus" meant that there was no protection or security for those who were forced to sell their labor.[52] So-called free labor was really slavery in disguise, a type of slavery far worse than the peculiar institution found in the South because Northern "slavery" had no organic bonds to mitigate it. In the view of many white Southerners, the oppression and exploitation of the white laboring classes in post-feudalist Europe demonstrated the horrific dangers of the industrial capitalism that was growing in North America. The two alternatives to it were socialism and slavery, and it was only slavery that was morally sanctioned in the Christian Bible and that had proven itself workable in ancient times up to the then-present.[53]

Socialism or slavery—a startling juxtaposition, especially for many contemporary Americans who think of their country as the global bastion of capitalism and freedom. But it is a juxtaposition that gets something right even though nineteenth-century Southerners made a devastatingly wrong choice in response to it. White slaveholders were right that the free labor industrial system blossoming in the North exploited and oppressed the white working class, and they were right that an alternative to it was needed. As they refined their arguments in favor of slavery, white Southerners increasingly turned to the history of the "humbler classes," insisting as did one Virginian that "the time is long past when they could be disregarded in the social organization."[54] Capitalism neglected the vast majority of people, "provid[ing] for the ascendancy of the strong over the weak and mak[ing] the rich richer and the poor poorer."[55] Unlike capitalism, which increasingly impoverishes families as their size and needs increase, slavery allegedly protects the lower (slave) class because masters are obligated to provide for all who are in their care. "By uniting the interest and sympathy of the superior white master with his property right in the slave, [slavery] protect[ed] and elevate[d] the black man" and thus "secure[d] the well-being of both races."[56] Indeed, according to Fitzhugh, slavery was not so much opposed to socialism as it was the fulfillment of its goals. Given that slaveholders provided food, clothing, and shelter to all their slaves, including the elderly and infirm, slavery was "a beautiful example of communism, where each one receives not according to his labor, but according to his wants."[57]

To be sure, the reality of slaveholders' treatment of slaves was very different than Fitzhugh's ideal. In addition to capturing the torment of mothers whose children were sold away as slaves, Harriet Jacobs recounts the sexual threats and abuse that many female slaves suffered at the hands of their licentious masters, as well as the formidable dangers they faced from their jealous mistresses.[58] Frederick Douglass also reveals the violence and terror at the heart of U.S. slavery in his autobiographical narratives.[59] He witnessed brutal whippings of his family members at a young age, was later brutally whipped himself, and was sold alongside livestock from one master to another before he was even a teenager. The contrast between the violent treatment of slaves and the affirmation of them as beloved family members likely produced extremely enigmatic messages for the white children in the household. The strong emphasis that slaveholders placed on the importance of family is especially ironic given that perhaps the most devastating effect of slavery was to tear apart black families.[60] When rethinking whiteness, critical philosophers of race need a very different conception of family than that held by white slaveholders. In particular, they need to dislodge the violence that often lies at the heart of family relationships.[61]

Rather than disregard what Fitzhugh and his peers said about slavery, "reading the unapologetic apologists for slavery can give us insight into the enduring effects of racism on white consciousness shaped within the family."[62] Caring and abuse were inseparable in slaveholding families, and thus it is not too surprising that Southerners' care for the white working class included exploitation. Fitzhugh and other white slaveholders used the history of the working classes primarily to bolster support for the ongoing enslavement of black people, and their concern for the "common people" was always mixed with a self-interested and harmful goal. Many Southerners who attacked the Northern system of free labor envisioned some form of personal or industrial servitude for the white working class in whose name they fought. Releasing white laborers from the clutches of industrial capitalism did not mean, in Southern eyes, that all white people would or could become equal to one another.

There is nothing pure to be found in the slaveholders' attacks on capitalism and atomistic individualism. But my embrace of white slaveholders as racial ancestors is not based on a quest for purity. Operating with mixed motives and often despicable intentions, white slaveholders nonetheless insisted that the needs of the white working classes be taken into consideration by those who governed a society. The propertied class of white people should not dismiss the interests of poorer whites, who were forced to sell the only thing they owned, their labor. The personal subsistence and security of all members of a society, including the non-laboring young, elderly, and ill, should be its first priority, and only then should it aim for material progress and economic profit.[63] This is a message retranslated for different ends than the slaveholders intended, and as such it is a message that contemporary white people can and should affirm. Put more generally, it is a message concerning the invidious effects of class hierarchies within whiteness, operating not only via economic, but also educational, moral, aesthetic, and other differences. Retranslated in this way, the white slaveholders' message about care for different classes of white people can loosen the tendency to other that is contained within that care.

When middle-class white people attempt to draw a sharp line between themselves and lower-class white people, they engage in a process of othering that replicates white slaveholders' attitude toward black slaves. They also reenact what historian Joel Williamson has called the "grits thesis," which is a view of politics and race strongly promoted by white elites in the turn of the century South that blamed racial violence on poor whites rather than examine racism as an institutional problem.[64] Here we can see, to paraphrase the Genoveses in the epigraph above, one significant measure in which white people today are the children of white racists who have gone before. Just as in 1900, contemporary white middle-class people who demonize white trash as intrinsically racist mask the pervasiveness of white racism, including their own role in it. The damnableness of slavery lives on, compulsively repeating itself in the unexamined habits of good white people.

Linda Martín Alcoff has argued that white people need to develop a double consciousness with regard to their racial past. This would be a double consciousness that acknowledges not just the negative, but also the positive aspects of white history: not just white racists, such as slaveholders, but also white people who challenged white domination.[65] I agree, but I want to complicate Alcoff's account by suggesting that white people also need a double consciousness with respect to white racists themselves. White slaveholders, for example, not only held despicable beliefs about black people and engaged in reprehensible acts toward them, but they also insisted that middle-class white people not discard lower-class white people in the trash bin of capitalist progress. When contemporary white people no longer other white slaveholders, they can develop a double consciousness with regard to their racist white ancestors, enabling white people to retranslate an important message about the need to connect across class lines.

Although this message has been sent by people of color, such as W. E. B. Du Bois in his monumental analysis of class and race in *Black Reconstruction in America*,[66] it is important also to receive it from white slaveholders. The complicated message sent by white slaveholders about caring across white class lines allows white allies to partially affirm, rather than absolutely dismiss their slaveholding heritage and racist past. This affirmation admittedly is dangerous because it could play into the hands of white supremacists who seek intellectual justification for their prejudice against and violent behavior toward people of color. In full recognition of that danger, I continue to think that the partial and critical affirmation of white slaveholders is important. It helps create the possibility for stronger ties between different classes of contemporary white people that are grounded in racial justice by undercutting the tendency to other those who are different from oneself. Granted, affirming connections with white slaveholders will not eliminate all racism or dissolve all enigmatic messages involving race. Every translation, including retranslations, involves repression of enigmatic remnants, and thus the retranslation of white slaveholders' message about classism will contribute to the unconscious habits of contemporary white people in ways that could need future loosening.[67] Although inevitably filled with risk, affirmation of white slaveholders can be an important step for contemporary white people to take as they struggle against the racist process of othering.

Calhoun argues that aspirational forgiveness cannot be obligatory because it's too burdensome to require that people sympathetically enter the lives of everyone and because we cannot demand that people refrain from morally judging other people's actions.[68] Perhaps this is why she chooses the adjective *aspirational* to describe genuine forgiveness: it is an ideal to which we should aspire, but it is too difficult a task to mandate universally. I find it helpful to think of genuine forgiveness as a difficult ideal to strive for, rather than an easily achieved accomplishment. I also appreciate Calhoun's reluctance to make aspirational forgiveness obligatory because doing so risks turning forgiveness into a moral duty that would undermine its vitalizing *ethos*. Yet at the same time, I want to say that all white people need to aspire to genuine forgiveness of their white slaveholding ancestors. The point is not that contemporary white people should never morally condemn white slaveholders, but moral(istic) judgment should not be the only way that contemporary white people relate to their racist white forebears. White people will be more effective allies to people of color in their struggles against white supremacy if white people can find a way to understand and respect, rather than merely condemn and resent their white slaveholding ancestors.

If this claim sounds preposterous, recall Barack Obama's comments about his white grandmother while on the campaign trail for the U.S. presidency. While Obama is not white, his relationship with his grandmother illustrates the aspirational forgiveness for which white people can and need to strive. In March 2008, Obama gave his so-called race speech, "A More Perfect Union," which addressed the political brouhaha that erupted after Obama's minister, Reverend Jeremiah Wright, made strong comments condemning the United States' racism and global imperialism. Obama made clear that he condemns the statements made by Wright as harmfully divisive and distorted. However, he also sympathetically placed the statements in the context of Wright's life story as a black man growing up in the United States: a story of care, service, love, and celebration, especially through the black church, but also of segregated schools, legalized discrimination, and lack of economic opportunity for black men. As Obama said, this story "helps explains, perhaps, my relationship with Reverend Wright. As imperfect as he may be, he has been like family to me. . . . I can no more disown him than I can disown the black community." And then Obama added,

> I can no more disown [Reverend Wright] than I can my white grandmother—a woman who helped raise me, a woman who sacrificed again and again for me, a woman who loves me as much as she loves anything in this world, but a woman who once confessed her fear of black men who passed her by on the street, and who on more than one occasion has uttered racial or ethnic stereotypes that made me cringe. These people are a part of me.[69]

It might seem obvious that a person concerned about racial justice, such as Obama, should disavow a white woman who fears black men and who views the world in terms of racist and ethnocentric stereotypes, especially if that person is black or mixed-race. But the situation is not that simple when the woman in question is a person's grandmother. Like Reverend Wright, Obama's grandmother helped make Obama who he is, and so even if he wanted to, he could not disown her. She will always be his family. And so Obama chooses not to morally condemn his grandmother—even though it is clear that he does not approve of her racist statements—and instead affirms her as part of himself. This affirmation is possible because of something like aspirational forgiveness. Obama is able to manage the complexity of treating his racist grandmother as a person deserving of respect because, as with Reverend Wright, Obama forgivingly understands the sense that his grandmother has made of her life.

    In a similar fashion, for white people to respect their white slave-holding ancestors as persons is for them to forgivingly understand the sense that they made of their lives. This is, in James Baldwin's words, to accept their history. As Baldwin explains in the epigraph above, accepting one's history doesn't mean wallowing or drowning in the past. Rather than becoming lost in or immobilized by the horrific aspects of their white ancestry, white allies need to figure out how to use it. And to use it effectively, they must understand the complexity of its transgenerational relationships. White people today are the children, grandchildren, and great-grandchildren of those who have come before them. This means that white people's working through history is "the work of owning up to who and what [they] are."[70] White people today cannot simply disown or separate themselves from their white ancestors because those ancestors are a part of them, just as Obama's grandmother is a part of him. White people's attempts to consider their white slaveholding ancestors and other racist forebears as persons are intimately connected to their ability to treat themselves and other contemporary white people as persons as well.

The task of learning how to use one's past isn't unique to contemporary times. As the Genoveses claim in the above epigraph, white slaveholders also were trying to figure out the meaning and usefulness of their history, asking themselves how they were implicated in the actions and lives of previous generations. When white allies accept their racial history and learn to use their racist past, they are behaving much more like their white slaveholding ancestors than they might have thought. This similarity is something for contemporary white people to affirm, rather than deny, as is white slaveholders' passionate belief in the importance of love and family relationships. While they need to be retranslated for the ends of racial justice movements, the messages sent by white slaveholders are something for which white people today can be grateful.[71] Those messages can help white people develop race/class habits that might dissolve the othering endemic to white racism.

3
_____

The Dis-ease of Color Blindness

Racial Absences and Invisibilities in the Reproduction of Whiteness

Our greatest responsibility is to be good ancestors.

—Dr. Jonas Salk

In today's world, open acknowledgment and discussion of whiteness often is considered inseparable from white supremacy, and so it might seem that to avoid white supremacy, non-supremacist white people should ignore both their and other people's races. This line of thought leads to the contemporary anti-racist strategy of color blindness, which is to "not see," that is, to not factor race into any of a person's considerations of others. On this approach, people are just people, and to treat them as raced is to treat them unfairly and even discriminate against them. Unlike white supremacists, white people who are not racist supposedly have moved beyond race. They do not see or discuss it. To do so would be to inject dynamics of race and racism into a situation where they did not previously exist.

Color blindness tends to be present across the spectrum of good white people's lives, for example, in their work places, community spaces, and family relationships. While each of these spaces deserves full analysis, this chapter will focus on the significant role that color blindness plays in the rearing of white children. Color blindness dominates white childrearing strategies so much that virtually no other credible strategy for good white people exists. (Unless it's explicitly developed in a critical form, multiculturalism is no exception because it almost always omits the ongoing realities of white domination. I'll return to the topic of

85

multiculturalism below.) If they care about racial justice, parents, teachers, and caregivers of all races, but perhaps especially white people, are supposed to teach white children that race does not matter or, in fact, even exist. As one recent study of white suburban parents in California confirmed, white parents "generally expressed the belief that we should all be color-blind, that they taught their children to be color-blind, and that they for the most part did not care about the color of someone's skin."[1] Everyone supposedly is equal, and it is only racists who think otherwise, manufacturing lies about the salience of race.

I understand why color blindness can seem like an attractive parenting strategy to non-supremacist white parents. It allows them to avoid clumsy and difficult conversations about race and white domination in which they fear they will say something inadequate, wrong, or harmful (from a perspective of racial justice) about race or racism. But color blindness is a very problematic strategy for fighting racial injustice. For starters, as the California study mentioned above also demonstrated, a person's alleged belief in color blindness can go hand in hand with racist worldviews in which some people are seen as more equal than others. Parents who claimed to be color-blind regularly voiced contradictory ideas at the same time, for example, explaining that if their white daughter were to marry a nonwhite person, they would be more comfortable with an Asian man than a black man because "Asians are just like— white."[2] Hiding behind color blindness makes it difficult, if not impossible, to see how white privileged beliefs and habits continue to function in one's life. The result is a strange kind of pride in one's interpersonal cluelessness. As José Medina explains, color blindness "requires being actively and proudly ignorant of social positionality, which involves a double epistemic failure: a failure in self-knowledge and a failure in the knowledge of others with whom one is intimately related."[3] Medina's analysis confirms that of James Baldwin, who charges that "whatever white people do not know about Negroes reveals, precisely and inexorably, what they do not know about themselves."[4] White people's epistemic failure is simultaneously spiritual because of the hubristic pride taken in white ignorance, camouflaged as moral innocence and goodness.

The strategy of not seeing race also is problematic because it implicitly seeks a racially pure space, and thus it enacts a form of white domination similar to white supremacy. Non-supremacist white people generally do not acknowledge whiteness as a race, and this is precisely the problem that color blindness allows to continue uninterrupted. For many white people, race tends to be something that concerns everyone but them (yet another epistemic-spiritual failure on their part). This view of whiteness explains the different emphasis—but to similar effect—that supremacists and non-supremacists place on race. While white supremacists stress a person's race whether or not it is white, non-supremacist white people tend to deemphasize or even "erase" it. Both groups' attitudes, however, have the effect of promoting the domination of white people over people of color because, whether explicitly or implicitly, they both consider race (read: nonwhiteness) to be a bad thing. Why else try to erase race—which only nonwhites are considered to have—unless it is a bad thing? Of course, white and nonwhite people handle this "badness" in different ways. In contrast to white supremacists, good white people respond to nonwhite people's race in a "kind" way by overlooking or negating it. But this form of "kindness" is just as corrosive to racial justice as the malevolence of white supremacy is.

Color blindness is especially problematic in the case of childrearing because childhood is a crucial time for the formation of a person's racial habits. Rearing white children in ways that will genuinely challenge racial injustice means helping them develop racial habits of believing and embodying that race, including whiteness, is okay: it is okay to notice race, to talk about race, and to be raced—and again, "race" here includes whiteness, perhaps more than anything. In the arguments that follow, I will concentrate primarily on parenting, but I also will address the role that teachers, daycare employees and other caregivers of white children, and white communities more generally, play in the education and nurturing of white children. While white parents often are the primary caretakers of white children, other adults also influence the way that white children learn to be white. Across the spectrum of white communities and caregivers, as we will see, a great deal of white allied work on raising white children is needed.

ᴄᴡ

How white children learn to be white is a matter of deep concern to racial justice movements—or at least it should be. This is because adults' racial habits, including those that function unconsciously, have their beginnings in childhood. In childhood, developing habits tend to be labile and capable of relatively easy redirection. Once sedimented in adulthood, however, habits (racial and otherwise) are relatively difficult to change. This is not to claim that it is impossible to change adult habits of white privilege.[5] But while I am not wholly pessimistic about the possibility of transforming habits of white privilege, I do think that such transformation will be very difficult and that it will take a great deal of time to see meaningful results. This is one important reason why it is crucial for critical philosophers of race and other critical race scholars to address how and when white habits are first developed in a white person's life. Rather than just trying to change white adults' habits of white privilege and domination—which I think can and should be attempted—critical philosophers of race need to explore how different white habits might be cultivated in the first place. And this means turning their attention to white children.

And yet, very few of them do. Perhaps this is not too surprising (although still disappointing) in the case of philosophy, which tends to assume an adult subject. With the occasional exception, such as Jean-Jacques Rousseau's *Emile* and John Dewey's mid-career work on education, the discipline of philosophy pays very little attention to the general question of how children develop, much less to the specific question of how they develop racial (and racist) habits.[6] Outside of philosophy, scholars in education, child development, and related fields have focused on questions of race, but this work almost always assumes children of color as its subjects. It tends to examine, for example, how to rear children of color so that they are not adversely affected by racism and white privilege.[7] Sometimes it injects the topic of whiteness by asking how, or even whether, white parents can successfully (from a perspective of racial justice) raise children of color.[8] But very little scholarly work asks how to rear or educate white children explicitly *as white* in ways that support racial justice.[9]

This is not to say that there is no material available on how explicitly to rear and educate white children as white. Ample advice is available online from white supremacist groups such as the Ku Klux Klan, World Church of the Creator, and Stormfront, but it promotes the superiority of the white race over all others. As white supremacist groups have begun to focus more attention on women's possible contributions to their efforts, the care of children and the home have assumed increasing importance to the project of "protecting" and promoting the white race. Nowadays, "children are a huge part of the Ku Klux Klan," for example, whose members "care deeply for their families" and "want to pass down their beliefs to their kids."[10] This is why, in the words of one white supremacist, "mothers and other women must be properly protected, cherished, and celebrated as the guardians of the next generation, the keys to the future of the White race."[11] White supremacy's current interest in children isn't new, however. At least since the eugenics movements of the early 1900s, white (married) women have been urged to aid in the reproduction of whiteness (and, by extension, nation) by literally bearing a high number of "pure" white children. No less than then-president of the United States Theodore Roosevelt chastised white middle-class American women in his 1906 annual message to Congress for their "willful sterility . . . the one sin for which the penalty is national death, race death."[12] While pressures for high fecundity still exist within contemporary white supremacist groups (sometimes accompanied by resistance from women members), those groups have broadened their notions of reproduction to explicitly include the social and cultural reproduction of whiteness in new generations.[13] As white supremacists understand, the continuance of white domination requires more than the birth of a high number of white babies. It also requires that those white babies be nurtured into children and adolescents who embody white pride and have been protected from the "contaminating" influence of a racially mixed world.

This task falls primarily to white mothers. Operating with a sharp—and sharply gendered—public/private divide, white supremacist groups tend to allot to men the work of fighting for white rights in a multi-cultural world and to women the work of securing a safe haven from it. White women are the gatekeepers between inside and outside the family, and thus their work as caretakers can be thought of as "a set of practices that ideally forge symbolic and physical boundaries around households," including the children that live in them.[14] "The real function of . . . [a] Klanswoman," for example, "is to indoctrinate the family—turning it into a Klan cell."[15] Without white women's domestic vigilance, racial impurities could seep into the home and lives of white children.

A logic of purity is central to white supremacist women's gate-keeping and mothering practices. White women are supposed to separate their children from polluting, contaminating influences, ensuring their purity. Home schooling, for example, is meant to provide white children with a physical barrier against literal contact with nonwhite children, as well as a symbolic or value-based barrier against exposure to "all the multi-cultural/pro-diversity crap going on in today's schools," as one Stormfront member explains.[16] Cooking with organic foods and avoiding artificial "junk" food is supposed to contribute to a pure home by promoting healthy living.[17] And white supremacist women's practices of domestic cleanliness help secure the racial (and class) status of their children by providing a place of purity for them. A truly white child allegedly would never come from a filthy home, and so keeping the home hygienic and clean both demonstrates and helps produce the child's white racial and class superiority.[18] In their everyday domestic practices, white supremacist mothers continually teach their children a myriad of lessons about what it means to be a racially pure white person. Limiting exposure to race-mixing "contaminants" and maintaining high standards of purity via healthy cooking and domestic cleanliness are crucial vehicles for those lessons.

White supremacists understand that it takes a great deal of hard work to cultivate white supremacist habits and beliefs in their children. A good portion of this process happens in unspoken and unreflective ways (a topic to which I shall return), but a significant amount of it also happens through explicit conversations and lessons about race. Explicit instruction is needed, according to one white supremacist, because we live in a subversive, media-filled environment that is ruled by Jewish interests and infused with antiwhite propaganda, all of which is difficult to detect because it tends to operate unconsciously.[19] On their view, in such a pernicious environment, "conscientious White parents must prepare their children with the analytical tools to see through the façade." White supremacist parents might develop those tools, it is asserted, by means of specific parent-guided exercises: pointing out the disparity between the number of dark-skinned doctors, lawyers, scientists, and other authority figures in reality and in mainstream television and movies; providing children with "a firm grounding in the relative achievements, behavioral tendencies, and capabilities of the races" so they won't fall for the portrayal of black as docile or passive; giving children a research project of comparing racial crime rates so that they understand the "color of crime;" teaching children the "shame of cosmic proportions [that] follows the squandering of fine White genes" through miscegenation; and taking children to museums to learn about the devastating effects on early Egyptian dynasties (allegedly ruled by white pharaohs) of allowing blacks and Arabs to mix in their royal bloodlines. This last assignment is to be paired with "query[ing] the young child if the election of the mulatto Barack Hussein Obama as President of the United States of American in 2008 signaled an analogous point in American history."[20]

I find these suggestions alarming, and not only because of their specific recommendations. Their content, which assumes and encourages white supremacy, is upsetting from a perspective of racial justice, but I think that there is another reason that many middle-class white people would find the suggestions shocking. It is that they so openly and explicitly acknowledge race in the context of childrearing in the first place. This is a separate matter from the suggestions' racist content, but those two issues can be difficult to untangle given good white people's high levels of discomfort with discussions of whiteness. It's as if merely saying the words "raising a white child as white" instantly transforms a good white person into a bad one, and most good white people want to avoid appearing bad at any cost—even the cost of successfully challenging racial injustice. Here we have a prime instance of what Charles Mills has called conceptual white flight: when it comes to children and race, white people flee as fast as they can from certain topics and concepts.[21]

This flight has allowed white supremacists to corner the market on discussions of white childrearing, but childrearing is too personally, socially, and politically important to let this happen. I am concerned that teaching white children to "not see" race means teaching them to ignore or disregard the power dynamics of white domination, and this in turn increases the likelihood that children will develop unconscious habits of white privilege, all in the name of supposedly being non- or anti-racist. Strategies of color blindness help create a racialized psyche for white children that is embedded in an epistemology of ignorance and that ironically perpetuates the existence of racism without racists.[22] Supposedly "blind" to color, children whose early racial awareness has been whitewashed will not be able to respond to the racially and racist-ly structured world in which they live and from which they benefit in ways that promote racial justice. Nor will they be able to see the active (though perhaps not consciously deliberate) role that they and other white people play as agents of racial inequality. This lack of understanding can be considered a cognitive dysfunction, yet because it is a dysfunction that allows white children to ignore their participation in racial oppression, it enables them to function extremely well as white privileged people in a white privileged world.

I also am concerned about the harmful effects of teaching nonwhite children color blindness.[23] Such lessons implicitly teach them that race is bad, which can encourage a self-deprecating internalization of white superiority given that nonwhite people are seen as quintessentially raced. When taught at daycare or school, lessons of color blindness also can conflict with the race-aware lessons regarding racism taught by nonwhite parents at home, producing confusion and a conflict of loyalties for a child and rendering her unable to legitimately name her oppression.[24] When children of color are told by their teachers that skin color doesn't matter, they don't necessarily take away the message of equality that the teachers presumably intend. They just as often are taught that race is something that should not be acknowledged or talked about, which makes it impossible for them to challenge their society's belief that white is good and everything not white (especially blackness) is bad.

One might object that young children don't yet understand the meaning of skin color and race and thus we need not worry about their misunderstanding adults' messages about color and equality. This objection corresponds with the thinking of some child development psychologists who hold that the preschool years are a "magical place" in which children are innocently ignorant of the meaning of race and racism.[25] This line of thought stretches back to nineteenth-century white abolitionist claims that "children are all born abolitionists. All we have to do is keep them abolitionists."[26] Because children allegedly do not lose their racial innocence until the early primary school years, nonwhite children in particular should be shielded from information regarding the existence of race and racism as long as possible and at least until the age of six.[27] On this view, early childhood is a place of purity, racial awareness is a contaminant, and the goal of parents, teachers, and other caretakers should be to keep children untainted by racial awareness for as long as possible.

But young children already are aware, at least in some basic but crucial ways, of the meaning and role of race in a white privileged society. They understand systems of racial purity at work in their world when, for example, they argue with each other about whether a black child can play the "good guy" in a game.[28] There is nothing magical or pure about early childhood, at least not in terms of its relationship to race.[29] By the age of three, children of all races tend to be aware of the existence and meaning of race and racism in fairly sophisticated ways. And recent research suggests that infants as young as six months notice, and perhaps even judge other people based on differences in skin color.[30] This is why, whether at home, daycare, or school, teaching color blindness tends to be an ineffective, and even counterproductive anti-racist childrearing strategy. Of course, children are not miniature adults, possessing the ability to manipulate racial categories and situations in the same way that most adults do. But "a highly developed, well-thought-out racial ideology is not necessary for children to make and develop racial distinctions in their everyday behavior."[31] While young children are not small adults, they are social beings and, as a result, are enmeshed in relations of reciprocal influence with others, not located in some pristine, asocial place outside them. Young children are not blank slates or passive recipients of adult action. They are active agents in the world who take up racialized (and other) ideas, behaviors, and habits from their caretakers and peers, reshaping and refashioning them to their own ends.[32]

The prevalence of cognitive theories of development in research on children helps explain why young children often are thought of as uninvolved in social relations and thus ignorant of race and racism. Influential theorists such as Jean Piaget and Lawrence Kohlberg stressed the development of individual intellectual abilities, which led many contemporary scholars to neglect the social dimensions of children's cognitive lives. In most child development research, children are posited as naturally egocentric. Incapable of focusing on anything but themselves and their own interests, children allegedly do not demonstrate an adequate awareness of social concepts or a sufficient ability to put themselves in the place of another person until around the age of seven. With regard to social matters, toddlers and preschool children tend to be thought of as empty vessels: unless and until adults pour into them ideas about race and other social phenomena, their minds will be devoid of them.[33]

But ample evidence exists that children are not mere imitators of adults, even as they are significantly influenced by them, and that children adapt and create meaning in transaction with the world, including each other.[34] In a daycare activity designed to help children recognize and value their racial differences, for example, children ages three to five were instructed to select and have their palms painted with a color of paint that looked like them and then press their palms against a large sheet of paper to create a "People Colors" handprint poster. While most children selected one color that "objectively" matched their skin, Corinne, a four-year-old girl with one African and one white parent, selected pale brown for one hand and dark brown for the other. When told that she had done the exercise wrong and needed to select a color that matched her skin, Corinne replied that she did and that she had two colors in her skin. Corinne's choice could be interpreted (and was, by her teachers) as cognitively inconsistent, as demonstrating her lack of understanding of race and color. But more illuminating is to see that the child, who on other occasions demonstrated her pride at her dual racial heritage, wanted to include both parents in her self-definition of skin color/race. Although her response did not conform to adult expectations regarding racial comprehension, it demonstrated a fairly complex understanding of color as more than just a matter of physical reality. While the teacher thought that the activity had failed in Corinne's case, we instead could conclude that Corinne creatively adapted the teacher's instructions and racial assumptions to fit her own goals and interests.[35]

Another situation at the same daycare shows how children actively use racial and racist concepts apart from immediate adult involvement.[36] Renee, a four-year-old white girl, was pulling Lingmai, a three-year-old Asian girl, and Jocelyn, a four-year-old white girl, across the playground in a wagon. The pulling was hard work, and Renee soon stopped, out of breath. Lingmai was eager to continue the game and so got out of the wagon and picked up its handle. As she did so, Renee repeatedly told her, frowning with hands on hips, that she could not do so because only white Americans were allowed to pull the wagon.[37]

Renee clearly understood how to use concepts of race as tools of social exclusion. Putting Lingmai "in her place," Renee gave her lessons in white purity: white and nonwhite people have different roles in the world and those roles are to be strictly enforced (by white people). Renee, moreover, merged racial and national identities by combining the concepts of white and American. Only white people are "real" Americans, and only real Americans can be in charge. These lessons obviously are ones that Renee learned from the adult world, but she was not mindlessly mimicking them. Even though she might not have fully understood the concept of "white American" as an adult does, Renee was able to creatively (and hurtfully) wield it in a play situation. She applied the concept of white American to the social occasion of wagon pulling, adeptly using it to maintain control over a nonwhite child. This is a striking instance of children teaching each other the power and meaning of racial and racist ideas.

Also striking is what happened—or, rather, didn't happen—after an authority figure became involved in the situation. When Lingmai began crying and ran to a teacher, she complained that Renee had hurt her feelings. When the teacher asked Renee if this was true, Renee gloomily admitted that it was. Renee was then instructed to apologize, which she somewhat unenthusiastically did, and then the teacher moved away after waiting a moment to make sure that the conflict did not re-erupt.[38]

Lingmai clearly understood racial concepts well enough to know that she had been hurt by Renee's comment, but she did not reveal to the teacher that race was involved in the incident. The teacher had no idea that the children were talking about race and apparently thought that some "standard" children's insult led to Lingmai's crying. Although Renee was made to apologize, in another sense she "won" in her struggle with Lingmai because her use of race-based exclusion worked. Lingmai did not succeed in gaining control over the wagon, and Renee's assertion of the superiority of white Americans went unchallenged. Renee learned from this incident the lesson that race-based exclusion can be an effective way to gain what one wants, especially when hidden from the eyes of a sanctioning authority.[39] Even more striking, perhaps, is that Lingmai also seems to have understood this destructive message. Although she cried and appealed to an authority figure for help, she apparently accepted Renee's pronounced "superiority" because she did not reveal the racial basis of Renee's comment, which would have landed Renee in much more trouble than a generic insult would. Lingmai's omission of the details of the wagon-pulling incident helped secure Renee's power as a white American, as well as perpetuate the common (white) adult belief that young children are innocently unaware of race and racism.

While the teacher's belief in children's supposed racial innocence worked against a child's (Lingmai's) best interests in this situation, it does not always do so. Children often use adult perceptions of their racial innocence and confusion to steer away from "dangerous" topics that get children in trouble because they make adults uncomfortable. For example, in a game designed once again to teach children the meaning and value of racial differences (as conceived by adults), a teacher at the same daycare instructed three- and four-year-old children to identify people in the room who had the same skin color as a black doll that was brought to class. The children reluctantly picked out a few black students in the room, but then fell silent even though several other dark-skinned black children had gone unnamed. Finally, the activity died out and the teacher moved on. While this activity might seem to have failed because of the children's inability to correctly identify race without heavy adult guidance, the children's frequent use of racial categories apart from the presence of sanctioning adults suggests that the children were deliberately avoiding a race-based discussion with their teacher. The children quickly had picked up that race was a highly sensitive subject for adults and that their teachers had a very particular way of viewing race and racism that was sternly enforced. Rather than risk a misstep and subsequent scolding, the children used their teachers' willingness to view them as racially ignorant to steer the classroom activity to a safer topic.[40]

These examples demonstrate that young children understand racial concepts and can manipulate both them and the adults in their world to achieve their own ends. Young children are not asocial, pure, or racially innocent, which is why teaching color blindness tends to backfire as a strategy for achieving racial justice. What might this impure and color-aware picture of young childhood mean for a white parent who is raising a white child? To begin, it points to the need to acknowledge the "white elephant" in white children's—and white adults'—lives.[41] Race and racism are not rendered nonexistent in white children's worlds just because middle-class white adults usually do not talk about those topics with them. If anything, when adults treat race as taboo, young children's curiosity about it only seems to increase, and they are "left to improvise their own conclusions [about race]—many of which would be abhorrent to their parents."[42] As one young white boy said to a white friend when they were talking about "skin like ours"—they hadn't been taught the names for races since their white parents never used them—"parents don't like us to talk about our skin, so don't let them hear you."[43]

The dis-ease that white parents, grandparents, teachers, and day-care workers experience around topics of race and white racism has harmful effects on children of all races by perpetuating the conditions for white domination. As in the case of one white woman who shut down her white grandson's questions about race by anxiously lecturing him when he commented that he didn't like black people, a message is sent "that some things are not 'polite' [= white] to talk about, that there is something uncomfortably emotional about talking about Black people, that grandma freaks out when you bring it up so don't bring this kind of stuff up."[44] It turned out that the white child in this situation had been teased by a black child at preschool that day, and while he did say something racially offensive in the aftermath of the event, his grandmother lost the opportunity to help the boy untangle his hurt feelings about being teased from his conclusion that he didn't want to be friends with any black people.

White parents and other white caregivers need to talk with white children about race, racism, and whiteness in particular. In many respects, this is a very basic guideline for white allied parents to adopt, but I want to underscore how difficult it is for many middle-class white people to follow. Most middle-class white adults today did not get much practice using race-based words and concepts as children, except perhaps as racist slurs. As a result, racial but nonracist words and concepts often are like a foreign—and forbidden—language that they do not know how to use without extreme discomfort.[45] And their discomfort tends to be passed onto their children in turn. Tense facial expressions, a subtle stiffness in one's posture, slightly stammered or unusually paced vocalizations: bodily signs of discomfort such as these that can occur as good white adults use race-based words and concepts can seduce children into unconscious habits of white privilege. Combating white discomfort when using words such as *race* and *black*—and knowing, for example, as many of my white college students do not, that "people of color" and "colored people" are not equivalent terms—is an important step in changing the idea and corresponding habits that any kind of talk about race is racist and that identifying a person as having a race is to insult him or her.

To appreciate how difficult it is for many middle-class white parents to talk about race with their children, consider the example of an early childhood development study conducted at the University of Texas in

Austin, in 2006.[46] The goal of the study was to learn if children's videos with multicultural storylines had an impact on five- to seven-year-old children's racial attitudes. Since the researchers knew from prior studies that the videos weren't likely to make much difference, some parents who volunteered their families were instructed also to use the videos as an occasion to discuss interracial friendships with their children. A third group of parents were instructed to have these conversations without watching any videos at all. What is interesting about the study is how it failed but in its failure revealed unexpected and significant results about the white parents. The researchers couldn't generate much conclusive data about the videos since very few families were willing to talk about race with their children. Five families who were supposed to have conversations but not watch videos quit the study altogether. As two of the families in this third group explained, "We don't want to have these conversations with our child. We don't want to point out skin color."[47] The researchers also discovered that most of the families who remained in the study barely mentioned race when talking with their children and "quickly reverted to the vague 'Everybody's equal' phrasing." Even though "every parent was a welcoming multiculturalist, embracing diversity" and understood from the start that the study would focus on white children's racial attitudes, most of them either dropped out or refused to cooperate with the researchers when they realized the study involved openly talking about race. They just couldn't—or wouldn't—talk about race. It's not what non-supremacist, middle-class white people are supposed to do.

And yet, when white parents in the study did talk openly with their children about race, their children's racial attitudes dramatically improved from a racial justice perspective. Since only six families out of the original one hundred that were recruited—only 6 *percent*—managed to have open conversations about race, I'm uncertain how meaningful the study is from an empirical perspective. But it is significant in my view that within a single week of conversations about race with their parents, the racial attitudes of children in these six families changed for the better. While many white parents failed—refused?—to comply with the study because "they just didn't know what to say to their kids, and they didn't want the wrong thing coming out of the mouth of their kids," the study demonstrates that even awkward, potentially "incorrect" conversations about race between white parents and children can make a significant, positive difference in white children's lives, countering beliefs and habits that support white domination.

That being said, there are some styles of conversations about race that white parents and other caretakers should try to avoid, and I mean

more here than the obvious point they that shouldn't make racist comments or use racial slurs. One style takes the form of talking about
race without really talking about it at all—as the "everybody's equal"
approach does. Another tempting style that many daycare centers and
schools succumb to, for example, is to engage in "cultural tourism" when
talking about race.[48] This well-intended but problematic approach tends
to focus on holidays as a time to celebrate different racial cultures and
heritages. For a day or perhaps more, a different racial group is learned
about in relationship to Thanksgiving (Native Americans), Hanukah
(Jews), Kwanzaa (Africans and African Americans), Cinco de Mayo
(Mexicans and Mexican Americans), and so on. Children pay tribute
to the racial group associated with the holiday in question by learning
about the food, song, and dress that tends to accompany it. While this
can seem like and, in some contexts, can be a respectful practice, it
too often reduces nonwhite groups to an exotic other and emphasizes
their entertainment value for white people. Its "celebration" of racial
difference tends to depoliticize it, flattening race into a nonthreatening
smorgasbord of interesting tastes and textures and erasing the history
of exploitation and oppression between racial groups. If the history of
injustice is mentioned in such celebrations, moreover, it tends to be
frozen in the past, as if it had no bearing on present-day inequalities.[49]
Multicultural tours of race also are problematic because they tend implicitly to present race as relevant to nonwhite people only. Children who
are cultural tourists might talk about race, but only nonwhite people
tend to be the topic of those conversations. In the name of anti-racism,
this approach to race thus tends to reinforce the view of white people
as raceless.

As difficult as it is for many of them to do, white parents need
to help their white children achieve a better contextualized and more
fully politicized understanding of race. The easy-to-pick-up souvenirs of
cultural tourism need to be replaced with what has been called critical
multiculturalism. In the classroom, "the goal [of critical multiculturalism]
is not merely, or primarily, about fostering an appreciation of diversity
but about ensuring equal access to the kind of education that trans-
lates into access to real opportunities."[50] Critical multiculturalism must
openly confront issues of power and white domination, in other words.
At home, critical multiculturalism might mean replacing, or at least
supplementing school-time holiday celebrations of diversity with books
and discussions that confront the realities of present-day inequalities
and connect them with the United States' and Western world's history
of racism and imperialism. In this context, it can be helpful to provide

important white allied role models to white children by learning about white people who actively have been opposed to racism (by fighting slavery through work on the Underground Railroad, for example). When doing so, however, white parents need to steer clear of children's books on multiculturalism that ultimately demean people of color, for example, by depicting African Americans as passive, spiritual-singing recipients of white people's heroic efforts to save them.[51]

More than anywhere else, however, an important place for children to find role models for their racial attitudes is in the lives and behaviors of their own parents. This makes most middle-class white adults' dis-ease with conversations about race particularly troublesome. Children learn a great deal about resistance to racism (or lack thereof) from their parents' responses (or, again, lack thereof) to racist situations. One of the most difficult of these to confront is racism within one's own family. How should a white parent respond, for example, when a grandparent makes a racist remark or joke in front of his or her child? Out of fear of confronting one's own parents, it can be tempting for the parent (perhaps especially white middle-class women) to change the subject, ignore the remark, or otherwise smooth things over so that additional conflict and tension are not injected into the situation. This is all the more true when one is fairly sure that the person who made the racist remark is not going to change his or her racist attitudes as a result of one's response to them. So why bother, one might wonder? One answer is that becoming a parent means that she or he is "now responsible for fighting racism 'for two.' "[52] A parent's struggle against racism is also his or her child's struggle in that the child learns a great deal about how and when to respond to white privilege and white domination by watching his or her parents. Resistance to racism does not have to involve yelling or physical threats, for example, nor does it have to humiliate the person who made a racist remark.[53] Quiet but clear challenges to racism can demonstrate to a child strength, courage, and "guts" in the face of an uncomfortable situation. They can demonstrate to a child a way of performing whiteness that disrupts white domination and privilege. In that way, "the power of resistance is to set an example: not necessarily to change the person with whom you disagree, but to empower the one who is watching and whose growth is not yet complete."[54]

The disruption of white privilege that white parents can model for white children includes interrupting the way that white class differences are used to buttress white domination across class-race lines. White parents need to realize that they are important models of love for other white people for their white children—or disdain and disgust, as too often is the case. Middle-class white children typically learn from their white parents the "appropriate" places to dump their racist inclinations while simultaneously appearing non- or anti-racist. As one cultural anthropologist notes, "white, middle-class liberals learn very young not to use epithets with racial connotations, but they receive quite different messages from their parents concerning labels for poor whites, the most naturalized of which is white trash."[55] The parent who is responsible for fighting racism for two also is responsible for fighting the abjection of poor whites. Teaching white children to deflect responsibility for white racism away from middle-class white people only helps them perfect their ability to abject people who aren't like them and pursue the quest for purity that middle-class white goodness shares with white supremacy.

Situations that call for a parent's challenging an individual insistence of racism or white abjection unfortunately are easy to come by, even if they are difficult for most middle-class white parents to deal with. More challenging but equally important is for parents to find ways to help children see the structural and asymmetrical aspects of race and racism. Children tend to see racism as something that operates only on the level of the individual and that impacts individuals of different races in commensurable ways.[56] But children need to understand that racism is the product of more than just deluded or scared individuals.[57] One simple activity that can help children see the structural asymmetry of racism is to count with them the number of white and nonwhite characters featured on television shows.[58] Combined with discussion of why most of the people on television are white when a large percentage of people in real life are not, this exercise can help children recognize racist imbalances in the world and to see the effects of an absence that otherwise might go unnoticed. (I'll return to this suggestion later in the chapter.)

Another example of both recognizing and failing to recognize racial absences comes from my experience with my oldest daughter at a major philosophy conference. The conference was held in Washington, D.C., in Fall 2009, a few months after a bedtime conversation she initiated about race. At the conference, my daughter remarked that she saw lots of black people as we milled around in the hotel lobby. I responded that both black and white people lived in D.C., and that her observation was right in that more black people live in D.C. than in our fairly white hometown. Later that evening, my daughter accompanied me for a few minutes to the conference reception. In retrospect, I realize that we walked into a room filled exclusively with white people, but at the time I wasn't thinking about race or our hotel lobby conversation. That quickly changed when the first thing my daughter asked me was why there weren't any black people at the reception. We then stopped to talk about how most philosophy departments don't include many black and other people who aren't white; that this is because they are made to feel like they aren't welcome; and that it's important to change philosophy so that black and other nonwhite people don't want to avoid it and can help shape the field.

In retrospect, what stands out about this event is what my daughter and I *didn't* talk about: our own whiteness. This absence became visible to me after reading Susan Raffo's account of walking into a coffee shop with her daughter when they were out running errands.[59] Raffo and her daughter are both white, and they have developed a habit of asking each other "Who is here?" when they walk into stores or down the street. When her daughter commented that there were only white people in the coffee shop, she and her mother asked why that might be so. Noticing that the store was in a predominantly white upper-middle-class neighborhood, they wondered if the shop drew only local traffic and if people of color wouldn't be comfortable there. What is most notable about Raffo's story is the next topic she and her daughter discussed. Unlike my daughter and me, they talked not just about the absence of people of color in the store, but also about what it was like for them as white people to be there: how they fit in with the other white people, which allowed them to not notice that they were white. Making visible the invisibility of their class status as well as their race, Raffo and her daughter cut through the "white noise" that enables white people to ignore the white privilege in their lives.

These examples demonstrate that even in the case of an event that doesn't focus on race or racism, parents sometimes will have opportunities to discuss with their children the role that race (and class) play in it. Even if they bumble through the situation as I did with my daughter, parents can identify and discuss with their kids the lack of explicit attention paid to race (and class) in a particular situation. In the case of political rallies, for example, why doesn't the topic of race often come up? When it does come up, are only people of color discussed? What is the effect of omitting white people from those discussions? These kinds of conversations between parents and children, which often are casual and even short (depending on the child's age), can be helpful to have about or at all sorts of events—community gatherings, county fairs, town festivals, and public library events—that do not explicitly center on race. Helping white children to see how race, and whiteness in particular, often functions invisibly (for white people) can be one of the most important lessons that a white parent can teach her child.

While this next suggestion likely will be very difficult for most middle-class white parents, they also might consider practicing "other-mothering" by discussing issues of race and racism with white children who are not their own. As Patricia Hill Collins explains, black women have a long tradition of informal and extended kin networks in which they have taken responsibility for other black children who are not "theirs." This tradition has helped black children survive and thrive in the midst of white domination and privilege. It also has deliberately refashioned the concept of family into something other than a white, patriarchal, nuclear unit. Given this refashioning, perhaps othermothering "could serve as a model for antiracist [sic] work" performed by white mothers, fathers, and other caregivers.[60]

This could take the relatively uncontroversial form of white parents' volunteering to give presentations on race and racial justice struggle at their children's school or their town's public library. But it also could take the more controversial and more existentially challenging form of othermothering white children in public settings, such as grocery stories, playgrounds, and public parks. Rather than care solely about the racial attitudes and behaviors of one's own child, white othermothers (including white fathers and grandparents) could respond to the offensive racial behavior of other white children. Given white, middle-class norms of the family as an isolated nuclear entity and the unconscious beliefs in white privilege of many white adults, this practice probably would be seen as offensive meddling by many of the parents of the white children who were othermothered. It also would seriously jeopardize a white parent's racial/class status as middle-class: it's just not what white middle-class parents do, in large part because of the individualism that pervades "proper" whiteness. A potential othermother would have to consider judiciously whether and how to intervene in any particular situation. And she or he would have to figure out how to do so without being preachy or moralizing, using the situation as an occasion for one's own racial redemption. This perhaps would be the trickiest aspect of othermothering for most middle-class white parents: How to intervene in a way that effectively reaches children, even if it doesn't particularly make the parent look good? If a white parent could figure out how to do that, her othermothering could serve as an example to other white children of how to be a white ally even if one's actions weren't appreciated by other adults.

I don't want these suggestions to make it appear that white allies must or do have all the answers, however. It's all too easy to play into a white fantasy of mastery when tackling questions of how white parents should deal with racism in their children's lives. In fact, perhaps one of the most important things that a white ally can do for her or his white child is to let the child see her parents struggle to figure out how to deal with racism in real life. Take the case of a white couple who regularly reads non-children's books to their two-year-old white son at bedtime and picked up Toni Morrison's novel *Sula* to read one evening. They quickly discovered that the word *nigger* appears multiple times in the first few pages of the book. As Arwyn, the white mother, explains, "After the third or fourth iteration, The Man [husband and father] abruptly stopped reading, and asked—more like demanded, desperate for an answer—'should I be reading that word aloud?' I said the only thing I could: 'I don't know.' "[61] The series of questions that Arwyn then asks of herself are ones that white parents need to wrestle with rather than avoid. After reflecting on the details of her family's white privilege, Arwyn writes:

> I think it is also white responsibility, stemming from that white privilege, to think about that language, to examine the role I play in perpetuating it, to act to counter it. I have a responsibility to teach my child about the word, about the larger evils it represents, yes: but I also have a responsibility to ensure that my child does not hurt those around him by repeating it before he knows better, do I not? So do we read the word aloud and hope he is able to understand our explanations? Substitute it with a euphemism more palatable but ultimately no less [oppressive]? . . . Put the book away until he's "old enough," whatever that is? If we do that last, are we white-washing his world, perpetuating racism-through-exclusions? Or would we be ensuring that in his formative years he only is exposed to positive images of people of color, friendly interactions between people of different races? I come around to the answer I gave that night: I don't know.

I don't know either. Perhaps Arwyn's questions are a little bit easier to answer in the case of an older child who is developmentally capable of understanding and discussing the varied uses of racial slurs, but her insightful question of what "old enough" means remains on the table. At what age is it most beneficial for racial justice movements to discuss racial slurs with white children? Probably much younger than many white parents would be comfortable with. Recalling the racialized tussle between three-year-old Lingmai and four-year-old Renee, we know that trying to shelter children of any race from racist language doesn't work for long, if it works at all. I don't think it would be crazy for Arwyn to begin to share some of her questions and reflections about "the N word" with her two-year-old son, although she will need to figure out how to do so in a simpler manner than she does in her blog. (Here is where help from education and child development specialists is sorely needed.) Whatever age a white parent decides is appropriate to discuss racial slurs with their white children, however, one thing is clear: "Don't assume you have to already know everything before you start trying to teach your children. . . . Figuring out how to be white is something [white parents need to] do together with our children."[62]

As they do so, white parents need to be emotionally and spiritually strong enough for what likely will happen. They have to be prepared to become visible as white people and be willing to put their white class status in jeopardy to be able to respond effectively to their children. Talking with children about race means that *they* will talk, and not always in ways that a white parent will welcome. As Susan Raffo remarks, "As soon as we encourage our children to reflect on the world around them, to say what they are thinking and feeling and to invite conversation, well, they start to talk. And they will say things just about everywhere. And in front of just about everyone. . . . We know the feeling in our bellies when we are walking through the world, thinking about our grocery list or the drive back home, when junior says something that immediately makes us feel exposed and visible. As white people. As potentially bad parents."[63] The sheer fact of having a child who makes a remark about race—even if the remark isn't racist—has the potential to mark a middle-class white parent as bad and thus also as not really middle-class. Doesn't your child know better than to say things like that? Didn't you teach her—that is, teach whiteness—better than that? This is the message a white parent often fears will be contained in the startled or uncomfortable expressions on nearby white parents' faces.

And this is why white allied parents have to "know [their] own shit" if they are going to encourage their children to talk with them about race and racism:

> Oh lovely shit, oh layered deep old stuff which gets triggered by the innocent voices of our children. The shame of it. The guilt. The embarrassment. What do I do if my child says something racist? What will others think of me? Will they look over at me, knowing what a horrible mother I am, because my son just came out with something funky

about that woman's hair, her skin, the way she talks? What will people say?[64]

Anticipating the next chapter, I would say that here is where white parents need the spiritual strength to not respond to a situation merely out of white shame or guilt. A white allied parent very well may feel ashamed, guilty, or embarrassed when her white child says something racially inappropriate or downright racist, but those emotions should not be the primary drivers of her response. When they are, they tend to steer a white parent in the wrong direction: toward what other people will say or think about his or her goodness as a (middle-class) white parent, toward shushing her child as he or she gives the other parents an apologetic smile. But a parent's goodness is not what should be at issue when a child says something racially offensive. What matters instead is what the child—and the other children around her—learn about race after the offending remark is made. And they tend to learn white invisibility and racial privilege when a white parent refuses to talk about race.

White supremacists are right about one thing: white parents need to openly discuss race, especially whiteness, with their white children. Of course, white allied parents need to do this in ways that challenge rather than promote white domination, but white supremacists nevertheless have something valuable to teach other white people about the importance of explicitly talking about whiteness with their kids. When providing examples of how white allied parents might do this, I was struck by their similarity to the suggestions made by white supremacist parents. Even though the content of the two sets of suggestions is different, their form is virtually identical: don't let whiteness be invisible, and identify and discuss race in all sorts of situations and places where it usually isn't done. And in some cases, the content of the two suggestions isn't even that different. For example, the worry about unconscious media messages concerning race and the resulting advice to count and discuss the number of people of different races portrayed on television are eerily similar to that of white supremacists. The difference in this case, of course, is that white allied and white supremacist parents have very different ideas about what is subversive about the racial environment provided by mainstream media and certainly about what count as desirable outcomes of discussing media portrayals of race. But what is the same is the belief that white parents should not leave the racial development of their white children to chance. White parents need to counter what contemporary society teaches about race by openly discussing racial matters with their kids.

As important as this advice is, however, it ultimately cannot be sufficient for racial justice movements. More discussion of race, as if white allies could talk the world free of racial oppression, cannot be the entire solution to problems of racism. As I have suggested, just as significant as the role of words in white parents' interaction with their white children is the role of their racially disciplined and normalized bodies. Not everything can be said, about race or any other topic, and the bodily unsaid—located in bodily habits and behavior—can convey a great deal. Many of the bodily messages conveyed about race will not be understood by a young child—although they can still impact her developing raced and racist unconscious—but a surprising number of them are.

This point is evident in the example of a white mother with two white children, ages seven and two and a half, who would wheel the toddler around the streets of New York in a stroller.[65] The mother habitually steered around the panhandlers on her neighborhood street, almost all of whom were black men. As she explains, she did so neither because she feared them nor because they aggressively approached her for money, but because she did not have change to give them and did not want her children to think that she was unkind. One day at home, the toddler suddenly announced to his mother that "black men are bad." The toddler's parents were horrified. They were good liberals who had never instructed their children to be blatantly racist, and the same could be said for their friends and other family members (all of whom presumably were white). Eventually, the mother realized that the child had taken up her and her husband's instructions to the toddler to stay away from "bad" things, such as stray dogs and electrical outlets, in an unexpected way. The toddler saw his mother carefully put bodily distance between themselves and the black panhandlers and reasoned that this must be because they also were bad.

This incident involves what Michel Foucault has called "a body totally imprinted by history," in this case, a racist history in which white women are disciplined and discipline themselves to fear black men.[66] Without saying a word about race, this white mother's bodily movements unintentionally taught her youngest child a lesson about blackness. In some respects, that this happened is not surprising. Children are notorious for adopting adult bodily behaviors and habits of which the adults are not consciously aware and which they assume their children do not notice—hence the enduring relevance of the clichéd phrase "Do as I say and not as I do." But it might be surprising to white adults who think of themselves as raceless and nonracist that children can and do learn a great deal about race and racism from their bodily habits. Bodily behavior and comportment regarding race can speak volumes. It can convey moral values, rigidly mapping them on to racial spaces that are split-separated into "pure" white and "impure" nonwhite categories.

Middle-class white children also learn a great deal about the abjection of white trash from their parents' bodily behaviors and habits. For example, when I was fifteen years old and dating a white boy from a lower socioeconomic class than my family, I had what I thought was a brilliant idea. Instead of paying top dollar to have Jiffy Lube change the oil in my truck, my boyfriend and I could do it. I had no idea what was involved, but he had done this many times for his own car and was happy to do it for mine, so the plan to save money seemed sound. When my parents saw the oil filter and quarts of oil that I had purchased, they asked what they were for. When I explained my plan, their faces looked uncomfortable or upset—some sort of emotion that was hard to identify—and they said no. There wasn't any additional conversation about the matter. I wasn't sure why, but it was clear from their tense reactions that changing the truck's oil in front of the house was somehow unseemly or inappropriate. This was puzzling given the pleasure my parents took (and take) in saving money, and we had (and have) a running family joke telling stories to each other about the great bargains we find on clothing, kitchen gadgets, airfares, whatever. But something different was going on with this instance of saving money, something that I was only vaguely aware of but couldn't comprehend at the time.

In retrospect, I realize that I had proposed an activity that was permissible for lower-class white people to engage in—like my boyfriend—but not "us." That "us" was white middle-class people, who lived on the "good" side of town in the country club estates. My parents didn't explain any of this to me, at least not via explicit conversation. Their facial expressions and body language instructed me on where the lines were between different classes of white people, and those lines were not to be crossed. (Dating across those lines was marginally acceptable, but this was because my parents feared I would run off with my boyfriend if they forbade me to date him.) I surely had received instruction on white class differences myriad times before from various sources, but this instance sticks out in my mind because it was so puzzling why this particular form of savvy bargain hunting was forbidden. While I was a teenager, not a young child, I didn't yet understand all the middle-class rules of distinguishing oneself from "white trash." But I learned a lesson that day that shaped my classed and raced self into adulthood.

Fast-forward twelve years to a conversation that I had with my department head in my first job as a philosophy professor. It was deer season, and while driving a few days earlier, I had been run into by a deer trying to race across the road. It was a low-speed collision that only damaged my side view mirror, which was left intact but dangling by a lone electrical wire. My car was old and I planned to replace it soon anyway, and thus I didn't want to pay several hundred dollars to replace the mirror. So I used duct tape to secure it back in place. When my department head and I were walking to the parking lot after work a few days later, he saw the "repaired" mirror and asked if that was duct tape holding it onto the car. I laughed, a bit embarrassed, and without thinking made a crack about how "white trash" the car now looked. And then I stopped short, embarrassed again, unsure whether that was something I was "allowed" to say. My department head, who also was white, seemed to be in a similar state of embarrassed amusement. I think neither of us knew if I had said something offensive. On top of this, my awkward embarrassment also was caused by my sudden uncertainty about my identity, especially in my department head's eyes. As the redneck joke goes, "You need only two tools: WD-40 and duct tape. If it doesn't move and it should, use WD-40. If it moves and it shouldn't, use the duct tape."[67] Was my use of duct tape a sign that I wasn't the respectable middle-class white professor that I presumed and presented myself to be? Or was it a sign that I was so secure in my raced and classed identity that I could afford to joke about it? After all, it's only those with sufficient distance from the stereotype of white trash who can enjoy being marked temporarily by it.[68] So maybe I should have laughed all the more confidently about the duct tape to prove that I wasn't really what I feared I was.

As I reflect today on these incidents from my teens and twenties, I'm struck at how I have learned to abject poor white people as a way of ensuring my identity as a middle-class white person. And I'm increasingly aware of the significant role that my parents played in the education of my raced and classed habits. This is not to pile blame on them, but to try to understand the lessons about race and class that I learned as a child and to point to a related lesson I need to learn now that I'm a parent of two white children. Just as my parents implicitly instructed me on how to help secure the family's white middle-class status—a recent achievement for my extended family accomplished only in their generation—I inevitably am teaching my daughters lessons about race and class through my habits, behaviors, facial expressions, and body language, as well as spoken words. What are the lessons that I am teaching them? This is a difficult question to answer since those lessons often are not ones that I consciously intend. But I nevertheless need to be able to respond to the way I unconsciously live my raced and classed beliefs through my bodily habits.

No one can ever fully comprehend the lessons about race and class that he or she was taught as a child. Unconscious habits don't give themselves up to conscious reflection that easily. But one thing I now realize is that my teenage pleasure at finding a bargain was about more than saving money. It was connected to the experience of receiving parental approval. While I was confused by my parents' disapproval of changing the oil on the front driveway, once I was aware of it, there was no question that I would spend the extra money to go to Jiffy Lube. Something as seemingly minor as where to change the oil wasn't worth upsetting my parents or straining my relationship with them.

Let me focus for a moment on the connection between strained parent-child relationships and white identity. Theologian Thandeka has argued that white identity—by which she means an identity for Euro-Americans compliant with white privilege and domination—is developed in a white child through the often unspoken parental threat of withdrawing love.[69] When a white child violates the (again, often unspoken) classed/raced rules for how white children are supposed to behave, they risk emotional abandonment and/or physical punishment. Or the flip side: it is when a white child obeys the rules of white domination that she is lavishly praised by her parents for being "a good girl" or "a good boy."[70] Because children—and young children in particular—are developmentally dependent on parents and other intimate caretakers for their survival, they usually choose to follow the rules of whiteness.[71] Jeopardizing their membership in the (white) community that nurtures and cares for them is to jeopardize their very lives: emotionally, psychologically, spiritually, and sometimes even physically. "It is," as George Yancy has argued, "[precisely] within the context of a *loving* white family structure that the vicious practices of white racism [often] are communicated and learned."[72]

Thandeka illustrates this point with the example of Sarah, a white girl who brought home her best friend from school and then was told by her mother never to do so again.[73] When Sarah asked why, the answer was that her friend was "colored." Sarah realized this, but didn't understand why that was a reason not to invite her over, and so she pressed her mother for the real reason. No other answer was given, but "the indignant look on her mother's face . . . made Sarah realize that if she persisted, she would jeopardize her mother's affection toward her."[74] This was shocking since Sarah and her mother were very close, and Sarah thought that nothing could ever come between them. Her friendship with a black girl, however, revealed "the unimaginable, the unspeakable—the unthinkable": she could lose her mother's love.[75] Sarah never brought her black friend home again.

We might say that Sarah was a coward, that she should have challenged her mother's racist attitude toward black people, and that she should have refused to abandon her friend. We might also point out how Sarah herself was harmed by her "cowardice." As Thandeka argues, children like Sarah suffer affectively and ontologically because of their decision to put aside both their feelings for nonwhite friends and their impulses to moral action in order to remain in good standing with their parents and white community more broadly. They are caught in a "hidden civil war" over what to feel toward whom, and they experience a "misalignment" within their (white) identity.[76]

But as Thandeka also points out, it is a very different matter to call for racial courage from children than from adults. Adults are not developmentally dependent on their caretaking communities to the degree that children still are. This means that adults can sever meaningful ties with those communities without jeopardizing their survival—although even in the case of adults, we should never underestimate the psychosomatic cost of breaking with communities that have sustained a person's life, even if in deeply flawed ways. And there also can be economic costs, sometimes severe, for breaking with church groups, financial partners, family members, and other local communities that help ensure one's day-to-day survival. These costs can be more difficult for poor than for financially comfortable white people to bear, and so class differences can make a significant difference in how much racial courage is required to sever ties with other white people. Whatever a person's class status, no human being can live without connections with others—psychological, spiritual, emotional, material, and otherwise. We necessarily are part of complex transactional relationships with other people. But adults usually have established life-sustaining communities beyond their family of origin, and so losing the love (or material support) of that family would not necessarily or as severely jeopardize their survival.

Not so with children. They are not in the same position of choosing the families and communities that sustain them. And so calling Sarah a coward misses the mark, as does calling her a racist because she abandoned her friend because she was black. In the case of children, "the standard racial categories of judgment and damnation," such as "racism," "prejudice," and "bigotry," don't adequately grasp the dynamics of a white identity compliant with white domination.[77] Thandeka proposes the concept of white shame instead, defining it as the "deeply private feeling of not being at home within one's own white community."[78] White shame clearly is not a positive phenomenon or an emotion to cultivate on Thandeka's view. It leads children to blame themselves, rather than their white parents or caretaking environment, for wanting something "wrong," such as a friend who is black. White shame might very well lead a child—and the adult that the child will grow into—to behave in ways that harm people of color, promote white domination, and otherwise produce racist effects. But the root of those behaviors and habits, according to Thandeka, is not necessarily or always hatred for nonwhite people. It instead can be fear of familial, social, and emotional perdition.[79] A profound sense of unlovability and a constant feeling of vulnerability lie behind a white identity compliant with white domination. Composed of shame, white identity is a child's defense against a white community that attacks it because it does not yet know and follow the rules of white domination. For this reason, Thandeka claims, white America's first racial victims are its own white children.[80]

The terms Thandeka uses to describe a child's developing white identity are provocative. She claims that "the crime of 'soul murder'" is committed against white children by white parents and white caretakers, who are guilty of "white racial abuse" that bears all the hallmarks of "psychological child abuse."[81] And while good middle-class white people might not find these phrases too strong to describe the parenting styles and choices of self-proclaimed white supremacists, those are not the white people Thandeka primarily writes about. It is the relationship between white children and white parents in many non-supremacist families that she depicts as one of racist abuse. According to Thandeka, many middle-class white families use fear of emotional abandonment and ostracism to cement their bonds and to develop the white compliant identities of the children in them.

I find some of Thandeka's claims about white racial abuse in non-supremacist white families to be too strong. As I'll argue below, not all parental influence on white children that produces racist habits is abusive. Furthermore, the type of emotional abuse she describes can and does take place within white (and other) families regarding all sorts of issues, not just race. Thandeka nevertheless is onto something important about white children and the mechanisms of white domination. People who care about racial justice long have known that white racism can be very damaging to black and other nonwhite children's developing sense of self. When young children of color are told by white adults that skin color doesn't matter, for example, they likely wrestle with a misalignment of their identities and experience a hidden civil war over what to perceive and to admit to their caregivers that they perceive. We have known, as Toni Morrison has argued, that finding a racial house that can also be a home often has been difficult for many black people.[82] But I think we haven't been very aware that something similar might be going on with white children. As Thandeka explains, in the racial abuse of many non-supremacist white families, no child is beaten or dies. The instances of "soul murder" are "*objectively* seamless events"—a kind of peaceful violence, as Franz Fanon might say—because no overtly violent rupture between child and parent occurs.[83] But something damaging nonetheless could be happening regarding the formation of a white child's racial and classed identity. That child likely is learning that habits of white domination are required to fully belong to her family.

Much of this damage occurs at unconscious levels, making the abusive lessons of a white identity compliant with white domination seem trivial, or even nonexistent. While many white adults interviewed by Thandeka initially didn't think that they learned any such lessons as children, after engaging in probing conversations with her, they often remembered incidents that had been forgotten for years. (It's an interesting question whether talking with a black person was central to unearthing their childhood memories about race, but I'll set aside that question here.) As the white people's accompanying tears and strong emotional responses suggest, their "forgetting" of these incidents wasn't an accident or a mere oversight on the part of their conscious memories. More likely is that "the experience of becoming white was too traumatic to retain in consciousness."[84] The formation of a racial identity out of threats from and fear of losing those who love one most "is too much for most persons to retain in conscious memory," and so it usually is repressed.[85] The more sedimented that white identity becomes, the less likely that the forgotten incidents will ever be remembered. "The success of the strategy renders the original injury invisible": nothing racially significant seems to have happened in most white people's childhoods because those children have become adults who are compliant with white domination.[86]

What also tends to be "forgotten" or repressed in the memories, lives, and habits of most white adults are the alternatives to white domination that they were aware of as children.[87] Although childhood is not a space of racial purity or innocence, it often is a time of greater plasticity and possibility since the etiquette and other habits of white domination haven't yet fully taken hold. As Jennifer Ritterhouse argues, childhood often is composed of " 'forgotten alternatives'—the ideas, impressions, and emotions that preceded and sometimes contradicted the lessons in white supremacy that their parents and the whole social world around them gradually taught."[88] The "forgetting" of these alternatives works hand in hand with the "forgetting" of childhood incidents in which a white person is taught how to be white. With all of these racialized aspects of childhood forgotten, a white identity compliant with white domination can seem to be the only available option, the only place a white person comfortably belongs.

As Morrison explains, "So much of what seems to lie about in discourses on race concerns legitimacy, authenticity, community, belonging. In no small way, these discourses are about home: an intellectual home; a spiritual home; family and community as home."[89] Discourses about whiteness also are discourses about family and home, and nowhere is that claim truer than in the case of white children. Just as black people need to figure out how "to convert a racist house into a race-specific yet nonracist home," white people—parents in particular—need to figure out how to create a race-specific yet nonracist home for white children.[90] Here I disagree with Thandeka's implied solution to the problem of white racial abuse, which is to raise white children as human, not white.[91] More options exist for a white person's racial identity than white supremacy, non-supremacist compliance with white domination, or raceless humanism, and I'm concerned that the raceless humanism suggested by Thandeka tends to operate as white domination in disguise. White parents and children can and need to create a critically raced home space that is allied with people of color's struggles for racial justice. White supremacist, nonwhite, and mixed-raced families have long explicitly focused on raising their children in what they perceive to be racially appropriate ways, by choice and of necessity. It is time that other white families do so as well in order to combat white racism.

A critically raced home needs to include parent-child relationships that aren't based on the withdrawal of love if a child doesn't comply with white domination. I wholeheartedly agree with Thandeka on this point, but I disagree with a possible implication of her account that all situations in which a child learns white domination from her parents are abusive. I think it is inevitable that in a racist world, a white child will learn racist habits from her parents (and others), and this doesn't always happen through threats of emotional abandonment. Through their bodily habits and behaviors—largely unspoken and often unconscious—white parents living in a white-dominated world can't help but model white privilege for their white children. This acknowledgment is not a manifestation of relativist despair; nor is it a claim that white domination and privilege is all that white parents can or should model for their children. It rather is a rejection of the white liberal conviction that "young children can be salvaged from racist beliefs, if [only] they are taught early enough" by parents who are good and try hard enough.[92] It is, in other words, a challenge to and rejection of the white need for purity—this time, the purity from racism desperately desired by many white people.

The attempt to be racially pure that characterizes white supremacy is manifest in non-supremacist white attempts to be perfectly pure of racism. My point here is not that non-supremacist white people should comfortably accept that they are racist. Rather, it is that the questions white allies are asking themselves about race need to be reoriented from ones of whether or not they have eliminated all the racism in their and their children's lives—in a world structured by white domination and privilege, they have not—to ones of how they might most productively deal with and even use the racist habits and beliefs that they and their children have. Are there, for example, ways that white people can utilize their white privilege against itself?[93] For white parents in particular, rejecting the white need for purity from racism means starting with the recognition that their white children eventually will learn racist habits and beliefs. This is not because of any genetic hardwiring, nor is it because of the inevitability of white racial abuse. It is because, like adults, children are social beings formed in and through transaction with a racist world. The issue then becomes one of how to deal with a white child's habits of white domination. And the answer is as simple—and as terribly difficult—as a parent's attempts to openly and honestly confront her own racism so that she can work together with her child to see and challenge the white privilege in both of their lives.

⌒

White supremacists are right that the reproduction of whiteness is not limited to gestation and birth. The perpetuation of whiteness, white privilege, and white supremacy depends on their social, psychological, and political reproduction as much if not more than on the physical reproduction of human beings with stereotypically white features. While children transact with a world much larger than the nuclear family, parents play a large role in the social reproduction of race and racism. The "thick relationships of family belonging" are not a distraction from a politics of racial justice; they are an intimate place in which that politics can take place.[94] This means that the deliberate and careful attention given by white parents to the raising of their white children should not be left to white supremacist parents only. White parents committed to racial justice can and should also engage in childrearing practices that focus on their child's race.[95] Here is where, to give a twist to the epigraph from Jonas Salk, white people's greatest responsibility is to be good ancestors. White parents pass down to their white children much more than genes for pale skin and other physical features associated with whiteness. They also pass down habits of whiteness through their conversations and silences, their bodily gestures and facial expressions, their unconscious desires and unspoken fears. The question in today's world thus is not whether, but how white parents will reproduce white children. It's not whether those children will develop habits of whiteness, but what kind of habits will they be? White parents, teachers, and other caregivers need to nurture forms of racial belonging that aren't dependent on quests for racial purity or superiority. Not just their children's future, but the kind of world all children will live in depends upon their doing so.

4

The Dangers of White Guilt, Shame, and Betrayal

Toward White Self-Love

Can the acknowledgement of whiteness produce only self-criticism, even shame and self-loathing?

—Linda Martín Alcoff, *Visible Identities*

White people in this country will have quite enough to do in learning how to accept and love themselves and each other, and when they have achieved this—which will not be tomorrow and may very well be never—the Negro problem will no longer exist, for it will no longer be needed.

—James Baldwin, *The Fire Next Time*

A particular joke was popular right after Barack Obama's historic 2008 election to the presidency of the United States: How many white people voted for Obama? Answer: A lot of guilt-ridden ones. Throughout and following Obama's presidential campaign, the American public seemed fascinated and sometimes puzzled by why white people might choose to vote for a black president. (In fact, when one Googles to find out how many white people voted for Obama in 2008, this joke, rather than news analysis of exit polls, is the first entry to pop up.)[1] Earlier in the political season, during Obama's victories in the Spring 2008 primaries, a syndicated political cartoon was printed that showed Obama seeming to walk on water. Just below the water's surface were white people with "white liberal guilt" written on their shirts, holding their breath as they held up their hands to be stepping stones for Obama's feet.[2] Obama's popularity and success may make him seem godlike, the cartoon tells us, but don't be fooled: guilty white liberals are responsible for his miraculous political results. Along with the political joke, this cartoon posits white guilt as the foundation of black success, a submerged and contentious belief that often is difficult for Americans consciously to grapple with except through humor.

I won't attempt to answer the question of whether white guilt was the main motivator for white Obama supporters in 2008 (or 2012, for that matter), but I am interested in the broader question of the political effects of white guilt, its close cousin white shame, and the related figure of the white race traitor. I'm also interested in the relationship between white middle-class liberalism and racialized affects and emotions. Do guilt and shame about whiteness and white domination help white people work for racial justice? Are white guilt, shame, and betrayal emotional comportments equally available to middle-class and lower-class white people? The latter is an important question, as we will see, because of the role of emotion and class in maintaining structures of racial injustice. I will argue that the answer to these questions generally is no, which means that critical philosophers of race need to rethink the role of white guilt, shame, and betrayal in racial justice movements. Offering an alternative to these emotions, I suggest that a critical form of self-love is a more valuable affect to be cultivated by white people who care about racial injustice.

ᴄᴧ

Affects and emotions help make up the selves that we are and thus also the capacities we have to act in and engage with the world. While I will use both terms, I tend to prefer "affect" to "emotion." This is because in the field of philosophy "emotion" often connotes an opposition to reason and the assumption of mind-body dualism. Given the hegemony of reason and mind in traditional Western thought, "emotion" thus tends to be treated dismissively as mere feeling. The term *affect* does a better job of interrupting conventional dismissals of the felt, embodied aspects of human life. The concept of affect also does a better job of recognizing that affects are constitutive of the self. Affects are not ontologically trivial or secondary to some other, allegedly primary part of the self, nor are affects layered on top of a rational core. They cannot be adequately understood in the traditional dualism between emotion and reason or feeling and thinking. Affects such as joy, love, gratitude, hate, resentment, shame, and so on dynamically constitute whatever is fundamental to the self, including its judgments of and responses to the world.[3]

This is not to say that the concept of emotion is adequately understood by the dualism of emotion and reason, either. Emotions are much smarter than this dualism allows. The so-called dumb view of emotion has been successfully challenged by feminist philosophers, such as Elizabeth Spelman, and they are joined by neuroscientists, such as Antonio Damasio, who provide non-reductivist accounts of the physiology of human emotions.[4] Emotions are not meaningless outbursts made by a body sharply separated from the mind. They contain judgments about the world and are suffused with intelligence and discrimination. They are forms of embodied thinking that primarily operate nonconsciously. We can become consciously aware of our emotions and the judgments they put forth, but the making of those judgments tends to happen apart from reflective thought. The nonreflective dimension of emotion does not make it irrational, however. The relevant distinction here is not between irrational emotion and rational reason but between nonconscious and conscious thought. It is a distinction rather than a sharp dualism, indicating that emotional and reflective thinking can be complementary and that emotions can infuse conscious deliberation.

I will use both "affect" and "emotion" to indicate a focus on the personal that is simultaneously political and that disrupts dichotomies between thinking and feeling. Above all, whichever term I use, I am speaking of something that is transactionally constitutive of the self. Emotions and affects are ways of taking in and responding to the world. They are part of a dynamic relationship with the world, including other people, in which the world helps constitute a person's emotional makeup, and in turn her engagements with the world, which are always inflected with some sort of emotion(s), help reciprocally shape it. For these reasons, emotion and affect can be considered instances of habit. They are predispositions for acting in and engaging the world that are woven together as the fabric of the self. They are ontological in such a way that the self is never sealed off from the world "around" it but is always affectively co-constituted with it. Given the ontological nature of affect and emotion, the question is not *whether* affect and emotion will impact a person's transactions with the world. It instead is *which* affects and emotions are or will be part of those transactions.[5]

The ontological dimension of affect and emotion also means that they are agential: affect and emotion are inherently related to a person's capacity or power to act in relation to the world. As the Latin root *movēre* suggests, emotions literally move us.[6] They have, as Theresa Brennan puts it, "an energetic dimension," and thus emotions or affects can be thought of as a kind of power that fuels the self's actions. Different emotions can move us in different directions, moreover, and some emotions are more powerful in terms of their ability to sustain ongoing, beneficial action. Here I'm in agreement with a philosophical tradition that makes a distinction between negative and positive affects that is not based on conventional moral judgment.[7] "Negative" here does not necessarily mean "morally bad," and "positive" does not necessarily mean "morally good." In some cases, affects that are considered morally good can be spiritually destructive. Likewise, affects that are considered morally bad in certain situations sometimes can be life-enhancing. While both positive and negative affects have an energetic dimension, negative affects ultimately seek to tear down people while positive affects attempt to build them up.

"Tearing down" and "building up" must be understood here transactionally, not atomistically. The genuine building up of a person can succeed only if those around her are built up too. To increase the ability of one person to harm another is not to build her up, but ultimately to tear her down. This is because in addition to harming others, her destructiveness also eventually harms herself by harming part of the environment that feeds back into her. She and her destructiveness, in turn, are part of the environment for others, composing a non-vicious circle between herself and others. As I will elaborate below, shame (as it functions in Western cultures) is an exemplary negative emotion that tears people down, and love is an exemplary positive emotion that builds people up. Depending on their different interpersonal effects, some emotions, such as anger, can be either negative or positive, or perhaps even both. The key question, in any case, is whether an affect is life-enhancing or life-deflating, with "life" understood as the psychosomatic totality of a human being's transactional existence in the world.

bell hooks's work on rage provides an excellent analysis of the different roles that a particular affect can play in people's lives, illustrating what I am calling the spiritual effects of emotion. Rage can be an expression and validation of racial hierarchies, as when white people experience "narcissistic rage" when their racial privilege is threatened. Or it can challenge white supremacy, as black people's "militant rage" does.[8] As hooks examines the nuances of black rage, she also distinguishes between the "constructive healing rage" of a black person who refuses to embrace racial victimization and the black rage that is "not processed constructively" and thus can lead to self-destructive behavior.[9] Rage is complex, all the more because as hooks surmises, "the rage of the oppressed is never the same as the rage of the privileged."[10] As she addresses the privileged, hooks suggests that white people's rage tends to take only negative forms, narcissistically working out of a sense of entitlement to tear down people of color. In the lives of black people, rage often is even more complicated. It can be a positive or negative affect, healing or corroding black people's souls depend on how they process their rage and whether they succumb to white people's efforts to pathologize it. Elite black people who have "made it" in the white world also can participate in the negative affect of narcissistic rage, which tends to result in the repression and trivialization of more positive, militant forms of black rage.[11] Whatever the type of rage, what is important on hooks' account is whether rage enhances or destroys the ability of oneself and others to flourish transactionally.

My focus in this chapter will be on the role that racialized emotions play in the lives of white people in particular, but my analysis will have significant implications for people of color also since affects are never isolated within an individual person or a particular group of people. As I will argue, white people qua white are ill in that their racial habits largely have been built out of negative affects such as greed, hatred, jealousy, fear, destructive anger, and cruelty. Their psychosomatic health has suffered and continues to suffer because of their toxic racial identities built out of these affects and emotions. Their effect is to exhaust or diminish white people's spiritual energies, leaving them weak and powerless, like a plant that is too sickly to put out new shoots and so effectively begins to die. This sickliness would seem to make white people innocuous, but the result tends to be the exact opposite. As we will see especially in the case of shame, people constituted by negative affects tend to be too psychosomatically depleted to do much that is active and yet extremely dangerous because they resents others' liveliness and health and so try to destroy them.[12] Fueled by toxic and enervating affects and emotions, white racist habits have been pernicious to both the white people who embodied them and the people of color who suffered from them.

People of color long have been aware of the toxicity of white people's affects and emotions. For example, in his classic manifesto on race, *The Fire Next Time*, James Baldwin urges black people not to retaliate against white people by attempting to debase or dominate them in return. The reason is that doing so would harm black people most of all. As Baldwin assures his readers, "I am very much concerned that American Negroes achieve their freedom here in the United States. But I am also concerned for their dignity, for the health of their souls, and must oppose any attempt that Negroes may make to do to others what has been done to them. I think I know—we see it around us every day—the spiritual wasteland to which that road leads. . . . I would not like to see Negroes ever arrive at so wretched a condition."[13] Likewise, when Martin Luther King Jr. counseled his black church members to love their white enemies rather than return their racial hate, he did so because he believed that "hate distorts the personality of the hater. We usually think of what hate does for the individual hated or the individuals hated or the groups hated. But it is even more tragic, it is even more ruinous and injurious to the individual who hates."[14] While Baldwin was an avowed atheist and King a Christian minister, both warned of the devastating effects of white racism on "the souls of white folk," and they pleaded and preached that black people should not stoop to white people's debased level.[15] Out of all the damage that white racism has done to African Americans and other people of color, the most damaging of all would be for it to turn them into the debilitated, deplorable people that white folk generally are.

We might say that on Baldwin's view, and perhaps also King's, that white people are the truly "wretched of the earth."[16] This claim is not an attempt to trump or erase the enormous physical, psychological, economic, spiritual, and other types of pain that white people have caused people of color around the world. Nor is it an assertion that white people are racially oppressed. It instead recognizes that white people's domination of people of color has not only harmed people of color; it also has impoverished and depleted the souls of white folk. In Baldwin's words, "The great, unadmitted crime is what [the white man (sic)] has done to himself."[17] While we might think that white people have spent too much time focused on themselves—adorning themselves with praise for being the sole source of beauty, truth, progress, and democracy, for example—the opposite is the case. White people have barely begun to constitute themselves with white affects and other habits that are worthy of admiration.

So much the worse for white people, we might say. But although understandable, this response would be misguided because of the contagiousness of affect. Affects not only constitute human beings; they also circulate through them in humans' relationships with one another. Because they are transactional, negative affects tend to simultaneously poison the person constituted by them and create toxic relationships with other people that in turn infect them with negative affects. Positive affects likewise are transactional, and for this reason as they nourish and enrich a person, they can render her strong enough to help build up others, who then experience increased positive affects themselves. Both positive and negative affects can be contagious; it is difficult, if not impossible, to isolate oneself completely from the emotions and affects of others. This means not only that the emotional habits of a particular person strongly matter to her own psychosomatic health, but that the emotional habits of other people are crucial to her well-being too.

Teresa Brennan captures well the contagious aspects of affect as she describes its transmission between people.[18] Focusing particularly on negative affects, Brennan debunks the belief that affects are self-contained. For example, destructive anger and aggression in one person often produces depression in another, which in turn can make the depressed person a greater target of additional aggression either because the depressed person herself becomes aggressive or because of the negative mood that her depression brings about in others.[19] Similarly, hatred tends only to fester and grow when it is returned, and so to free oneself of hatred, one has to free others of it as well. Martin Luther King makes a similar observation when he claims that "at the very center of Jesus' thinking is this: that hate for hate only intensifies the existence of hate and evil in the universe." This is why "somebody must have religion enough and morality enough to cut [the chain of hate] off and inject within the very structure of the universe that strong and powerful element of love."[20] (I'll return shortly to King's strategy for disrupting chains of hate and other negative affects with love.)

The contagiousness of affect has been demonstrated empirically. The recent work of sociologist and physician Nicholas Christakis and political scientist James Fowler, for example, argues that people's good and bad health, including their behaviors and emotions, can be passed to others around them as if it were an infectious virus. Interestingly, positive emotions, such as cheerfulness, appear to be more contagious than negative ones. According to Christakis and Fowler, "each happy friend boosts your good cheer by 9 percent, while each additional unhappy friend drags you down by only 7 percent."[21] Perhaps even more relevant for my purposes here is the research of social psychologist Dacher Keltner and his colleagues that documents the emotional convergence of "low power" and "high power" individuals.[22] Low power individuals move toward the emotions and attitudes of high power individuals, and this holds true for both positive and negative emotions. Working with a definition of power as greater position in a social hierarchy, this research suggests that people of color's emotions will tend to converge with white people's emotions, which underscores my claim that white people's emotional health matters to those around them, as well as to themselves.[23]

Admittedly, how to combine empirical research on the contagiousness of affect into a coherent whole isn't always clear. If cheerfulness is more contagious than despair, for example, then shouldn't cheerful low power individuals lift up depressed high power individuals? Or does position on a social hierarchy trump emotional contagion, all else being equal (which of course it rarely is in practice)? We don't have to have complete answers to these questions, however, to conclude that Brennan and King are right: emotion and affect tend to be contagious. They often are transmitted between individuals, in many cases without their being aware of it, and their transmission can result in a mutually reinforcing spiral of emotion.

Given such mutual reinforcement, we might wonder how affective spirals can be interrupted. If negative (as well as positive) affects tend to reproduce themselves, how can one manage to respond to hatred with something besides hatred, or destructive anger with something other than more anger and/or depression? How can one get free of the poisonous affects of others? King provides an important answer with his invocation of love. While Jesus is the primary exemplar of love for King, one does not have to be a Christian or other religious follower to cut off chains of hate. A supernatural being need not be invoked to account for the disruption of negative affect even though the disruption may well be experienced as divine. A spiritual but naturalistic understanding of King's answer can be found in a transactional type of self-love. This would be a love of oneself that doesn't want to be burdened with negative affects, and so—understanding affect's contagion—it would try to make it such that other beings aren't constituted by negative affects either. This kind of self-love is very different from that of narcissism, whose atomistic focus on the self megalomaniacally disregards others.[24] A spiritually healthy self-love in contrast can interrupt a chain of negative affect, helping generate positive rather than negative affects in others, which can fuel further positive emotions in oneself, and so on.

Complementing King, Brennan also recommends love as a powerful affect that can transform the emotional economy that circulates between people. As Brennan explains, "When we love those who are not like us, even though they don't think like us or read the same books or read at all, those others feel it. Sometimes the other even listens, because the love allows them to lower their own shield (or projected [negative] affects or judgments) and permit entry to a new idea."[25] Love is a form of living attention, as Brennan calls it, which caringly focuses on another person and, in so doing, energizes and refuels her.[26] Living attention can help a destructively angry, defensive person loosen the fierce grip of her negative emotions and redirect her energy toward discerning the cause of her anger.[27] This is the first step in gaining freedom from destructive forms of anger and hate.

Lest this discussion of self-love sound suspiciously selfless, as if benefiting oneself were merely a means to the ultimate goal of benefiting others, let me emphasize the importance of focusing on oneself. Brennan captures this point well. Speaking of the "loop" of negative affects, she claims, "To love or forgive is to remove oneself from the loop. This is why the act of real forgiveness can be entirely selfish. *The forgiver* is the beneficiary, insofar as he or she is then free of transmitting a negative affect, and so free from attracting more of the same. . . . Really love those that hate you; do good to them that persecute you. There is no better escape, no clearer path to freedom. There is also no better revenge."[28] I'm skeptical that seeking revenge through love has the same effects as a spiritually healthy love. But Brennan's suggestion that the forgiver, not the forgiven, is the primary beneficiary of her forgiving love is right on target. The forgiver benefits most of all because she has freed herself from the toxic spiral of hate and ill will. The forgiven also has a greater chance of freeing herself from negative affects, but how she responds to the act of forgiveness is a separate matter. In forgiving—genuine loving forgiving—the forgiver already experiences the vitality of positive affects and increases her spiritual power and freedom no matter what the forgiven one's response.

In the end, however, sharp distinctions between selfishness and selflessness break down due to the transactional nature of human existence. Helping myself might seem selfish, but it's the best way to benefit others, and helping others is the best way to benefit myself. This means that negative affects can be resisted without violence, and positive affects can be used to reorder aggression.[29] This reordering happens when I have first reordered myself through love. Love can change one's constitution, in other words, such that one thinks, acts, and desires in different ways than when one hated. When bodies are in agreement with one another such that they reciprocally increase each other's power, they acquire a new constitution. They are constituted by positive affects, which leads them to believe, desire, and act differently. Love indeed can change the world by changing the self and its relationships with others.

Love has not been the dominant affect that characterizes white people. White people long have been constituted by negative affects, and it's probably safe to say that negative affects are what gave (and continues to give) birth to whiteness in the first place. The specific negative affects that constitute white people have changed somewhat over the years, however. White fear, for example, is one of the primary affects that historically has constituted whiteness. As Steve Biko argued in the context of South Africa, "One must not underestimate the deeply imbedded fear of the black man so prevalent in white societies."[30] In the case of the United States, we also could describe one of the central emotions of white people qua white as fear of people of color. In the seventeenth through the first half of the nineteenth century, for example, white slaveholders increasingly feared the uprising and rebellion of their black slaves and so created a plethora of slave codes and laws to punish slaves who attempted to run away from their slave owners or resist capture after they had fled.[31] White people have been particularly afraid of black men, casting them as hypersexual animals who threaten the purity of white women. The results of this fear can be seen in the lynching of approximately 3,500 black people from the late nineteenth century through the first half of the twentieth century, many whom were black men who were ritualistically castrated after they were lynched.[32]

Today, white fear of black people and black men in particular tends to manifest itself in a more peaceful form of violence.[33] Riotous lynching generally has disappeared in the United States, for example, but white people, and white women in particular, often are still afraid of black men. In the 1980s, Brent Staples described the protective march that white women assumed whenever he would take a walk after dark along Chicago's downtown streets. With their faces neutrally composed and their purses firmly clutched to their sides, white women would purposefully stride as if bracing for a tackle whenever they saw Staples on the sidewalk.[34] Jump to the twenty-first century and not much has changed. As George Yancy explains, when he walks across the street, he constantly "endure[s] the sounds of car doors locking as whites secure themselves from the 'outside world,' a space that is raced as nonwhite. . . . The *clicking* sounds are always accompanied by nervous gestures and eyes that want to look but are hesitant to do so."[35] Consider also the example of white behavior on elevators. White fear of black people perhaps is even stronger there than on the street since the elevator doesn't provide an automotive layer of glass and steel to "protect" white people from black people. As Yancy insightfully depicts "the elevator effect" of white fear, he explains that when he walks into an elevator that a white woman is on, he can tell by her bodily reactions that "she feels apprehension. Her body shifts nervously and her hearts beats more quickly as she clutches her purse more closely to her. . . . There is panic, there is difficulty swallowing, and there is a slight trembling of her white torso, dry mouth, nausea."[36] Even if white people don't consciously think of themselves as afraid of black people, their bodily reactions and habits often reveal that they are.

And their fear is not innocuous: it tends to result in significant harm to black people and other people of color. Contemporary white fear may be peaceful in that it usually does not produce a bloody body hanging from a tree, but it does bodily and psychological violence to people of color nonetheless. It harms the embodied, affective being of people of color, often by forcing negative affects onto them. In the transmission of affect, some people carry negative affects for others. Those tend to be feminine or feminized beings, namely women but also people of color when racism is a factor.[37] People of color often are instances of "affective marginalities," the affective Other who is the repository for the negative passions of the One who is in a position of domination.[38] In fact, we could say without much exaggeration that a war on affect is currently taking place in which negative emotions such as guilt and fear are being unequally distributed along racial (and global) lines.

As Yancy explains the harm done to him by white fear, the *clicks* of white people's car locks and white women's tightened grips on their purses confiscate his body and return it to him as something dangerous, animal-like, even evil. White fear of black people constitutes Yancy's "Black body [as] a site of enduring white semiotic constructions and historical power relations that inscribe and mark it as a particular *type* of body, an indistinguishable, threatening, evil presence, the so-called black bugaboo."[39] Yancy rightly talks about the need and the struggle to disrupt the way that white domination tries to constitute blackness, and such disruption is possible. But it is not always successful. When it is not, the greatest form of violence occurs, which is that people of color come to believe and experience themselves to be the dangerous, worthless evil that white racism says they are. This violence occurs, for example, when Pecola, the young black protagonist of Toni Morrison's *The Bluest Eye*, goes insane to escape her wish to be white with blue eyes in a world that finds her blackness ugly.[40] It occurred when James Baldwin self-destructively believed for many years that it was better to be white than black.[41] In instances such as these, white domination becomes victorious. Indeed, the racial contract established by white domination fully succeeds when people of color themselves become affective signatories to it.[42]

Fear is not the only negative affect that historically has been central to the constitution of whiteness in the United States and elsewhere. Other destructive emotions, such as vengeful anger, hatred, greed, and jealousy, also have played an important role in the makeup of whiteness.

White mistresses often were jealous of their black female slaves, and white masters often were jealous of the alleged sexual prowess of the black men they lynched and castrated.[43] The racial fears of both white men and women generally intensified into hatred as slave resistance increased before the Civil War and as Reconstruction began and then collapsed afterward.[44] In the twentieth century, as W. E. B. Du Bois argues, jealousy and greed were the main motivations for World War I, in which white people "struggle[d] for the largest share in exploiting darker races."[45] More recently, white anger over racial situations in the United States, such as alleged reverse discrimination and illegal immigration, continues to grow. This anger, which often is male anger in particular, is best understood as a form of resentment generated out a sense of loss of culturally normative identities, such as whiteness and maleness.[46]

The history of white affects deserves more detailed treatment than I have provided here, but I set it aside since my purpose is not to provide a comprehensive account of the emotions that have constituted whiteness. I instead have sketched a backdrop against which we can better understand the affects involved in contemporary efforts to remake whiteness. Those efforts have focused on guilt, shame, and betrayal, which, I will argue, function as negative affects much in the same way that fear, hatred, and greed do. Let me begin with guilt and, in particular, shame, the latter of which has emerged as *the* recommended emotion for white people today who care about racial justice. White people often feel very guilty when they face up to their racial history of degradation, violence, and death, and they struggle with how to respond to ongoing racism. Some feminist philosophers even have enthusiastically defended guilt as an effective motivation for political action.[47] But increasingly critical philosophers and other theorists of race have criticized white guilt as a paralyzing emotion that impedes, rather than assists racial justice movements.

To take one such example, Amy Edgington explains her realization that her well-intentioned effort to challenge desegregation in the 1950s by sitting next to a black girl at the back of the bus put the black girl in a great deal of danger. Whether the black girl remained in the seat or moved, she risked violence and humiliation. Reflecting on this incident, Edgington reveals how she was paralyzed with guilt for some time afterward. Still determined to do the right thing regarding racism, as she worked in the civil rights movements of the 1960s she often wasn't sure what the right thing was. The result was that "[she] felt stuck on that bus where there was no moral place to sit or stand. Guilt was keeping [her] from learning anything useful or doing anything effective."[48]

Edgington's experience demonstrates how, because of their guilt, white people sometimes feel incapable of making moral decisions about racial matters. The paralysis associated with white guilt can inhibit not only action, in other words, but also judgment. For this reason, Shelby Steele has gone so far as to define white guilt as "the *vacuum of [white people's] moral authority* that comes from simply *knowing* that one's race is associated with racism."[49] Steele argues that contemporary white people who acknowledge the existence of white racism "step into a void of vulnerability . . . [that] leaves no room for moral choice."[50] White guilt obligates white people to black people "because they needed the moral authority only black people could bestow."[51] This obligation merely reverses the previous situation in which only white people could possess moral authority. While that reversal might seem like a good development from a perspective of racial justice, it tends to make black and other nonwhite people responsible for white redemption and deliverance from racism.

Steele's analysis of white guilt and racial discrimination more broadly is problematic in several ways, including its atomistic individualism and its dismissal of systemic racism. But Steele accurately portrays a danger that many white allies need to avoid. If white guilt results in white people's inability to make moral and other judgments when issues of race are involved, it undermines white attempts to fight racism. A white identity that contributes to racial justice should not take the form of ducking obligation to make decisions about racial matters or positing nonwhite people as the only possible moral agents when it comes to race. As activist Sheila Wilmot argues, white people can fall into a "patronizing trap . . . if we do not deal well enough with guilt and fear," always deferring to the opinion of people of color and thus failing to treat them as equals.[52] "Being a [white] ally does not mean [merely] doing what we're told," as Wilmot explains, "it means respecting people of color and ourselves enough to disagree sometimes."[53] This does not mean that white people always know what the right thing is to do or that their decisions will result in racial justice. What it means is that even though white people often are unsure how to make a right decision when involved in a situation infused with race, they nonetheless need to be responsible for making the best decision that they can in genuine dialogue with people of color. White guilt often interferes with white people's assuming that responsibility. This is why, as Edgington concludes, white people who want to be effective against racism need to replace their collective guilt with concepts of collective privilege and collective responsibility.[54]

Critical whiteness scholar Audrey Thompson recounts a powerful story that underscores the need for white people's action rather than their guilt. When she was temporarily caring for the children of friends who lived in another state, Thompson realized that her friends had forgotten to leave her a key to their car. No neighbors had a spare car key, and Thompson needed the car to get around town with the children. After Thompson left a message at her friends' hotel, she "received daily, anguished phone calls about how dumb it had been to forget the key, how guilty [the parents] felt, and how lucky it was that [she is] a bus person and could make do without a car." At one point, one of the parents even urged Thompson to no longer mention the issue to the other parent because it was ruining their vacation by making her feel guilty. Thompson's replied calmly, "Everything's fine. These things happen. Stop feeling guilty. Just send me the key." But the key never came, and Thompson was cast into the role of being a potential troublemaker (vacation ruiner) because of her requests for the key. To preserve the friendship, Thompson shifted to making their phone conversations pleasant and alleviating the parents' guilt.

White people are like the friends who made Thompson's life difficult and then responded to that difficulty with guilt rather than action to improve the situation. It would have interrupted the parents' vacation for them to find a post office from which to mail the key, just as it would disrupt white people's enjoyment of their racial privilege for them to take action against racial injustice. The analogy between Thompson's childcare experience and white domination isn't perfect, as Thompson readily acknowledges, but it hits the nail on the head in one important respect. People of color aren't particularly interested in how white people feel about white racism. They especially don't want to hear about white guilt when that guilt is offered as a substitute for action. They instead want white people to do something to eliminate white domination. In some respects, the situation is very simple: "They just want us to send the key."[55]

Other criticisms of white guilt involve its connection with cultural theft and its irrelevance to contemporary racism. Terrence Macmullan argues that white guilt leads to white people's plundering the culture of nonwhite people out of an attempt to fill a perceived void in white people's lives. White guilt makes white people want to focus on the traditions and practices of other people, rather than their own, and this focus often takes the form of cooptation and commodification.[56] In contrast, Naomi Zack argues white guilt is irrelevant to racial justice struggles since institutional racism is the main problem of contemporary racism.

The fight against racism is supposed to be about nonwhite people—how they are treated, for example—not about white people.[57] For all their differences, however, Macmullan and Zack agree with Edgington that white responsibility for past and present white racism is a better alternative to white guilt.[58]

In my view, the move away from white guilt in critical philosophy of race is beneficial to racial justice movements. Unfortunately, however, this move has not been also a shift away from promoting white people's negative affects more generally. The supposed importance of white people's negative emotions hasn't been eliminated with the demotion of white guilt, it's just been relocated: white guilt has been replaced by white shame. This is because of shame's alleged ability to promote greater responsibility for racism on the part of white people. White guilt may be ineffective for racial justice struggles, but some sort of negative affect is seen as needed to motivate white people to change. As Alexis Shotwell claims, "A certain kind of feeling bad can be important for producing meaningful solidarity across difference, particularly for individuals who benefit from racist social/political structures."[59] Some of those negative emotions might include "guilt, anger, sadness, panic, shame, embarrassment, and other emotions not easy to name."[60] These negative affects often are tangled together for many white people, and guilt is too reductive a concept to do justice to the tangle, in Shotwell's view. Shame, in contrast, can help white people understand their negative feelings about race, including whiteness, in ways that can increase their feelings of racial responsibility and their solidarity with people of color.

To see how shame allegedly does this, we need to understand the differences between guilt and shame more generally. Shame typically is distinguished from guilt in that guilt involves something that a person did or did not do, while shame concerns who a person is. Guilt is about acting; shame is about being.[61] As Shotwell explains, "Shame represents being thrown into the self you are that you also repudiate, a self you don't want to be."[62] Shame also has a social dimension that guilt does not. Unlike guilt, shame allegedly "opens a potential space for thinking adequately about a constitutive relation between self and other."[63] While both guilt and shame concern the failure to live up to expectations that can originate with others, shame is linked more tightly to how other people judge oneself. As Michael Morgan argues, "Shame is a feeling we have about how we see ourselves *in terms of how others see us.*"[64] Jean-Paul Sartre's famous example of person peeking through a keyhole illustrates this point: a wave of shame washed over the Peeping Tom once he was seen by another person squatting outside the door.[65] In the case of guilt, the standards by which I judge myself also might have originated from other people and the broader world around me, but guilt does not involve embarrassment that another person sees me failing to uphold those standards. Shame does. In that sense, shame allegedly is more other-oriented than guilt is (a claim to which I will return). Shame connects my being the failed, inadequate person that I am to other people through their witnessing my failures and inadequacies.[66]

The ontological and social dimensions of shame explain why Shotwell and other scholars claim that shame can be an emotion that encourages positive moral development. According to Morgan, because shame involves the whole person and not a particular act, shame can help bring about self-transformation. Recognizing yourself as a self that you don't want to be implies a different kind of self that you do want to be. Shame is the appropriate moral reaction to a world full of both great suffering, such as the genocides in Nazi Germany, Cambodia, Bosnia, Rwanda, and Darfur, and great indifference to that suffering.[67] In those situations, we who have been indifferent need to cultivate our feeling of shame: a feeling of embarrassed inadequacy tied to the loss of other people's respect for us because of our indifference. This feeling of demeaning failure supposedly will lead to criticizing oneself for who one is, and that self-criticism can jar us out of our indifference and spur us to productive action that will change the world for the better. Shame-fueled self-evaluation can lead to a change in our relationships with others so that we no longer feel debased in their eyes.[68]

This is how shame allegedly can lead to a change in the self that results in greater responsibility. To feel shame, as Macmullan claims, is for white people to take responsibility for their feeling of emptiness and the racist wrongdoing to which it has led.[69] Guilt also is associated with responsibility, perhaps even more essentially than shame since with guilt there is a specific action at issue that one can be guilty of doing or not.[70] But it is all too easy for a person to deny guilt in the case of suffering that her actions did not directly cause. Morgan's examples of genocide are relevant here, as are the protestations of contemporary white people that they did not own slaves and so should not be blamed for slavery. James Baldwin captures the latter perfectly: "'Do not blame me,' white people contradictorily plead, 'I was not there. I did not do it. My history has nothing to do with Europe or the slave trade. Anyway it was *your* chiefs who sold *you* to me.'"[71] As psychologists have demonstrated, guilt can lead to responsible interpersonal behavior, such as apologies and reparations for wrongdoing, but only when there is a particular behavior, specific action, or "bad thing done" that could have been done differently by the guilty person.[72]

In today's post–Jim Crow world, however, there often are not particular behaviors or actions of racial injustice to directly connect to a individual white person—or at least, individual white people have a difficult time recognizing any of their actions as racist. The notion of white guilt is too narrow and tends to be fruitless, as shame-advocates argue and I would agree. Morgan and others thus work with a broadened notion of responsibility as the ability to respond to rather than ignore or neglect other people who need care, arguing that shame can result in this type of responsibility. It can "lead to lives committed to preventing such atrocities [such as genocide] from continuing to occur."[73] In Macmullan's words, if "the habit of guilt is to wallow in self-disgust," then in contrast "the habit of shame is to see this disgusting past and then 'live so as never to do such a thing again.'"[74] Because of shame's relational characteristics, "white people's shame response to racism may mark and create a kind of responsible attention to racial formation as structural and systemic within the context of changing who and how we are in relation to race."[75] Even if our responsibility cannot meet the demands placed upon it, shame can expose our responsibility for situations "that are great and even beyond satisfaction but that still require our attention if we are to maintain a sense of integrity and self-worth, in short if we are to do what we can to overcome the shame which we now may have come to acknowledge."[76]

Perhaps the most influential recent endorsement of shame, which also focuses on its ontological dimensions, can be found in Eve Kosofsky Sedgwick's account of queer performativity. While Sedgwick does not explicitly directly address shame's connection to responsibility, she does claim that shame has positive political effects. According to Sedgwick, shame is formative of identity as performative rather than essential, and "queer" is the identity most in accord with the shame that grounds performativity. Sedgwick strongly suggests that shame might be formative of all performativity, but even if shame is irrelevant to some instances of non-queer performativity, "at least for certain ('queer') people, shame is simply the first, and remains a permanent, structuring fact of identity."[77] This means that efforts to eliminate shame—think here of gay pride movements—can't be what people often think they are. Given that shame structures identity, "the forms taken by shame are not distinct 'toxic' parts of a group or individual identity that can be excised."[78] Affirming the alleged permanence of shame, Sedgwick detaches it from "the moralisms of the repressive hypothesis," which praise shame's ability to preserve privacy but condemn shame's support of self- and social repression, and argues that understanding shame as (per)formative of identity can open new doors for identity politics.[79] For Sedgwick, "shame consciousness" and "shame creativity" can support an effective political activism that does not rely on essentializing queer (or other) identities.[80]

I agree with proponents of shame on a number of points: When a person experiences shame, the affect is constitutive of, rather than superficially excisable from the self; white people's ability to respond effectively to racial injustice is important and must be cultivated; improving white responsibility is an ontological and social matter; and white guilt is insufficient to do the affective work needed by racial justice movements. I disagree that any particular emotion, including shame, is necessarily a permanent component of the self. More significantly, I also disagree that cultivating white people's shame is the best way to promote white responsibility or to conceptualize white people's co-constitutive relationships with others, including people of color.[81] I am wary of the claim that a person's ability to respond to others in generous, enriching ways can be fueled by impoverishing, enervating emotions. As empirical studies in psychology demonstrate, shame tends to be "accompanied by a sense of shrinking or of 'being small,' . . . [and] a desire to escape or to hide—to sink into the floor and disappear."[82] This sense of shrinking is not equivalent to humility, which we might very well wish more white people felt. Instead, it is a narcissistic retreat from other people and interpersonal situations into an "egocentric, self-involved" focus on oneself.[83] In fact, it is not shame, but guilt that is credited in social scientific literature with being "other-oriented" and "foster[ing] empathic connection" as long as it is connected with a specific act of individual wrongdoing.[84] Shame's broader engagement with the entire self leads instead to feelings of worthlessness and powerlessness that undercut rather than enhance responsibility within interpersonal relationships. Shame tends to beat down an ashamed person, and a beaten-down person doesn't usually have the psychosomatic resources to engage with others in uplifting ways.

These are not claims that white people should never feel shame or guilt about their roles in racial injustice. They often do, and there is much in their collective and perhaps also individual history to feel ashamed or guilty about. And perhaps at times, shame and guilt in the face of this history can result in motivation to do something different, something more effective with regard to race and racism. For example, even if the step was small, I think that racial justice took a step forward in the United States when Obama was elected and then reelected president. Children often take as a given the way that the world is as they grow up, and millions of children in the United States, white and nonwhite alike, now are likely to find it a routine matter of fact that a black person could hold the highest political office in the country. Thus, if (alleviating) their guilt was the main reason white people voted for Obama, then white guilt probably had a positive effect on the budding racial habits of American children. Perhaps also, queer shame has been a source of creativity that fuels queer activism, even without conversion to queer or gay pride. But I'm concerned that more often than not, shame tends to deflate a person, to rob her of the vitality and energy it will take to make a sustained kind of change in herself or the world. The experience of a shrunken self doesn't motivate beneficial action. It kills it.

Beyond the passive-sounding conditions of depression, despair, and feelings of worthlessness, very aggressive and even violent reactions toward others also can be the results of the shrinking feeling of shame. The person who wishes to sink into the floor doesn't usually disappear; he or she tends to do just the opposite. When I think of the effects of shame, especially queer forms of it, I can't help but think of the gay teen suicide rate, which is five times higher than that of heterosexual teens.[85] I also think of the 1995 "Same Sex Secret Crushes" episode of the tabloid talk show *The Jenny Jones Show*, which led to the murder of Scott Arnedure. Arnedure was a gay man who revealed on television his crush on his best friend Jonathan Schmitz. "Ambushed . . . with humiliation," Schmitz retaliated by purchasing a shotgun and shooting Arnedure.[86] Psychological studies demonstrate that shame of all types regularly leads to destructive forms of hostility and rage, which in turn tend to generate more anger in response.[87] The result often is what psychologist Helen Lewis called the shame-rage spiral: a negative spiral of contagion in which my destructive emotions encourage your destructive emotions, which feed back into my increasing destructiveness, and so on. As sociologist Thomas J. Scheff's research indicates, shame tends to lead to blame and violence, which threaten social ties. This means that rather than strengthen positive connections between people, "shame marks social fragmentation, one person turning away from each other."[88]

Extending Lewis's landmark work, psychologist Jane Tangney and her colleagues have demonstrated that "the tendency to experience shame was significantly positively correlated with measures of trait anger and indexes of indirect hostility, irritability, resentment, and suspicion."[89] As these indexes suggest, ashamed anger is not healing rage. It is better described as "humiliated fury."[90] No wonder then that shame-prone individuals "appear to have significant liabilities in their management of interpersonal hostility and anger."[91] Not only are they more likely to feel shame, but "once angered, they are also more likely to manage their anger in an unconstructive fashion."[92] The array of toxic actions and emotions empirically related to shame is devastating: "malevolent intentions; direct, indirect, and displaced aggression; self-directed hostility; and projected negative long-term consequences of everyday episodes of anger."[93] Far from promoting greater responsibility on the part of wrong-doers, shame tends to motivate them to harm other people even more.

More empirical work on different forms of various emotions, such as anger, needs to be pursued, particularly work that examines emotion in relationship to various social and political hierarchies. For example, are the affective outcomes of shame gendered, making a shame-rage spiral more likely for men and a shame-depression spiral more likely for women? Empirical studies by psychologists suggest so,[94] but they don't often consider how race and class intersect with gendered emotional expectations and demands. Are, as hooks claims, the racially privileged generally more prone to pathologically destructive anger than to constructively healing rage in the context of race? I suspect hooks is right, but the social science literature does not provide definitive answers to these questions. Nonetheless, there is ample empirical evidence to conclude that white shame is highly likely to be harmful to racial justice movements. Cultivating the negative affect of shame on the part of white people—perhaps especially because they tend to be positioned at the top of racial/social hierarchies—is misguided because it will tend to produce destructively angry white people who have malevolent intentions toward people of color and who will act with hostility toward them (as well as toward themselves). In the end, white shame cannot be considered radically different in kind from the negative affects that historically have constituted white people: white hatred and fear of people of color. Shame instead tends to represent merely a difference of degree in the negative affects with which white people are racially constituted.

My assessment of shame—as well as most of the scholars cited above—is implicitly generated from an American/Western perspective that tends to prioritize the individual self. This is in contrast to an Asian perspective that tends to value social cohesion and a person's harmonious relationships within family and other social groups.[95] In China, for example, the use of shame (and guilt) tends to be organized around social reintegration in the wake of unwanted behavior. It has very little to do with stigmatizing a person because of her undesirable identity, the motivation that generally organizes the use of shame in the United States.[96] It's important to realize that shame can function differently in different cultures and contexts, and it's doubtful that any use of shame is universal or context-independent. In some cultures, such as China, shame appears to be an affect that strengthens rather than fragments social ties. But even though true, this fact does not change the situation for cultures that have a higher regard for the individual than for social harmony and proper fulfillment of social roles. In those cultures, shame almost always concerns the worth of the individual self. Acknowledging this reality is not the same thing as endorsing atomistic individualism, let me hasten to add. The individual prioritized in American/Western culture can and should be understood as transactional. While one might wish that American/Western culture didn't prioritize the individual in the first place, however, the simple truth of the matter is that it does, and a person cannot simply decide, as if by fiat, not to be shaped by her culture and other environments. This means we need to reckon with the overwhelming evidence that as it functions in a Western context, shame tends to be a destructive affect.

Given that we have ample reason to conclude that both white shame and white guilt are counterproductive for racial justice movements (at least in the Western world), we might wonder why they have been so heavily promoted in critical race theory and critical philosophy of race. I trust that good intentions lie behind their promotion, but conscious intent is not the entire story when it comes to the operations of white domination. The overwhelming evidence that white guilt and shame do not help and even harm racial justice movements suggests that unconscious habits of white privilege are at work. In this case, I think that those habits are heavily influenced by white class hierarchies as well. Even though good white liberals might not consciously intend it, their promotion of and participation in white guilt and white shame functions to exacerbate insidious class divisions between white people that simultaneously support white racism.

White shame and guilt are not socially or politically neutral emotions. (Indeed, perhaps no emotions are.) They are located in terms of class, privileging middle-class white people in ways that ultimately support white domination of people of color.[97] As educational theorist John Preston has demonstrated, "Displays of [white] guilt and shame are a form of cultural capital" possessed by the white middle class.[98] White working-class students, for example, generally do not feel ashamed of being white in the way that white middle-class students do. Does this mean that they are callous racists? Not necessarily. Guilt and shame aren't helpful measuring sticks in this case because white working-class students often have to monitor their selves in ways that preclude their emotional expressions ("outbursts") in the classroom. Open displays of guilt and shame tend to jeopardize working-class students "rightful" membership in the college classroom since emotional displays undercut the careful monitoring of their bodily selves that working-class students continually have to perform.[99] For these reasons, white guilt and white shame tend to have little value for white working-class people.[100] Guilt and shame about being white does not enable working-class white people to accrue symbolic capital in their communities in the way that it generally does for middle-class white people.

Encouraging white people to feel ashamed of their whiteness as a response to racial injustice implicitly caters to the hegemonic and narcissistic interests of middle-class white people. It encourages middle-class white people to experience a raced emotion that buttresses their class/race supremacy, and it keeps lower-class white people "in their place" by promoting an emotion that is unavailable to them. This helps explain why Jim Goad caustically exclaims, "I've finally figured out why I can't get rid of my white guilt. It's because I have none."[101] This statement is somewhat shocking, and there admittedly are sections in Goad's *Redneck Manifesto* that are dismissive of the severity or even the reality of white racism. At one point, for example, Goad reductively claims, "Economics. That's all it was, is, or ever will be. Racism is only a smoke screen, a cynical diversionary tactic. . . . It ain't about skin, it's about class. It ain't epidermal, it's hierarchical."[102] I nonetheless want to listen to Goad's (deliberately) provocative remarks about white guilt because they capture its class-based dynamics and should not be dismissed as the racist ravings of a white redneck. Goad's manifesto perceptively explains how the guilt and shame of the white liberal, "Mr. Multicultural . . . serves a definite psychological purpose for him, and he wouldn't ever want to get rid of it [through reparations to Native Americans, in Goad's example]. The Guilty White Male takes pride in his own shame. But guilt only serves the guilty."[103] White guilt tends to serve the white middle class, rather than people of color, and it does so by deflecting white racism onto lower-class white people.

Let me turn now to the third affect often recommended for white people who care about racial justice. This affect is betrayal, in the form of the white race traitor. Of course, betrayal also is an event or an act, not just an emotion, but it has a significant affective component associated with losing trust and feeling tricked or misused. Along with guilt and shame, betrayal via the race traitor is prevalent in scholarly literature that discusses white people's appropriate roles in racial justice struggles. In her 1991 *Whose Science? Whose Knowledge?*, Sandra Harding provides perhaps the earliest racial justice–oriented instance of calling a white person who challenges white racism a traitor to her race.[104] I say "racial justice–oriented" since racist instances from the 1960s abound. The term *race traitor* appears to have originated during the civil rights movement in the United States, when white Southerners who opposed voting rights and equal education for black people verbally attacked white supporters of black civil rights by calling them traitors to their race. The origins of the term clearly are maliciously destructive in their intent. Aware of this origin, Harding reclaims the idea of traitorous identities for feminist and racial justice purposes. In doing so, she builds on Adrienne Rich's 1978 essay "Disloyal to Civilization: Feminism, Racism, Gynephobia," which calls on white women to become disloyal to a patriarchal civilization that teaches them to solipsistically misperceive women of color and their experiences as insignificant and unimportant.[105] Harding argues that white people should develop "traitorous identities and social locations" that are supported by "traitorous agendas," such as "provid[ing] 'traitorous' readings of the racial assumptions in texts . . . written by whites."[106]

These disloyal identities, social locations, and agenda are crucial to racial justice movements for at least four reasons, according to Harding. First, they combat white people's immobilization by helping them concretely figure out what they might do to fight racism. Second, learning to think critically out of a traitorous identity or social location helps white people avoid an exclusive focus on people of color that arrogantly refuses to examine the role of whiteness in racism and class exploitation. A third, related reason given by Harding is that, speaking as a white person, "learning about my race *only* from racists, or quite differently, *only* from people of color, I deprive myself of *my* perspective on myself. I fail to take an active role in defining what my racial identity can be."[107] And finally, recruiting white people to racial justice movements is not likely to be very successful if white people "are constantly told that they are the wrong kind of people to speak in this group" or otherwise actively participate in the movement.[108] White people need a racial identity and a related agenda that allow them to make positive contributions to racial justice struggles.

I think Harding is exactly right on all four of these points, and I am interested in the positive valence that she gives to white identity in her third and fourth points in particular. Those two points demonstrate why white allies need to develop a racial identity alternative to what a white racist society demands of them, but not necessarily one that is characterized as traitorous. A traitor is one who betrays others, who violates the confidence and trust that another has placed in her. In effect, a traitor attempts to destroy the social fabric that binds people together. I do not have much confidence in the positive effects of building an identity exclusively on destruction, nor do I think that asking people to conceive of themselves as treacherous destroyers is likely to be a fruitful recruiting device in most cases.[109] One might respond that our current social fabric needs to be ripped up since it is woven together out of racism, sexism, and other forms of oppression, and so destroying this fabric should not be conceived of negatively. I agree that oppression is part of the warp and woof of society's political, cultural, aesthetic, economic, and other relationships. But the social fabric does not so much need ripping up as it needs reweaving. This creative act will involve a great deal of unraveling of what currently exists, but such unraveling should not be the final goal of racial justice and related liberatory projects. Something new needs to be created and, as Harding hints, that something new includes a positive racial identity for white people.

Another well-known example of an anti-racist endorsement of the notion of white race traitors can be found in Noel Ignatiev and John Garvey's journal, *Race Traitor*. As the journal's motto states, "Treason to whiteness is loyalty to humanity."[110] The journal's editors view race as a product of social discrimination in which whiteness has meant and can mean nothing but the domination of people of color. For that reason, the journal seeks to abolish the white race. This doesn't mean physically exterminating white people, but instead encouraging white people to defect from whiteness by trying to tear it apart. From the journal's perspective, whiteness is a club that white people can quit, and if enough of them quit, then the club will dissolve. Given that most white people belong to the club without having deeply or consciously committed to it, according to the journal we can have faith that they would quit the club if it were convenient to do so.[111]

Race Traitor clearly uses terms such as *treason* in ways that oppose the aims of white supremacist groups, and for that reason I label its endorsement of race traitors "anti-racist." But strictly speaking, the journal wouldn't classify its goal as anti-racist since, its editors claim, anti-racism assumes the natural existence of different races even though it opposes hierarchy and oppression based on race. According to the journal, anti-racism isn't enough. The more radical work of abolition is required. "So long as the white race exists, all movements against racism are doomed to fail," Ignatiev and Garvey argue.[112] Only if whiteness is eliminated is there any hope that discrimination against and the oppression of people of color can be ended.

While I disagree with Ignatiev and Garvey that anti-racism (even the liberal variety) assumes the natural existence of race, I agree with them (for different reasons) that anti-racism can be problematic. My concern about anti-racism is not that it fails to abolish whiteness, but that it often operates with a liberal framework that uses class differences to bolster white domination, in the deceptive guise of fighting for racial justice. Even though I share some of the journal's concerns about anti-racism, however, I object to its mission because it underestimates the significance of whiteness to many white people's identities and habits, and not just those who are avowed white supremacists. While that significance often is unconsciously experienced, it can constitute a deep commitment. Or better put: precisely because whiteness and white privilege often operate unconsciously, commitment to them tends to run very deep. Ignatiev and Garvey's faith that white people will quit the white club once it is convenient for them to do so is naive. Using the metaphor of a club to describe white people's relationship to whiteness and the ways that racial habits help constitute the self also is misleading because club membership is easy to eliminate quickly. Whiteness and white privilege are not. In this way, as Linda Martín Alcoff explains, "the issue of convenience unfortunately misses the point." The point is that "if the collective structures of identity formation that are necessary to create a positive and confident sense of self . . . require racism, then only the creation of new structures of identity formation can redress this balance."[113] As constitutive of the self, habit—racist or otherwise—doesn't disappear. Either particular habits are replaced by new ones or the old habits quickly settle back into place.[114] But in the case of *Race Traitor*, there's never the opportunity to raise the question of whether white identity and habits will be constituted by positive or negative affects. Unlike feminists' uses of "race traitor," Ignatiev and Garvey's appropriation of the term does not offer an alternative white identity for white allies to embody. Instead, it represents the abolition of any and all kinds of white identity. This has the effect, if not the intention, of granting victory to white supremacist understandings of whiteness.[115]

Another major objection I have to the figure of the race traitor is that, similar to the emotions of white guilt and white shame, it implicitly operates with insidious class/race hierarchies. While the race traitor allegedly is a figure open and available to all white people to embody, in fact it is not equally welcoming of lower-class white people and white trash in particular. This is because they already have betrayed, or failed to live up to the (middle-class) standards of proper whiteness. The event of betrayal associated with the race traitor is possible primarily for those in a secure position within whiteness. That security is what makes possible the "radical" break with whiteness that seeks to abolish it. In this way, the race traitor's act of betrayal is essentially an exercise of class privilege. If one has already been pushed to the margins of whiteness, a break with it doesn't function in the same way. This doesn't mean that white trash aren't able to desire and work for the end of white supremacy, but it does mean that their efforts are only awkwardly thought of as abolishing whiteness. Or if we want to retain the language of abolition, we ought to recognize that merely existing as white trash already opens up the possibility of white abolition because it already troubles the stability and meaning of whiteness. In that sense, white trash might be thought of as the true "race traitors" among white people, but their destabilizing of whiteness usually is not acknowledged. Instead, white trash tend to be dismissed as irrelevant to racial justice movements.

One example of this can be found when Ignatiev criticizes whiteness studies for allegedly assuming that whiteness can mean or be something other than white supremacy. As Ignatiev ridicules attempts to locate white culture in things such as Wonder Bread, fast food, and daytime television game shows, his attacks implicitly reveal class relations and hierarchies within the journal's version of neo-abolitionism.[116] Ignatiev is right to criticize attempts by an uncritical whiteness studies to essentialize and depoliticize white culture, but his particular criticism deracializes white lower-class people as not really white or white enough, implicitly affirming other (middle-class) white people as the "real" whites. As Preston explains, "in naming the absent (white culture) [the editors of *Race Traitor*] reveal the ability to recognize white working class cultural forms, and form a shared recognition between themselves and the reader, whilst ignoring white middle class ones. This is because white working class cultural forms are more recognizable to academic audiences as there is a shared recognition between the (largely middle class) author and reader."[117] Perhaps unintentionally, *Race Traitor*'s neo-abolitionism nonetheless presents itself as a club that lower-class white people are discouraged from joining. The journal implicitly judges middle-class white people to be the only legitimate white people who can work against white supremacy by dismantling whiteness.

A final influential example of the white race traitor is more promising, but this is because, as I will argue, betrayal ultimately is not the most accurate or compelling emotion with which to describe it. Mab Segrest's 1994 *Memoir of a Race Traitor* helped firmly establish the race traitor as the model identity for feminists opposed to white racism (and perhaps lesbians and American Southerners especially). Instead of betrayal, however, Segrest's "race traitor" points us to an alternative comportment for white people that relies on positive rather than negative affects. In particular, Segrest's attempts to wrestle with family relationships in the context of white racism highlights the important place for love in racial justice movements.

In her gripping memoir, which she calls a "treatise on the souls of white folks," Segrest describes her work as a white, lesbian racial justice activist in Alabama and North Carolina in the 1980s, weaving that description together with stories about race and racism from her child-hood and family history in the American South.[118] Segrest recounts the ostracism, fear, and violent threats she experienced as she worked for North Carolinians Against Racist and Religious Violence (NCARRV) to bring white supremacists, such as White Patriot leader Glenn Miller, to court. As she does so, she explains, "I had begun to feel pretty irregularly white. Klan folks had a word for it: *race traitor*. Driving in and out of counties with heavy Klan activity, I kept my eye on the rear-view mir-ror, and any time a truck with a Confederate flag license plate passed me, the hair on the back of my neck would rise. My reaction was more like the reactions of Black people I was working with than of a white woman with three great-grandfathers in the Confederate Army."[119] Seg-rest continues to reveal some of the disturbing psycho-ontological effects of her racial justice work, describing her fear of "the possibility of being caught between the worlds of race, white people kicking me out, people of color not letting me in" and admitting that she "often found [her]-self hating all white people, including [her]self."[120] Segrest's identity as a white person clearly changed as a result of her work for racial justice, and that change often was painful and frightening.

As she wrestles with her racial identity as a "race traitor," Segrest also wrestles with guilt over her family's racist history. At one point, she tries to reassure herself: "I'm not acting out of guilt [by working for the NCARRV], I would tell myself, just working on the Segrest family karma."[121] Wrapped up with her guilt on behalf of her white family, and perhaps on behalf of white people more generally, are Segrest's equivocal feelings about the notion of betrayal. When a friend of hers, Leah, tells her that the title of her book is wrong because "that's not what you were doing," Segrest explains, "I flush. I do struggle with betrayal. My Klan folk had me spotted: a race traitor. . . . [But] it's not my people, it's the *idea* of race I am betraying. It's taken me a while to get the distinction."[122] Interestingly, Segrest here uses "race traitor" in its original, Klan-intend-ed sense: as a racial identity of which one should feel ashamed. Segrest's flush reveals that on some level, Segrest believes she should, and she does, feel ashamed for her betrayal of her (white) family. Her love for her family makes it difficult for her to accept that she is a race traitor. And yet at the same time, her deeply felt commitment to racial justice makes it difficult for her not to think of herself as a race traitor, that is, as someone who works against white racism, white supremacy, and white privilege. How can she both work against ("betray") white racism and love her white racist family? Does her betrayal of whiteness mean that she also must betray her white family?

The solution to this dilemma proposed by Segrest is to distinguish between white people and the idea of race. Her answer is that one can love white people even as one betrays the white race. In my view, this answer involves a problematic divorce between theory and practice, between ideas and lived reality. It assumes that the idea of race can be construed as a bloodless abstraction from the lives, activities, habits, and practices of people who are categorized as white. Given that the idea of whiteness is intimately bound up in the intimacies and intricacies of white people's identities, the idea and the people cannot be neatly separated in practice. Just ask any member of the Klan: if you are challenging dominant ideas of whiteness, you are challenging white people.

My objections to feminist appropriations of the race traitor are not based on the fact of appropriation itself. I am not concerned, as is Naomi Zack, that the origins of the term are malign. While Zack says that for this reason "it's not clear to me that [the term *race traitor*] can be reclaimed," I think that it can and, to a limited extent, already has been successfully taken back by some feminists and white allied activists and scholars.[123] My objection also is not that the white racists who originated the term *race traitor* are like comic book villains in that they are not socially significant enough to use the weighty term *treason* to describe someone who breaks their rules. This origin gives the term a bizarre and overblown character, according to Zack, and she asks why someone who is seriously committed to anti-racist work would want to use it.[124] Segrest's memoir suggests a powerful answer to this question. When it is members of your own family whom you love who call you a race traitor, your accusers are very significant to you and their denunciations can pierce deeply into your being. Reclaiming the slur that they sling at you is one way to reckon with and attempt to minimize its destructive power.

Challenging dominant ideas of whiteness does not have to be interpreted or experienced as an act of treason (which is not to say that Klan members won't still see it that way). A more satisfactory solution to Segrest's dilemma about how to love her racist family and fight against racism is for feminists, critical philosophers of race, and other white allies to set aside the notion of betrayal as the primary motivation for work against white domination and as the main component of a white identity grounded in racial justice. This also means challenging the assumption that love and criticism are incompatible, as I will elaborate in the book's conclusion. I think Segrest's friend Leah was right when she said that being a race traitor wasn't what Segrest was doing. Of course, Leah might have merely meant that Segrest wasn't a race traitor in the Klan-intended sense of the term. In other words, Leah might have been trying to help Segrest resist understanding herself from a Klan perspective and to reassure Segrest that her work was a good, not bad, thing to be doing. But Leah also was right, perhaps without intending to be, that Segrest should not view herself as a race traitor even in the reclaimed, feminist sense of the word. Segrest's racial justice activity and criticisms of white supremacy are better described as forms of love for herself and her family members: loving herself and them enough to challenge their self- and other-destructive racialized habits of domination and violence, loving herself and them enough to try to transform white habits into something different and better than what they generally are today. With this understanding of Segrest's racial justice work, loving herself and her white family members is not something that conflicts with Segrest's relationship to whiteness. It's another crucial place where her critical, transformative love is needed.

What would this white self-love look like? For starters, a spiritually healthy self-love would enable a self-relation for white people that is not based on trying to flee their white selves. Given whiteness's history as a racial category of violent exclusion and oppression, one might think that white people need to focus less on their whiteness, to separate themselves from it. But just the opposite is the case. White people's flight from their whiteness is not necessarily the opposite of white narcissism. It instead tends to be another manifestation of it. Given that distance from racial identification tends to be the covert modus operandi for contemporary forms of white privilege, white people who wish to fight racism must become more intimately acquainted with their whiteness in order to transform it. White people who want to work toward racial justice need to stop overly focusing on people of color and turn to themselves to clean up their own house. While white people myopically have engaged in "white solipsism," in which only white people and their interests are recognized or seen as important, the best corrective for white solipsism is not necessarily for white people to do the opposite and focus only on people of color.[125] White self-denial and self-hatred can be the flip side of the same coin of white solipsism and narcissism, after all. What is needed instead is for white people to develop a different kind of relationship to their whiteness.

This different relationship would require rethinking many of the moral virtues that are associated with the good white liberal. As Audrey Thompson has argued, dominant modes of "morality [can be] one of the main obstacles to racial change."[126] In that case, white people may need to "relinquis[h] our cherished notions of morality . . . [including] how we understand what it means to be a good person."[127] Like many other facets of whiteness, white notions of goodness currently tend to be saturated with white supremacy. A set of virtues different than the ones generated by white liberalism is needed to govern white people's involvement in racial justice movements, virtues that neither seek reassurance of moral goodness nor orient their lives around goodness through simple opposition to it.

Consider earnestness, which is fairly mandatory on the part of white people who involve themselves in racial justice movements. While African Americans have long used laughter and humor as a subversive form of social critique, white people fighting against racism have tended to use sober argumentation and direct expressions of earnest commitment. As Cris Mayo thoughtfully observes, this has been for good reason since "the break entailed by humor is potentially a break that can too easily convert intentioned white antiracist action back into the all-too-easy-to-assume gestures of white superiority."[128] When it comes to race, white people generally don't have the interpretative skills to hear humor's complex messages that black and other nonwhite people tend to have. Even though she admits white earnestness can too easily convert to an expression of mastery, Mayo argues that it's probably the best that white people can do at this point. She concludes that "while earnest white antiracist philosophizing has its shortcomings, it may remain the only path to white intervention in white racism until the structures of racism have been dismantled."[129]

But I think this gets the relationship backward: we need alternatives to white earnestness so that we have the best chance of dismantling white racism. Or rather, it's not so much a question of which comes first since alternatives to white liberalism need to be developed hand in hand with strategies for destroying structures of racism. Efforts to eliminate white racism will be much more successful if we don't wait to address the spiritual toxicity that can infuse earnest white people's involvements in racial justice movements. This is because white earnestness often turns out to have little to do with fighting racial injustice and a great deal to do with maintaining existing class and race hierarchies. The earnestly intense focus on securing one's moral standing as a white person can produce what Charles Scott has called "the awful sobriety inspired by an over-heated sense of goodness."[130] White people's somber seriousness about race sometimes is taken as proof that they are one of the good white people, not one of the bad white trash. Ironically, an overheated sense of goodness on the part of some white people is less about taking responsibility for racism than deflecting it onto lower-class white people. In this way, middle-class white people's seriousness about race sometimes can interfere with, rather than aid struggles to end white racism. Their earnest seriousness turns out to be more of a white class marker than an effective response to white domination of people of color.

It's a problem for racial justice movements when white people take up their responsibilities regarding racism solely as a grim, serious burden.[131] This probably will seem like a strange thing for me to say since responsibility customarily is seen as a serious moral matter. In that sense of the term, however, my project does not strive for moral responsibility. Am I then claiming that white people—middle-class or otherwise—shouldn't try to do the right thing when it comes to race? That they shouldn't try to be good? No, not exactly. What I'm attempting to do instead is carve out a different way of thinking about white people's relationship to issues of race. White people who are concerned about racism need a different set of virtues, a different *ethos* for their racial justice efforts, one that is not centered on dominant, liberal understandings of moral goodness.[132] As Scott has argued, "To say that goodness is bad would be absurd. The badness of goodness [is] not . . . the problem. . . . 'Goodness' names the problem."[133] He continues: "When we tell stories and engage in thinking without revenge [and other negative affects], options to orders in the name of goodness can emerge. . . . [and] the heavy-handed seriousness that often characterizes western morality and universalization decreases. Another kind of entertainment of options and differences emerges with an altered type of concerned energy—not so much beyond good and evil as different from the polarization and its ordering force. It is an issue . . . of attitudes and options . . . outside the sanction of goodness' name."[134]

Instead of "selflessly" and "earnestly" working to "benefit" of people of color, a white ally might seek to support others' flourishing by turning to herself first. She would understand that the white person who is best able to work against white racism in solidarity with people of color isn't seeking goodness. Neither is that person bad or evil in the sense of flippantly disregarding racial matters or deliberately committing racist acts. We might say instead that a white ally is a person who is constituted by a loving affirmation of herself that exercises and strengthens her positive affects regarding race and thus allows her to digest, rather than resentfully fester over, impotently avoid, or evasively deflect her and other white people's roles in racist institutions and histories.[135] Admittedly, from a dominant moral perspective, this self-affirmation might look bad, or at least extremely inappropriate. But I think it is one of the tools that white people most need if they are going to be useful and effective in struggles against white racism. White people need to become spiritually healthy enough that they do not poison other races when interacting with them but instead reciprocally nourish each other. They need to adorn their souls with genuine treasures, rather than the counterfeit gems of white supremacy. Only then will they be in a psychosomatic position that allows them to fairly, generously, and even lovingly engage with others rather than respond to them out of a soul-starved stinginess.[136]

I wish to be as clear as possible on this point: what I am advocating is *not* that white people need to uncritically feel better about themselves. There's been far too much of that already, even within racial justice movements. The connections I am making here are between affect, ontology, and personal and political agency. Affects are not about "mere" feeling, and positive affects in particular do not necessarily involve feeling happy or good. While spiritual health may sometimes feel good—and it does not always, as Brennan discusses[137]—its good (or bad) feeling is somewhat irrelevant to the matter at hand. The relevant question is how does a particular affect animate a person? What does a particular affect move a person to do? Calling for white people to be constituted by self-love is not a call for them to feel delighted about being white racists or benefiting from white privilege. In the mix of negative and positive affects that make up white people—even, or perhaps especially, when the negative far outweigh the positive—it is a call for them to nourish their positive affects with regard to whiteness so that a different kind of political and interpersonal action on their part will be possible. As bell hooks has argued, "To return to love, making it a central issue in our efforts for collective recovery and healing is not a move away from political action. Unless love is the force undergirding our efforts to transform society, we lose our way."[138]

Spiritually positive emotions are an effect—as well as a cause, in an ongoing transactional spiral—of an affective-ontological reconfiguration of a being's relations with other beings in which the active thriving of one is intimately linked to the active thriving of others. From that perspective, we could say, to paraphrase James Baldwin, that what is truly sinister about white people is their lack of positive affect.[139] Writing about the destructiveness of white people's guilt in particular, Baldwin claims, "The fact that [white people] have not yet been able to do this—to face their history, to change their lives—hideously menaces this country [the United States]. Indeed, it menaces the entire world."[140] It's likely that multiple kinds of positive affect will be needed to fully change white people's lives and drastically reduce their menace to the world. The task probably is that large. Instead of being constituted by negative affects, even the seemingly beneficial ones of white guilt and shame, white people need to develop a spiritually healthy form of self-love. That "selfish" affect will be beneficial to both white people and people of color, and perhaps even the entire world.

Conclusion

Struggles over Love

I haven't said much in this book about strategies for directly improving relationships between white people and people of color. This isn't because I think those relationships are unimportant, but because I'm wary of many white attempts to use them to prove—to themselves? other white people? people of color? a divine being?—that they are not racist. In many cases, white people need to do some spiritual work on themselves to be capable of respectful, nonabusive relationships with people of other races. Such work must begin in the middle since white people and people of color are already in relation with each other. This book thus might serve as a kind of warning post for people of all races in the midst of various relationships with white people. What is at stake for many liberal white people in their dealings with people of color seems to be achieving a self-righteous distance from whiteness and obtaining relief from the affective burdens of white guilt and shame. It should go without saying, but it is inappropriate and harmful for white people to use people of color in this way. As Thurgood Marshall once said, "You know, sometimes I get awfully tired of trying to save the white man's soul."[1] White people's souls may indeed need saving, but to demand that black and other nonwhite people be the vehicle for white salvation merely replicates the racial inequalities and abuses that led to their damnation.

That is why I turned to white people's self-love in chapter 4, arguing that white people should stop trying to flee their whiteness and that white racial identity should not be based on the toxic emotions of guilt, shame, and betrayal. White people can find ways to live in their own skins *and* help bring about more racial justice in the world. To do so, white people need to develop different "virtues" than the ones they've cultivated as masters of white domination. These would be virtues that aren't concerned with the conventional morality of white people since those conventions tend to be steeped in white domination. They would be virtues that challenge the narcissistic self-loathing at the heart of white people's racial quest for moral goodness. If good white liberals can learn to love themselves, then they might have a shot at eliminating many of the habits, emotions, and beliefs that have fueled white exploitation, oppression, and domination of people of color.

I realize that when the word *love* is used in the context of whiteness, there is an inevitable and significant risk that it will be heard as an endorsement of white supremacy. In no way do I want to endorse the domination of people of color by white people. But I'm willing to take the risk of being misunderstood—indeed, I think it must be taken—because even though there is nothing ahistorically essential about whiteness, it is not likely to disappear any time soon. Rejecting racial essentialism, as most contemporary scholars do, does not mean that problems associated with whiteness simply evaporate. Of course, white people do not have sole control over their whiteness, and they might not have much control over it at all. Other racial groups certainly have contributed and will continue to contribute to the meaning of whiteness.[2] But white people are uniquely responsible for their whiteness, even if they do not uniquely control it. The question for them—us, me—is how can white people live their whiteness in ways that actually challenge white domination?

Trying to answer this question has involved me in what Sara Ahmed calls "a struggle over who has the right to declare themselves as acting out of love."[3] As Ahmed documents, many so-called white hate groups now claim that they are not based on hatred of other racial groups, but on love for "our White Racial Family."[4] For example, the Aryan Nation Web site claims "the depths of Love are rooted and very deep in a real White Nationalist's souls and spirit, no form of 'hate' could even begin to compare. . . . It is not hate that makes the average White man look upon a mixed racial couple with a scowl on his face and loathing in his hear[t]. . . . No, it is not hate. It is Love."[5] According to the Aryan Nation and other white supremacist groups, love is the emotion that fuels their work on behalf of white people. On their view, hatred comes from the people who inaccurately label so-called hate groups as hate groups in the first place. The Aryan Nation and other similar groups are not hate groups, but hated groups. It is anti-racists and racial justice activists, not white supremacists, who allegedly inject hatred into the emotional economy that circulates between different races.

Ahmed's thoughtful analysis of the politics of love is wary of struggles over the emotion, going so far as to "challenge any assumption that love can provide the foundation for political action, or is a sign of good politics."[6] One reason for her skepticism is that, on her account, love is either multicultural or oppositional, and both forms of love are highly problematic. As I will explain, I agree with her on the latter point, but I think that forms of white self-love are possible that are neither multicultural nor oppositional. For that reason, Ahmed's well-placed skepticism about these two forms of love need not mean that love has no positive role to play in racial justice movements. "Love is profoundly political," as bell hooks has argued, and what she calls a "love ethic" can ground effective resistance against white domination.[7]

It's easy to see why oppositional love is extremely problematic from the perspective of racial justice and other libratory struggles. The love in oppositional love is formed out of strong, even vicious opposition to those whom one doesn't love. Oppositional love openly and deliberately pits a person against others who are different from herself. In the specific case of race, oppositional love would mean white people loving themselves and other white people to the exclusion of anyone who didn't count as white, reinstating rather than challenging the marginalization and oppression of nonwhite people. As Ahmed rightly asks of oppositional love, "what does it mean to stand for love by standing alongside some others and against other others?"[8] I would add that it's not clear in what sense oppositional love even should count as love since, to paraphrase the Aryan Nation, it openly has loathing at its heart. In any case, it is clear that oppositional love is not an emotion on which racial justice movements should be based.

In contrast to the oppositional "love" of the Aryan Nation and other white supremacists, multicultural love can seem very appealing. Rather than oppose those who are different than oneself, multicultural love understands itself to be a love of difference.[9] Instead of taking a hostile stance toward people of color, a white person engaged in multicultural love would be open to and embrace otherness. But as Ahmed rightly argues, this form of love often is the product of a humanist fantasy that assumes that distance between people of different races necessarily produces hate and that bringing different racial or cultural groups closer together automatically will eliminate their conflicts.[10] This is a fantasy in the sense of fulfilling an unrealistic, self-aggrandizing, and often unconscious wish of liberal humanists, which is a separate matter from the historical question of whether intercultural closeness occasionally has eliminated conflict.

In educational settings, the humanist fantasy often takes the form of the Diverse Environment Theory, which holds that "diversity breeds tolerance . . . [and] if you raise a child with a fair amount of exposure to people of other races and cultures, the environment becomes the message."[11] But in fact, "increased opportunities [for people of different races] to interact are also, effectively, increased opportunities to reject each other."[12] As recent research on more than ninety thousand teenagers at 112 different schools across the United States demonstrates, the more diverse the school, the more likely it is that kids tend to segregate themselves along racial lines. This doesn't mean that racial diversity necessarily is antithetical to racial justice struggles, or that schools should never be racially integrated. But it does mean that diversity and integration shouldn't be considered panaceas for a society's racial problems. This is precisely what humanist fantasies promoted by liberal white people's ideas of multicultural love tend to do. For many white people, the rhetoric of diversity tends to have a "talismanic power," but often "it is little more than another form of white noise" generated by white people who see themselves as "hip, trendy, and 'down with the program,' even if the program is 10 [or more] years out of date."[13]

In addition to operating with a misguided humanist fantasy, multicultural love tends to resemble what Ahmed labels the liberal politics of charity and Du Bois called the philanthropy of high descent. Nearly one hundred years ago, Du Bois scathingly criticized white philanthropists who thought of themselves as benefiting poor, ignoble people of color across the world. As Du Bois bitingly charged, these "worthy souls in whom consciousness of high descent brings burning desire to spread the gift abroad" receive a great deal of "mental peace and moral satisfaction" when "humble black folk, voluble with thanks, receive barrels of old clothes from lordly and generous whites."[14] But when black recipients of white charity begin to challenge white authority and accept white "gifts" sullenly rather than gratefully, "then the spell is suddenly broken" and the true, even if unconscious purpose of white charity is revealed.[15] It has very little to do with genuinely increasing the flourishing of black people, and everything to do with covertly using black people to generate middle-class white people's moral sense of goodness.

Like liberal philanthropy and charity, multicultural love tends to erect an ideal of all-inclusive sympathy that focuses on reaching out toward and caring for those who have been marginalized, mistreated, and hated by a society. In a racist society, the marginalized often are people of color, who then are dependent on benevolent white people to charitably extend their good will toward them. This charitable love often results merely in making white people feel better about helping people of color, but it does little to change the power relations that support the need for charity in the first place.

For these reasons, I would caution against assuming that love between white people and people of color necessarily will eliminate racism. Of course, white people sometimes have loved and do love people of color in ways that are not instances of white charity. White people's ability to love people of color in healthy ways might even be considered an ultimate indication of successful struggle for racial justice. Nonetheless, bypassing intermediate steps toward the goal of healthy cross-racial relationships is likely to be counterproductive. Those steps involve a great deal of work that white people need to do on their relationship to their white identities. To put the point bluntly, the historical, psychological, sociological, and other evidence thus far suggests that many white people currently aren't spiritually capable of loving people of color in healthy ways. Racing breathlessly toward that love can be a symptom of white domination, not a cure for it.

Another problematic version of multicultural love can be found in the white fantasy of interracial friendships that are filled with warmth and intimacy. (Warm interracial friendships do exist, but again the fantastical white desire for them is another issue.) The fantasy of fulfilling interracial friendships is an illusion that reigns in the United States, in which images of interracial friendship are ubiquitous. Popular cinema, television, and advertisements often present black and white people, in particular, as best buddies whose personal ties overcome or sidestep any racial tension. The 2006 Oscar-winning film *Crash* is an exception in its portrayal of interracial relationships as ambivalent and conflicted,[16] but for every *Crash* there are many more *Pulp Fictions*, *Lethal Weapons*, *Forrest Gumps*, and *Driving Miss Daisys*.[17] Political oratory also contributes to the cultural messages in the United States that friendship is the solution to the nation's racial problems. As then-presidential candidate Bill Clinton explained immediately after the 1992 Los Angeles riots, "White Americans are gripped by the isolation of their own experience. Too many still simply have no friends of other races and do not know any differently."[18] Scholarly research in social psychology sometimes supports these cultural messages, claiming that "opportunities for stigmatized and nonstigmatized individuals to become friends may be the primary route to the reduction of prejudice."[19] Workbooks for white anti-racism groups often do the same, breezily reminding white people, "Don't forget to make friends with people of color," as one of the "steps toward breaking free of racism."[20]

A few years ago, the breakfast cereal company Kashi debuted a new brand of high fiber cereal called "Good Friends," which prominently displays a smiling, snuggling pair of white and black women on one box front and a similarly posed white woman and black man on another.[21] "Fiber and Taste Buds. Be Friends," declares the back cover, which offers a recipe for "Kashi Friendly Fiber Muffins" to further that friendship. "For all the good things fiber does for you, it deserves to be loved. So we created great tasting, convenient recipes to make it easy for you to make fiber your good friend" (back cover). I cannot help but wonder who the "you" is that needs to love her good friend Fiber. Is it the black person who needs to acknowledge all the good things that white Fiber has done for her? Or—more likely, given that the cereal is marketed primarily to white, middle-class, "progressive" women—is "you" the white woman who needs to recognize that, while often distasteful, black Fiber makes positive, not just negative contributions to white life and health? My point with these cynical questions is that oppressive hierarchies and stereotypes can be perfectly compatible with some forms of friendship. Kashi's "Good Friends" fails to recognize this fact, operating on the assumption that all problems with interracial tensions and hostilities have been or can be solved through the warm friendships of white and nonwhite people and playing into white people's desire for the painless elimination of interracial friction.

The friendship orthodoxy, as cultural critic Benjamin DeMott has called it, is dangerous for at least two important reasons.[22] First, it ahistorically ignores the economic, legal, and other institutional causes of the United States' racial problems, suggesting that changes in interpersonal relations alone can eliminate racism and white privilege. Second, it is dangerous because it makes those changes in interpersonal relations seem both necessary and easy. White people just need more warm interactions with nonwhite people, and then all racism will disappear—so promises the friendship orthodoxy. This belief overlooks both the way that economic and other structural inequalities between white and nonwhite people can profoundly affect their interpersonal relations and the fact that racism and white privilege often function unconsciously and thus are not always readily available for conscious examination. By eliminating the hard work of solving thorny racial problems, the friendship orthodoxy can appeal especially to white people who feel guilty about racism and vaguely want to do something about it, but who do not want to have the basic structure of their selves changed.

White people need to stop narcissistically looking for redemption in the warm and easy smiles of "Good Friends." Solidarity with people of color does not necessarily depend on white people's intimacy or closeness with people of color, and too quickly seeking that intimacy can be a way for white people to avoid the more difficult task of grappling with their whiteness. I say this in full realization that feminists of color, such as María Lugones, have emphasized the importance of friendship between Latina and Angla women when theorizing and practicing coalitions against gendered, raced, and other forms of oppression. But even as she endorses interracial friendship, Lugones cautions that such friendships will not be easy or pleasant for most white women.[23] In fact, from the perspective of the friendship orthodoxy, the relationships between white and Latina women depicted by Lugones might not look like friendship at all because they are not composed primarily of warm intimacies. For Lugones, relationships between Angla and Latina women (and women of color more generally) are just as likely to include difficult distances and uncomfortable separations, especially as experienced by Angla women. As Lugones might agree, rather than necessarily see this lack of closeness as a failure, white allies need to view it as a positive form that interracial relationships can take when white people aren't using them as a vehicle for their racial redemption. As Lugones says to white women, "Out of obligation you should stay out of our way, respect us and our distance, and forego the use of whatever power you have over us."[24] When equated with intimacy, friendship between white and nonwhite people can be an obstacle to racial justice. In contrast to what the friendship orthodoxy tells us, distance between white and nonwhite people can be a positive and important component of interracial relationships. In situations where the elimination of distance means only the increase of a damaging white influence on people of color, interracial friendships are part of the problem, not the solution.[25]

Yet another form of multicultural love can be found in the assumption of good white liberals that trust across racial lines is a necessary factor in white people's ability to work for racial justice. As I think about white fantasies of interracial trust, I'm reminded of an astute comment made by Donna-Dale Marcano, who discussed at a recent philosophy conference the reasons given by white people decades ago that black philosophy cannot or should not exist. Explaining why young black women philosophers need to know these reasons, Marcano playfully but truthfully exclaimed, "I know [white] philosophers are all liberal [nowadays], but you can't trust that."[26] History supposedly has changed, and white philosophers today supposedly are accepting of "alternatives" to the tradition, but black people shouldn't fall for this liberal facade. As Marcano and other black women philosophers know, there still are significant obstacles for them—and anyone else who isn't white and preferably male, able-bodied, and straight—who want to join and transform the discipline.

Marcano's claim that black people shouldn't fully trust white people is right on target, but white people still can and need to work for racial justice, as I believe Marcano would agree. The assumption that white people must have nonwhite people's trust before they can fight white racism is yet another harmful manifestation of multicultural love, part of white people's toxic quest for racial redemption and freedom from self-hatred through relationships with people of color. White people can make significant contributions toward achieving racial justice by getting their own house in order. People of color don't need white people to save them, and they don't need to use up their energy and resources trying to save white people in return. As Tim Wise, a white activist for racial justice, has argued, "It's not about trying to save others. I'm really trying to save and redeem the community that I live in so that that community can join with communities of color in a real sense of equity and not a paternalistic arrangement. . . . We have to be able to clean up the crap between whites."[27]

This is not something that most good white people want to hear. Wise recounts a story that underscores this point, as well as highlights Marcano's insight into the lack of trust across race lines. When Wise was giving a presentation on whiteness to a predominantly white college audience, a young white woman asked him how his work was received by black people and admitted that she didn't think she could do the same sort of work because black people wouldn't trust her. Wise replied that while there occasionally was some mistrust, he never felt hated or resented once black people had seen him work and "walk the walk," not just "talk the talk." At that point, an extremely agitated black woman raised her hand and sharply responded, "Make NO mistake . . . we do hate you and we don't trust you, not for one minute!"[28] The young white woman was so distressed that she nearly fell apart. The black women's response apparently confirmed all her worst fears as a good white person. Wise, however, calmly replied to the black woman that he was sorry to hear this, but it was okay since he ultimately wasn't fighting racism for the sake of nonwhite people. Upon hearing this, the entire audience snapped to attention as if a bomb had been dropped in the room, and even the agitated black woman looked puzzled. So Wise continued, "I mean no disrespect by saying that. . . . It's just that I don't view it as my job to fight racism so as to save you from it. That would be paternalistic. . . . I fight [racism] because it's a sickness in my community, and I'm trying to save myself from it."[29]

On a dominant understanding of morality, Wise sounds like a bad, perhaps even a supremacist white person. His reply appears to selfishly care for himself and his racial group more than he cares about the black woman and other black people. This is why his audience was shocked by his reply to the black woman's mistrust. In addition to seeming uncaring and selfish, Wise doesn't prioritize the establishment of close, trusting relationships between himself and other people of color as a goal, or even a means of his activist work. On a conventional understanding of how white antiracism should operate, the distance Wise allows between himself and people of color makes his activism ineffective at best and scandalous at worst. But we can view Wise's reply and his activist work through the lens of a different *ethos*, one that encourages white people's "selfish" attention to their own race and understands the importance of white self-love to their work for racial justice. Wise is fighting for white people's racial health, rather than their racial goodness, and he sees that their improved health will make them better able to join with communities of color in a relationship of genuine respect, rather than paternalistic domination.[30]

Wise models a type of spiritually healthy self-love that provides white people an alternative to both multicultural and oppositional love. Ahmed is right that a great deal of the "love" that exists today, perhaps especially on the part of white people, entails opposing, even hating other people. But love does not have to generate an us-versus-them relationship in which love for oneself is indistinguishable from hate for other people. Other forms of love exist besides multicultural and oppositional love, which often are just two sides of the same coin, and to fail to explore other forms is to hand over the exclusive meaning and function of love to white supremacy. White allies cannot afford to do that. Love is too important to racial justice to let it go.

As part of a transactional spiral, love for oneself can be also an important source of love, rather than hatred for other people. The love that I give myself can build up affective resources that enable me to be generous and loving with others, which in turn can make it more likely that they will return my positive emotions in kind. The contagious quality of love can break down sharp boundaries and rigid divisions. This alternate form of love is not multicultural, however, even as it avoids being oppositional. Its primary focus is not on people who are different from oneself, nor is it based on the assumption that distance between groups of people necessarily breeds antagonism and conflict. It allows embracing, rather than fleeing from, oneself to be the basis of one's relationships with others.

A central reason that multicultural and oppositional love turn out to be two sides of the same problematic coin is that neither makes room for criticism within love. Multicultural love's embrace of difference tends to romanticize the lives of those who are seen as "different," assuming that a warm and fuzzy relationship with them demonstrates that their marginalization and oppression have been overcome. In a strangely similar fashion, oppositional love does the same thing flipped around: it also prioritizes warm and fuzzy noncritical relationships, but those relationships are reserved only for people like "us." All "others" are subject to destructive criticism born out of negative affects such as hatred. Neither form of love can conceive of love as including a critically constructive relationship to the person or thing that one loves.

Such a form of love is precisely what white allies need to transform their relationship with their whiteness. An alternative to multicultural and oppositional forms of love must include room for criticism of that which one loves. Even stronger, it requires such criticism as part of spiritually healthy loving. Understanding love in this way is not a new development, of course. It has a rich philosophical history. As Wendy Brown notes, it harkens back at least to Socrates in the *Apology*, where "we have an argument that dissent from existing practices, even wholesale critique of the regime, is not merely compatible with love and loyalty to a political community, but rather is the supreme form of such love and loyalty."[31] Socrates's criticism of Athenians as caring more for wealth and reputation than for their souls was strong and unrelenting even as the city-state condemned him to death. His criticism, however, was always for the aim of improving Athens, not merely destroying it. Harsh though it was, Socrates's dissent never positioned him as external to Athens, and he literally refused to move outside of Athens even when doing so would have saved his life. Socrates's critique was always internal, always the product of someone who was passionately invested in Athens and who had something to lose—and not just his life—if Athens did not change.

Socrates's dissent was generated out of love, and dissent born of love operates in different ways than dissent born of hatred. Of course, the presence of love does not necessarily make dissent a gentle or warm-feeling practice. Dissent born of love, as Brown explains, can be an outlet for hostility felt toward the loved object.[32] It can be, for example, the enactment of the ambivalence of love and hostility about which

Sigmund Freud and other psychoanalysts rightly caution. Rather than being a drawback, however, this characteristic makes practices of dissent particularly important to the preservation of a loved object, given that hostility can—perhaps must, on many psychoanalytic accounts—accompany love. Even though it might be intertwined with hostility, dissent generated by love can give that negative affect a productive outlet. This is because the ambivalent expression of hostility through dissent born of love is different in its effects from dissent born of hostility. The former has a transformative function while the latter has a purely destructive function. Dissent born of love seeks the ongoing and improved life of that which it criticizes, not its death.

The challenge in the case of dissent born of love is to ensure that dissent perpetuates, rather than extinguishes, the love that produces it. "How far can critique go," as Brown asks, "and in particular how aggressive can it be . . . before it ceases to be loyal where loyalty is defined as love?"[33] She answers that a clue is found in the *Crito*, where Socrates warns against destroying Athens by destroying the laws that hold it together. Dissent that would dismantle a loved object all at once, rather than transform it piece by piece, would be dissent that is disloyal to that which it criticizes and thus be dissent that is not animated by love. Destructive dissent admittedly might be a purer place from which to criticize something. This is because in the case of purely destructive dissent, the risk of complicity with the criticized object is low or even nonexistent because the criticized object is eliminated. For that reason, destructive dissent might seem to be the more attractive option. But playing it safe has its consequences, ones that racial justice movements might not be able to afford. Dissent born of love, in contrast, is willing to risk complicity with the criticized object because of the love felt toward it. It might not be pure, but dissent born of love deeply cares for that which it criticizes, and for that reason it can make a more powerful difference in the world than purely destructive dissent can.

Dissenting with whiteness out of love means a white person's being willing to risk complicity with white privilege and white supremacy—the dominant meanings and effects of whiteness to this point—out of a loving relationship with oneself. These are very real and dangerous risks, but taking them offers one of the best opportunities for transforming white identity in ways that support racial justice. In part, this is because dissent born of love tends to be received differently than if it were generated out of hate or out of a position external to the loved object. Criticism of oneself and others offered as an act of love can "appear less threatening to those who, consciously or unconsciously, experience it as assaulting their love object and as undermining the collectivity rallied around this love object."[34] White people who experience criticism of whiteness as assaulting something dear to them and as undermining their personal identities—and this includes more than the obvious examples of members of white supremacist groups—are likely to feel less threatened by criticism of whiteness that comes from people who are personally invested in whiteness and have something significant at stake in its preservation and transformation. There are no guarantees of this, and at least some feeling of threat probably will remain. But what is certain is that, undertaken without love, the task of transforming whiteness into a white allied identity is likely to fail.

Cleaning up the unhealthy crap between and among white people is one of the best ways that white people today can live their whiteness as an identity that challenges racial injustice. In Lucius Outlaw's terms, it is an important way that whiteness can be "rehabilitated," or returned to a condition of good health.[35] I'm not sure that whiteness has ever been very healthy, as I think Outlaw would agree, so the return here is very much in question. But the sickness and need for better health are not. White people have been ill from white domination for centuries. If they are to recover, they need answers to the question of what a healthier whiteness might be, answers "that must be taken up and lived by folks who identify as 'white.'"[36] This is not work white people can ask or demand that people of color do for them, which is not to say that white people don't have a great deal to learn about themselves from nonwhite people. They do.[37] They also have a great deal to learn from people of color about how to accept and interact with "bad" white people, as Barack Obama's aspirational forgiveness of his grandmother and Daryl Davis's respectful conversations with the Klan demonstrate. While they cannot do it in a white solipsistic vacuum, white people need to figure out new ways to take up their white identities. No one else can live their whiteness for them. So what will they—we, I—do with it? The best answers to this question will be ones that emerge apart from the abjection of white trash, the othering of white ancestors, the distancing strategy of color blindness, and the dominance of white guilt, shame, and betrayal. By developing a critical form of self-love that helps transform whiteness, white people can make positive contributions to struggles for racial justice.

Notes

Introduction

1. See, e.g., Merrill Proudfoot, *Diary of a Sit-In* (Chicago: University of Illinois Press, 1990).

2. http://www.cnn.com/ELECTION/2008/results/polls/#val=USP00p1, accessed March 30, 2011. See also accounts of the election that claim many white supremacists voted for Obama because they believe a black presidency would be so disastrous that it would drive many white people to their cause. http://www.splcenter.org/blog/2008/06/11/president-obama-many-white-suprem-acists-are-celebrating/, accessed March 21, 2013; and http://www.esquire.com/the-side/feature/racists-support-obama-061308, accessed March 21, 2013.

3. Malcolm X, *The Autobiography of Malcolm X* (New York: Ballantine Books, 1964), 312.

4. Shannon Sullivan, *Living Across and Through Skins: Transactional Bodies, Pragmatism and Feminism* (Bloomington: Indiana University Press, 2001). See also chapter 1 of Shannon Sullivan, *Revealing Whiteness: The Unconscious Habits of White Privilege* (Bloomington: Indiana University Press, 2006).

5. bell hooks, *Feminist Theory: From Margin to Center* (Boston: South End Press), 81.

6. At the national level, France recently provided a striking example of this hocus-pocus. Following François Hollande's 2012 pronouncement as a presidential candidate that "there is no place for race in the [French] Republic," the French National Assembly voted on May 16, 2013, to remove the word "race" from all French legislation (Enora Ollivier, "Le mot 'race' indésirable," *20 Minutes*, May 16, 2013, 6, my translation; Pierre Andrieu, "L'Assemblée nationale supprime le mot 'race' de la legislation," *Le Monde*, May 16, 2013, http://www.lemonde.fr/politique/article/2013/05/16/l-assemblee-nationale-supprime-le-mot-race-de-la-legislation_3272514_823448.html, accessed May 17, 2013). Instances of the word "race" (*race*) in approximately fifty French legislative articles addressing the French penal code, laws regarding work and sports, and so on, will be replaced by "ethnic group" (*ethnie*) or "lineage" (*origine*) (Ollivier, "Le mot 'race' indésirable," 6). So that the elimination of "race" from the documents does

not incriminate France as racist, the following statement also will be added to the first legislative article: "The Republic combats racism, anti-Semitism and xenophobia. It does not recognize the existence of any so-called race" (Andrieu, "L'Assemblée nationale supprime le mot 'race' de la legislation," http://www.lemonde.fr/politique/article/2013/05/16/l-assemblee-nationale-supprime-le-mot-race-de-la-legislation_3272514_823448.html, May 17, 2013, my translation).

7. See Michael Lind, "The Beige and the Black," *New York Times Magazine*, Aug. 16, 1998, section 6, p. 38; and Eduardo Bonilla-Silva and Karen S. Glover, "'We Are All Americans': The Latin Americanization of Race Relations in the United States," in *The Changing Terrain of Race and Ethnicity*, ed. Maria Krysan and Amanda E. Lewis (New York: Russell Sage Foundation, 2004), 149–83. Thanks to Charles Mills for bringing these essays to my attention. Mills provided the term *beige supremacy* in discussion after his presentation, "The Racial Contract and Beyond," at Penn State University, July 25, 2007.

8. Linda Martín Alcoff, *Visible Identities: Race, Gender, and The Self* (New York: Oxford University Press, 2006), 207.

9. Crispin Sartwell, *Act Like You Know: African-American Autobiography and White Identity* (Chicago: University of Chicago Press, 1998). See also Audrey Thompson, "Tiffany, Friend of People of Color: White Investments in Antiracism," *Qualitative Studies in Education* 16, no.1 (2003): 7–20.

10. See, for example, Charles Mills, *The Racial Contract* (Ithaca: Cornell University Press, 1997).

11. I explain my use of the terms *white supremacy* and *white privilege* in more detail in Sullivan, *Revealing Whiteness*, 5.

12. Steve Biko, *I Write What I Like* (Chicago: The University of Chicago Press, 1978), 23.

13. George Yancy, *Look, a White! Philosophical Essays on Whiteness* (Philadelphia: Temple University Press, 2012), 17–18.

14. Wendy Brown, *States of Injury: Power and Freedom in Late Modernity* (Princeton: Princeton University Press, 1995), ix.

15. Sarita Srivastava, "'You're calling me a racist?' The Moral and Emotional Regulation of Antiracism and Feminism," *Signs* 31 no. 1(Autumn 2005): 50.

16. Ibid. 45.

17. María Lugones, *Pilgrimages/Peregrinajes: Theorizing Coalition against Multiple Oppressions* (Lanham, MD: Rowman and Littlefield, 2003), 73.

18. Steph Lawlor, "'Getting Out and Getting Away': Women's Narratives of Class Mobility," *Feminist Review* 63 (Autumn 1999): 4. See also sociologists Richard Sennett and Jonathan Cobb, who argue "the activities which keep people moving in a class society, which make them seek more money, more possessions, higher-status jobs, do not originate in a materialistic desire, or even sensuous appreciation of things, but out of an attempt to restore a psychological deprivation that the class structure has effected in their lives" (Sennett and Cobb, *The Hidden Injuries of Class* [New York: Vintage Books, 1973], 171).

19. See John Preston, *Whiteness and Class Education* (Dordrecht: Springer, 2009), 13–16, for a helpful explanation of Bourdieu on class.

20. http://en.wikipedia.org/wiki/Wealth_inequality_in_the_United_States, accessed March 21, 2013.

21. See, for example, the insightful analysis of Preston's *Whiteness and Class Education.*

22. James Baldwin, *The Fire Next Time* (New York: Dell Publishing Company, 1963), 35.

23. The phrase "tough love" might come to mind here, but it would be misplaced given the term's primary association with an unregulated billion-dollar industry of military-style boot camps, many of which are aggressively confrontational and sometimes deadly to the teenagers they are supposed to help (Maia Szalavitz, "The Trouble with Tough Love," *The Washington Post,* Jan. 29, 2006, B01; www.washingtonpost.com/wp-dyn/content/article/2006/01/28/AR2006012800062.html, accessed March 21, 2013).

24. John Hartigan Jr., *Odd Tribes: Toward a Cultural Analysis of White People* (Durham: Duke University Press, 2005), 208.

25. On Great Britain, see women.timesonline.co.uk/tol/life_and_style/women/body_and_soul/article1557903.ece, accessed Sept. 16, 2010.

26. http://en.wikipedia.org/wiki/Multiracial_American, accessed March 21, 2013.

27. Ronald Sundstrom, *The Browning of America and the Evasion of Social Justice* (Albany: State University of New York Press, 2008), 131.

28. See Elizabeth A. Wilson, *Psychosomatic: Feminism and the Neurological Body* (Durham: Duke University Press, 2004).

29. Mab Segrest, " 'The Souls of White Folks,' " in *The Making and Unmaking of Whiteness,* ed. Birgit Brander Rasmussen, Eric Klinenberg, Irene J. Nexica, and Matt Wray (Durham: Duke University Press, 2001), 65. See also bell hooks's claim that "white supremacy . . . promotes mental illness and various dysfunctional behaviors on the part of whites" (hooks, *Killing Rage: Ending Racism* [New York: Henry Holt, 1995], 30).

30. W. E. B. Du Bois, *Darkwater: Voices from Within the Veil* (New York: Harcourt Brace, 1999), 19, 22.

31. Thanks to Lucius Outlaw (personal communication) for providing the term *soul work.*

32. Du Bois, *Darkwater,* 28.

33. Alcoff, *Visible Identities,* 223.

34. Judith Butler's *Gender Trouble: Feminism and the Subversion of Identity* (New York: Routledge, 1990) offers probably the best-known criticism of gender identity and identity politics. See also María Lugones and Elizabeth Spelman's excellent criticism of the category of "woman" in "Have We Got a Theory for You! Feminist Theory, Cultural Imperialism, and the Demand for 'The Woman's Voice,' " *Hypatia* (WSIF) 1: 573–81. The first four chapters of Alcoff's *Visible Identities* provide a very helpful explanation of (and response to) the political and philosophical pathologizing of identity.

35. Alcoff, *Visible Identities*, 287.

36. Ibid.

37. Rachel E. Luft, "Intersectionality and the Risk of Flattening Difference," in *The Intersectional Approach: Transforming the Academy through Race, Class and Gender*, ed. Michele Tracy Berger and Kathlenne Guidroz (Chapel Hill: University of North Carolina Press, 2009), 103.

38. For literary, poetic, and historical accounts of white bonding through terror, see respectively James Baldwin, "Going to Meet the Man," in *Black on White: Black Writers on What It Means to Be White*, ed. David R. Roediger (New York: Schocken Books, 1998), 255–73; Claude McKay, "The Lynching," in *Black on White*, 335; and Harriet Jacobs, "Muster," in *Black on White*, 336–37).

39. hooks, *Killing Rage*, 41.

40. Harriet A. Jacobs, *Incidents in the Life of a Slave Girl* (Cambridge: Harvard University Press, 1987).

41. Nell Irvin Painter makes this argument in "Slavery and Soul Murder," in *Black on White*, 328.

42. Once again, France offers a striking example of this problematic tendency; see note 6 above. For further discussion of the use of white ethnicity to evade race, see Charles A. Gallagher, "Playing the White Ethnic Card: Using Ethnic Identity to Deny Contemporary Racism," in *White Out: The Continuing Significance of Racism*, ed. Ashley W. Doane and Eduardo Bonilla-Silva (New York: Routledge, 2003), 145–58.

43. Terrence MacMullan, *Habits of Whiteness: A Pragmatist Reconstruction* (Bloomington: Indiana University Press, 2009), 201.

44. MacMullan, *Habits of Whiteness*, 202; emphasis in original.

45. For a fascinating account of how middle-class white people use history to manage race and class lines, see John Hartigan Jr., *Racial Situations: Class Predicaments of Whiteness in Detroit* (Princeton: Princeton University Press, 1999), 191–208.

46. Linda Martín Alcoff, plenary discussion at conference on "The Supremacy of Whiteness: Systemic, Ethical and Intrapersonal Explorations," Allegheny College, April 2008.

47. http://www.census.gov/Press-Release/www/releases/archives/population/012496.html, accessed July 10, 2009.

48. Sonia Kruks, "Simone de Beauvoir and the Politics of Privilege," *Hypatia* 20, no.1 (Winter 2005): 181.

49. Ibid., 181–83.

50. See note 4 above.

51. Lisa Tessman, *Burdened Virtues: Virtue Ethics for Liberatory Struggles* (New York: Oxford University Press, 2005), 12.

52. Sullivan, *Revealing Whiteness*, 10.

53. Greg Tate, *Everything but the Burden: What White People are Taking from Black Culture* (New York: Harlem Moon, 2003).

54. Lugones, María C., "Playfulness, 'World'-Traveling, and Loving Perception," *Hypatia* 2, no. 2 (1987): 3–19. See also Shannon Sullivan,

"White World Traveling," *The Journal of Speculative Philosophy* 18, no. 4 (2004): 300–304.

55. Lisa Heldke, "A Du Boisian Proposal for Persistently White Colleges," *Journal of Speculative Philosophy* 18, no.3 (2004): 226.

56. Ibid., 232; emphasis in original.

57. Ibid., 231.

58. Noel Ignatiev, "Abolitionism and the White Studies Racket," *Race Traitor* 10 (1999): 5.

59. Ibid.

60. The mission paragraph on the center's home page says nothing about racism or white privilege, an omission that supports Ignatiev's concern (http://www.euroamerican.org/, accessed July 13, 2009). The center's home page also fits with Heldke's experience at a predominantly white university, at which there is a great deal of talk about diversity and multiculturalism without ever mentioning words such as "racism" (Heldke, "A Du Boisian Proposal for Persistently White Colleges," 228).

61. Lucius Outlaw, "Rehabilitate Racial *Whiteness?*" in *What White Looks Like: African-American Philosophers on the Whiteness Question*, ed. George Yancy (New York: Routledge, 2004), 161.

Chapter 1. Dumping on White Trash

1. Mike Hill, *After Whiteness: Unmaking an American Majority* (New York: New York University Press, 2004), 1; http://www.amren.com/conference/2002/index.html, accessed Feb. 26, 2010.

2. Ibid.; Mike Hill, "America's Biennial Gathering of Academic Racists: The 2002 American Renaissance Conference," *The Journal of Blacks in Higher Education* 35 no. 2 (Spring 2002): 94.

3. Hill is the editor of *Whiteness: A Critical Reader* (New York: New York University Press, 1997).

4. Hill, "America's Biennial Gathering of Academic Racists," 94–99.

5. http://www.amren.com/siteinfo/index.html, accessed Feb. 26, 2010.

6. Hill, "America's Biennial Gathering of Academic Racists," 94.

7. Hill, *After Whiteness*, 2.

8. Ibid., 3.

9. Ibid.

10. Ibid., 4.

11. Ibid., 3.

12. Ibid., 7.

13. Jim Goad, *The Redneck Manifesto: How Hillbillies, Hicks, and White Trash Became America's Scapegoats* (New York: Simon and Shuster, 1997) 18.

14. Hartigan, *Racial Situations*, 8.

15. Hill, *After Whiteness*, 6.

16. Ibid., 1; 218, note 16.

17. http://dictionary.reference.com/browse/etiquette, accessed March 21, 2013.

18. Bertram Wilbur Doyle, *The Etiquette of Race Relations in the South: A Study in Social Control* (Chicago: University of Chicago Press, 1937).

19. Ibid., xvii–xviii.

20. Ibid., xix.

21. Ibid., xx.

22. Jennifer Ritterhouse, *Growing Up Jim Crow: How Black and White Southern Children Learned Race* (Chapel Hill: University of North Carolina Press, 2006), 15.

23. Doyle, *The Etiquette of Race Relations in the South*, xvii, 172.

24. Ladelle McWhorter, *Bodies and Pleasures: Foucault and the Politics of Sexual Normalization* (Bloomington: Indiana University Press, 1999), 211. See also Michel Foucault, *The History of Sexuality: Volume I*, trans. Robert Hurley (New York: Vintage, 1978); and Foucault, "The Ethics of the Concern for Self as a Practice of Freedom," in *Ethics: Subjectivity and Truth*, volume 1 of *The Essential Works of Foucault, 1954–1984*, ed. Paul Rabinow (New York: New Press, 1997) 281–301.

25. Doyle, *The Etiquette of Race Relations in the South*, 11.

26. Ibid., xviii.

27. Ibid., 12.

28. Ibid., 159.

29. See Joseph Margolis, "Personal Reflections on Racism in America," in *On Race and Racism in America: Confessions in Philosophy*, ed. Roy Martinez (University Park: The Pennsylvania University Press, 2010), 29–37. In apparent contradiction with the conclusion of his essay, Margolis himself says that the "well-intentioned, natural etiquette that I've learned to share with all my neighbors . . . mediates every encounter along the street (and leaves the world unchanged). It exacts no tribute, and it has no deeper purpose. But it fills the air very nicely" (31–32).

30. Martin Luther King Jr., "Letter from a Birmingham Jail," www.africa.upenn.edu/Articles_Gen/Letter_Birmingham.html, accessed March 21, 2013.

31. Doyle, *The Etiquette of Race Relations in the South*, xviii–xix.

32. Ritterhouse, *Growing Up Jim Crow*, 15, 32–33, 48.

33. Ibid., 54.

34. Ibid., 19. See also Kristina DuRocher, *Raising Racists: The Socialization of White Children in the Jim Crow South* (Lexington: The University Press of Kentucky, 2011).

35. Hartigan, *Racial Situations*, 17, 46–47.

36. Hartigan, *Odd Tribes*, 19.

37. Ibid., 90.

38. Ibid., 110.

39. Hartigan, *Racial Situations*, 28, 33, 88–90.

40. Charles Mills, "Comments on Shannon Sullivan's *Revealing Whiteness*," *Journal of Speculative Philosophy* 21, no. 3 (2007): 225. This is why, accord-

ing to Mills, the eradication of class can be more radical than the eradication of race.

41. Beverley Skeggs, *Formations of Class and Gender: Becoming Respectable* (London: Sage, 1997) 82.

42. Quoted in Lawlor, " 'Getting Out and Getting Away': Women's Narratives of Class Mobility," 5.

43. Hartigan, *Odd Tribes*, 124.

44. See, for example, Jeff Foxworthy, *You Might Be a Redneck If . . . This is the Biggest Book You've Ever Read* (Nashville: Thomas Nelson Publishers, 2004).

45. Hartigan, *Odd Tribes*, 122.

46. Ibid., 99.

47. Ibid., 78; see also 85, 103–104.

48. Ibid., 18.

49. Julia Kristeva, *Powers of Horror: An Essay on Abjection* (New York: Columbia University Press, 1982), 1.

50. Ibid., 1.

51. Hartigan, *Odd Tribes*, 113; see also Matt Wray, *Not Quite White: White Trash and the Boundaries of Whiteness* (Durham: Duke University Press, 2006), esp. p. 2.

52. Goad, *The Redneck Manifesto*, 22.

53. Kristeva, *Powers of Horror*, 3.

54. Goad, *The Redneck Manifesto*, 100.

55. See Genesis 3:19: "For dust thou art, and unto dust shalt thou return."

56. Kristeva, *Powers of Horror*, 2.

57. Ibid., 90–132.

58. Ibid., 4.

59. Ibid., 14.

60. Ibid., 10.

61. Goad, *The Redneck Manifesto*, 100.

62. http://www.fortogden.com/foredneck.html, accessed March 21, 2013; Goad, *The Redneck Manifesto*, 90.

63. Goad, *The Redneck Manifesto*, 91.

64. Here I also disagree with John Hartigan when he claims, "It is not clear that psychoanalysis has any effective insight into collective processes, especially the intense contests over belonging that are constitutive of cultural orders" (Hartigan, *Odd Tribes*, 13). Hartigan's concern is that psychoanalysis cannot deal with the classed and raced complexities of white identity and that it lumps together white people "as uniform ideological subjects all operating under a shared perception of Difference" (13).

65. Goad, *The Redneck Manifesto*, 91.

66. Hartigan, *Odd Tribes*, 61.

67. George Weston, quoted in ibid., 63.

68. Ibid., 67.

69. Ibid., 68.

70. Kirby Moss, *The Color of Class: Poor Whites and the Paradox of Privilege* (Philadelphia: University of Pennsylvania Press, 2003), 53.

71. Ibid., 52.

72. Toni Morrison, "The Talk of the Town: Comment," *The New Yorker,* Oct. 5, 1998. http://www.newyorker.com/archive/1998/10/05/1998_10_05_031_TNY_LIBRY_000016504?currentPage=all, accessed March 21, 2013.

73. Andrea Sachs, "10 Questions for Toni Morrison," *Time.com*, May 7, 2008, http://www.time.com/time/arts/article/0,8599,1738303,00.html, accessed March 21, 2013.

74. Quoted in Goad, *The Redneck Manifesto*, 90.

75. Hartigan, *Racial Situations*, 28.

76. Ibid., 27–28.

77. Ibid., 88.

78. Quoted in ibid., 33.

79. Ibid., 88, 89.

80. Thanks to Samuel Findley for sharing this saying with me at the March 2012 meeting of the West Virginia Philosophical Association.

81. Quoted in Doyle, *The Etiquette of Race Relations in the South*, 120. South Carolina and North Carolina had similar codes as well (138).

82. Doyle, *The Etiquette of Race Relations in the South*, 150. See also Ritterhouse, *Growing up Jim Crow*, 30, 42.

83. Neil McMillen, quoted in Ritterhouse, *Growing Up Jim Crow*, 15.

84. Hartigan, *Racial Situations*, 28.

85. See Daniel Hundley's account of "poor white trash" in his 1860 *Social Relations in our Southern States*: "They are about the laziest two-legged animals that walk erect on the face of the Earth. Even their motions are slow, and their speech is a sickening drawl . . . while their thoughts and ideas seem likewise to creep along at a snail's pace. . . . [They show] a natural stupidity or dullness of intellect that almost surpasses belief'" (quoted in Goad, *The Redneck Manifesto*, 81).

86. Hartigan, *Racial Situations*, 90.

87. Ibid., 197, 198, 206.

88. For example, middle-class white people often prefer to work politically against racism alongside people of color than poor white people (Anna Stubblefield, *Ethics Along the Color Line* [Ithaca: Cornell University Press, 2005], 173). See also Lerone Bennett's claim that "the fundamental trait of the white liberal is his desire to differentiate himself . . . from [other] white Americans on the issue of race" (Lerone Bennett Jr., "Tea and Sympathy: Liberals and Other White Hopes" in *The Negro Mood and Other Essays* [Chicago: Johnson, 1964], 77).

89. Andrew Hacker, *Two Nations: Black and White, Separate, Hostile, Unequal* (New York: Scribner, 2003); and Philip J. Mazzocco, Timothy C. Brock, Gregory J. Brock, Kristina R. Olsen, Mahzarin R. Banaji, "The Cost of Being Black: White Americans' Perceptions and the Question of Reparations," *Du Bois Review: Social Science Research on Race* 3, no. 2 (2006): 261–97. The variation in money depended on factors such as whether participants were given informa-

tion on racial wealth disparities and how the study scenarios were set up. For example, in Hacker's study, participants generally demanded a great deal more money ($1 million per year) if they had to change their skin color and bodily and facial features to appear stereotypically African American. If they were told that they had been passing as white but would now have the knowledge that they were black, the participants demanded less money. Mazzocco's study demonstrates that when white people understand racial wealth disparities in the United States, they tend to ask for much more compensation for becoming black.

90. Alison Jones insightfully discusses her (Pakeka/white) desire to work alongside Maori colleagues in Jones, "Limits of Cross-Cultural Dialogue: Pedagogy, Desire, and Absolution in the Classroom," *Educational Theory* 49, no. 3 (1999): 303.

91. For more on the black middle class, see Karyn R. Lacy, *Blue-Chip Black: Race, Class, and Status in the New Black Middle Class* (Berkeley: University of California Press, 2007); and Mary Pattillo-McCoy, *Black Picket Fences: Privilege and Peril among the Black Middle Class* (Chicago: University of Chicago Press, 1999).

92. Moss, *The Color of Class*, 77.

93. Ibid.

94. Thompson, "Tiffany," 19.

95. Goad, *The Redneck Manifesto*, 23.

96. Noëlle McAfee, *Democracy and the Political Unconscious* (New York: Columbia University Press, 2008), 26.

97. Ibid.

98. Ibid., 21.

99. Ibid.

100. Ibid., 19.

101. McAfee, Ibid., 17; emphasis added. See also Iris Marion Young's criticism of deliberative democracy for operating with too narrow an understanding of what reasonableness is (Young, *Inclusion and Democracy* [New York: Oxford University Press, 2000]).

102. Baldwin, *The Fire Next Time*, 131–32.

103. Sullivan, *Revealing Whiteness*.

104. McAfee, *Democracy and the Political Unconscious*, 15.

105. Ibid., 24.

106. Ibid., 30.

107. Robyn Marasco, "Comments on *Democracy and the Political Unconscious* by Noëlle McAfee," presented at the Society for Phenomenology and Existential Philosophy, Oct. 29, 2009.

108. McAfee brought out this point in her reply to Marasco; see note 107 above.

109. http://www.africa.upenn.edu/Articles_Gen/Letter_Birmingham.html, accessed March 21, 2013.

110. McAfee, *Democracy and the Political Unconscious*, 87; emphasis in original.

111. Ibid., 88.

112. Ibid., 70–71.

113. I take the term *sub-person* from Mills, *The Racial Contract*.

114. McAfee, *Democracy and the Political Unconscious*, 90.

115. Marilyn Frye provides an illuminating account of how the concept "crazy" works in chapters 5 and 7 of Frye, *The Politics of Reality* (Berkeley: The Crossing Press, 1983). In the context of the Tea Party movement in the United States, see also Chip Berlet's criticism of the "constant demonizing rhetoric coming from the Democrats and their liberal allies, rhetoric that portrays the majority of Americans who are angry at the government as crazies and fools" (Berlet, "Taking Tea Partiers Seriously," *The Progressive*, Feb. 2010, 26).

116. McAfee, *Democracy and the Political Unconscious*, 90.

117. Ibid., 155. See also Young, *Inclusion and Democracy*, 52–80, for a model of inclusive political communication that emphasizes the importance of storytelling, rhetoric, and rituals of respectful greeting.

118. John Preston, *Whiteness and Class in Education* (Dordrecht: Springer, 2009) 186.

119. Daryl Davis, *Klan-Destine Relationships: A Black Man's Odyssey in the Ku Klux Klan* (Far Hills, NJ: New Horizon Press, 1998), 308.

120. http://www.amazon.com/Klan-destine-Relationships-Daryl-Davis/dp/0882822691/ref=sr_1_2?ie=UTF8&s=books&qid=1248885109&sr=1-2, accessed July 12, 2012.

121. http://www.amazon.com/Klan-destine-Relationships-Daryl-Davis/product-reviews/0882822691/ref=cm_cr_dp_all_helpful?ie=UTF8&coliid=&showViewpoints=1&colid=&sortBy=bySubmissionDateDescending, accessed July 7, 2012.

122. Ibid.

123. Davis, *Klan-Destine Relationships*, 308.

124. Thanks to Phillip McReynolds for bringing up these issues and to Noëlle McAfee for helping me respond to them.

125. Sheila Wilmot, *Taking Responsibility, Taking Direction: White Anti-Racism in Canada* (Winnipeg: Arbeiter Ring Publishing, 2005), 15.

126. hooks, *Feminist Theory*, 67–81.

127. Quoted in Kathy Hytten and John Warren, "Engaging Whiteness: How Racial Power Gets Reified In Education," *Qualitative Studies in Education* 16, no. 1 (2003): 76. See also Thompson, "Tiffany," 7–29, for an excellent criticism of white people—and white college professors in particular—who claim to "get it."

128. Cooper Thompson, Emmett Schaefer, and Harry Brod, *White Men Challenging Racism: 35 Personal Stories* (Durham: Duke University Press, 2003), 77.

129. Ibid., 94.

130. Ibid.

131. Ibid., 94–97.

132. Ibid., 98.

133. Preston, *Whiteness and Class in Education*, 179.

134. Ibid., 179–82.

135. Ibid., 181.

136. Ladelle McWhorter, *Bodies and Pleasures: Foucault and the Politics of Sexual Normalization* (Bloomington: Indiana University Press, 1999), 167–75.

137. Ibid., 172.

138. Ibid., 173.

139. Ibid., 174.

140. Ibid.

141. Ibid.

142. As John Preston asks, "What should educators do about white supremacists in the classroom?" (Preston, *Whiteness and Class in Education*, 107). Paul Taylor also asks, "How can unreconstructed [white] privilegists be made to confront and overcome themselves?" (Taylor, "Race, Ethics, Seduction, Politics: On Shannon Sullivan's *Revealing Whiteness*," *Journal of Speculative Philosophy* 21, no.3 [2007]: 206).

143. Thanks to an anonymous reviewer for suggesting this particular condition and for pressing the issue of conditions for inclusion more generally.

144. Jones, "Limits of Cross-Cultural Dialogue," 299.

145. Lugones and Spelman, "Have We Got a Theory for You!," 573–81.

146. Jones's students speak very powerfully about this need—sometimes without realizing it, as in the case of her Pakeha (white) students—in Jones, "The Limits of Cross-Cultural Dialogue," 301–303.

Chapter 2. Demonizing White Ancestors

1. Jacobs, *Incidents in the Life of a Slave Girl*, 23; emphasis in original.

2. Ibid., 70.

3. William Faulkner, *Requiem for a Nun* (New York: Random House, 1951), 92.

4. *Sullivan, Revealing Whiteness*.

5. Jean Laplanche, *Essays on Otherness* (New York: Routledge, 1999).

6. Sigmund Freud, "Three Essays on Sexuality," in volume VII of *The Standard Edition of the Complete Psychological Works of Sigmund Freud*, ed. and trans. James Strachey (New York: W. W. Norton, 1960).

7. Laplanche, *Essays on Otherness*, 128. Laplanche's version of psychoanalytic theory thus is much more transactional than is Freud's.

8. Peter Osborne, *Philosophy in Cultural Theory* (New York: Routledge, 2000), 209.

9. Laplanche, *Essays on Otherness*, 91.

10. For a fuller explanation of Laplanche's psychoanalytic theory, especially in connection with race and racism, see chapter 3 of Sullivan, *Revealing Whiteness*.

11. Leon F. Litwack, "Hellhounds," in *Without Sanctuary: Lynching Photography in America* (Santa Fe: Twin Palms Publishers, 2003), 8–17. For additional discussion of the "excess of enjoyment" that executioners and death squads sometimes take in inflicting pain and death on others, see Slavoj Zizek, "Love thy Neighbor? No, Thanks!" in *The Psychoanalysis of Race*, ed. Christopher Lane (New York: Columbia University Press, 1998), 154–75.

12. W. E. B. Du Bois, *Black Reconstruction in America* (New York: The Free Press, 1962), 11.

13. See, e.g., Eduardo Bonilla-Silva, *Racism without Racists: Color-blind Racism and the Persistence of Racial Inequality in the United States* (Lanham, MD: Rowman and Littlefield, 2003).

14. Mills, *The Racial Contract*, 84.

15. See Bonilla-Silva, *Racism without Racists*, especially p. 2.

16. Cultural anthropologist John Hartigan Jr., has charged that "whiteness studies . . . is dominated by the enormously influential model of Otherness," which ignores "the social dynamics of establishing, comparing, and ranking similarities [and differences within whiteness] is as fundamental to the operation of racial identities as is the projection of [nonwhite] Otherness" (Hartigan, *Odd Tribes*, 12). Either I would disagree with Hartigan that analyses of othering necessarily do this, or I would consider my analysis of othering, both here and in chapter 1, to offer an alternative to dominant models.

17. Albert Taylor Bledsoe, *Liberty and Slavery: Or, Slavery in the Light of Moral and Political Philosophy*, in *Cotton Is King, and Pro-Slavery Arguments Comprising the Writings of Hammond, Harper, Christy, Stringfellow, Hodge, Bledsoe, and Cartwright, on this Important Subject* (New York: Negro Universities Press, 1969), 272. See also William Garrott Brown, *The Lower South in American History* (New York: Greenwood Press, 1969) 91–92.

18. http://www.antislavery.org/english/slavery_today/what_is_modern_slavery.aspx.

19. Jean-Paul Sartre, *Anti-Semite and Jew: An Exploration of the Etiology of Hate*, trans. George J. Becker (New York: Schocken, 1976), 16.

20. Think here of the 1994 genocide in Rwanda, when as many as one million Tutsis were killed by their Hutu neighbors and compatriots (Mahmood Mamdani, *When Victims Become Killers: Colonialism, Nativism, and the Genocide in Rwanda* [Princeton: Princeton University Press, 2001]). Even in this case, however, white atrocities were involved since colonialism's politicization of indigeneity laid the groundwork for the genocide.

21. Michelle Anderson, *The New Jim Crow* (New York: The New Press, 2010).

22. Kim Q. Hall, "My Father's Flag," in *Whiteness: Feminist Philosophical Reflections*, ed. Chris J. Cuomo and Kim Q. Hall (Lanham, MD: Rowman and Littlefield, 1999), 32.

23. Warren Read, *The Lyncher in Me: A Search for Redemption in the Face of History* (St. Paul: Borealis Books, 2008).

24. Ibid., 10.

25. Ibid., 11.

26. Osborne, *Philosophy in Cultural Theory*, 109.

27. Laplanche, *Essays on Otherness*, 164–65.

28. Jean Laplanche in John Fletcher and Martin Stanton, eds., *John Laplanche: Seduction, Translation, and the Drives*, trans. Martin Stanton (London: Institute of Contemporary Arts, 1992), 35; see also Laplanche, *Essays on Otherness*, 244.

29. Laplanche, *Essays on Otherness*, 244.

30. Ibid., 230.

31. Laplanche in *John Laplanche*, 170.

32. Ibid., 177, 172; and Laplanche, *Essays on Otherness*, 101.

33. Laplanche, *Essays on Otherness*, 214.

34. Cheshire Calhoun, "Changing One's Heart," *Ethics* 103, no. 1(1992): 87, 89.

35. With regard to Hitler, see Ursula Mahlendorf's explanation of why she wants her students to identity with the Hitler Youth, "to see this generation as humanly understandable despite spending their formative years under Nazi training . . . so that they would not, with the clarity of perfect hindsight, dismiss who [Mahlendorf] almost became with a facile 'this would never happen to me'" (Mahlendorf, *The Shame of Survival: Working Through a Nazi Childhood* [University Park: Penn State University Press, 2009], 4). Nicknamed "prime evil," Eugene de Kock was the commander of the South African government's death squad, "Valkplaas," during apartheid (Samantha Vice, "How Do I Live in This Strange Place?" *The Journal of Social Philosophy* 41, no. 3[2011]: 323–43, and http://en.wikipedia.org/wiki/Eugene_de_Kock, accessed March 21, 2013).

36. Calhoun, "Changing One's Heart," 89.

37. Ibid.

38. Ibid., 92.

39. Ibid., 95.

40. Ibid.

41. Probably many people of color would feel the same way, but their refusal to use words such as *respect* for, and their corresponding condemnation of white slaveholders tends to operate in different ways and to different effects. It might be part of a broader condemnation of all white people as racist, for example. In any case, it generally would not function to (try to) absolve contemporary white people of their complicity with white domination.

42. Quoted in Elizabeth Fox-Genovese and Eugene D. Genovese, *The Mind of the Master Class: History and Faith in the Southern Slaveholders' Worldview* (New York: Cambridge University Press, 2005), 407.

43. Ibid., 312.

44. Ibid., 676.

45. Ibid., 3; Drew Gilpin Faust, *Southern Stories: Slaveholders in Peace and War* (Columbia: University of Missouri Press, 1992), 55.

46. Faust, *Southern Stories*, 98.

47. Fox-Genovese and Genovese, *The Mind of the Master Class*, 312.

48. Ibid., 110, 112.

49. Ibid., 672.

50. Ibid., 109.

51. George Fitzhugh, *Sociology for the South: Or the Failure of Free Society* (New York: Burt Franklin, 1965), 33.

52. Fox-Genovese and Genovese, *The Mind of the Master Class*, 313.

53. Ibid., 62–63, 174.

54. Ibid. 173.

55. Eugene D. Genovese, *The World the Slaveholders Made: Two Essays in Interpretation* (Hanover, NH: Wesleyan University Press, 1988), 168.

56. Faust, *Southern Stories*, 23.

57. Fitzhugh, *Sociology for the South*, 29.

58. Jacobs, *Incidents in the Life of a Slave Girl*, 31–36.

59. John W. Blassingame, John R. McKivigan, and Peter P. Hinks, eds., *Narrative of the Life of Frederick Douglass, An American Slave Written by Himself* (New Haven: Yale University Press, 2001).

60. Du Bois, *Black Reconstruction in America*, 11; see also Cynthia Willett, *The Soul of Justice: Social Bonds and Racial Hubris* (Ithaca: Cornell University Press, 2001).

61. For various feminist criticisms of the violence of family, see Cheshire Calhoun, *Feminism, the Family, and the Politics of the Closet: Lesbian and Gay Displacement* (New York: Oxford University Press, 2000), 133; Marilyn Frye, *The Politics of Reality: Essays in Feminist Theory* (Freedom, CA: Crossing Press, 1983), 52–83; Luce Irigaray, *This Sex Which Is Not One*, trans. Catherine Porter (Ithaca: Cornell University Press, 1985), 142; and Ladelle McWhorter, *Racism and Sexual Oppression in Anglo-America: A Genealogy* (Bloomington: Indiana University Press, 2009), esp. ch. 6.

62. Mab Segrest, "'The Souls of White Folks,'" in *The Making and Unmaking of Whiteness*, ed. Birgit Brander Rasmussen, Eric Klenenberg, Irene J. Nexica, and Matt Wray (Durham: Duke University Press, 2001), 51.

63. Eugene D. Genovese, *The Slaveholders' Dilemma: Freedom and Progress in Southern Conservative Thought, 1820–1860* (Columbia: University of South Carolina Press, 1992), 56.

64. Hartigan, *Odd Tribes*, 118.

65. Alcoff, *Visible Identities*, 222–23.

66. Du Bois, *Black Reconstruction in America*.

67. Laplanche, *Essays on Otherness*, 112.

68. Calhoun, "Changing One's Heart," 95–96.

69. http://www.huffingtonpost.com/2008/03/18/obama-race-speech-read-t_n_92077.html, accessed March 21, 2013.

70. Vincent Colapietro, "The Eclipse of Piety: Toward a Pragmatic Overcoming of a Theoretical Injustice," *Journal of Chinese Philosophy* 24 (1997): 478.

71. On the need for gratitude toward one's ancestors and the relationship between this gratitude and care for young children, see Colapietro, "The Eclipse of Piety," esp. p. 478.

Chapter 3. The Dis-ease of Color Blindness

1. Amanda E. Lewis, "Some Are More Equal than Others: Lessons on Whiteness from School," in *White Out: The Continuing Significance of Racism* (New York: Routledge, 2003), 160. For an example of a parent explicitly instructing his ten-year-old daughter to be "color blind," see Tahar Ben Jelloun, *Racism Explained to My Daughter* (New York: The New Press, 1999), 25–26.

2. Lewis, "Some are More Equal than Others," 160.

3. José Medina, *The Epistemology of Resistance: Gender and Racial Oppression, Epistemic Injustice, and Resistant Imaginations* (New York: Oxford University Press, 2012), 37.

4. Baldwin, *The Fire Next Time*, 63.

5. Some readers misunderstood me to be making this claim in *Revealing Whiteness*.

6. See Thomas D. Fallace, *Dewey and the Dilemma of Race: An Intellectual History, 1895–1922* (New York: Teachers College, 2011) for an explanation of why Dewey's work on children is problematic.

7. See, for example, Marguerite A. Wright, *I'm Chocolate, You're Vanilla: Raising Healthy Black and Biracial Children in a Race-Conscious World* (San Francisco: Jossey-Bass, 1998).

8. See, for example, Susan Bordo, "Adoption," *Hypatia* 20, no. 1 (Winter 2005): 230–36; Jane Lazarre, *Beyond the Whiteness of Whiteness: Memoir of a White Mother of Black Sons* (Durham: Duke University Press, 1996); Shelley Park, "Mothering across Racial and Cultural Boundaries," in *Everyday Acts Against Racism: Raising Children in a Multicultural World*, ed. Maureen Reddy (Seattle: Seal Press, 1996), 223–37; Maureen T. Reddy, "Working on Redemption," in *Everyday Acts Against Racism*, 238–56; and Becky Thompson, *Mothering without a Compass: White Mother's Love, Black Son's Courage* (Minneapolis: University of Minnesota Press, 2000).

9. This is confirmed by child development specialist Stacey York, who explains that "the vast majority of studies related to racial identity development have focused on black and white children. The studies of white children have emphasized their awareness of attitudes toward other races but have not investigated how white children form their own racial identities" (York, *Roots and Wings: Affirming Culture in Early Childhood Programs* [St. Paul: Redleaf Press, 2003], 42). In the field of philosophy, one exception to my claim is Rebecca Aanerud, "The Legacy of White Supremacy and the Challenge of White Anti-racist Mothering," *Hypatia* 22, no. 2 (Spring 2007): 20–38. While not scholarly, "White Noise" is a group recently established by white parents to help them raise their white children in anti-racist ways (see Susan Raffo's "White Noise: White Adults Raising White Children to Resist White Supremacy," http://loveisntenough.com/2009/08/05/white-noise-white-adults-raising-white-children-to-resist-white-supremacy/, accessed March 21, 2013).

10. James Edward Bates, "The Modern-Day Ku Klux Klan," *The Chronicle Review*, May 20, 2011, B18.

11. Christian Miller, "Mind Wars: Raising Healthy White Children in a Subversive Environment," in *The Occidental Observer: White Interests, Identity, and Culture*, http://www.theoccidentalobserver.net/2011/02/mind-wars-raising-healthy-white-children-in-a-subversive-environment/, accessed March 21, 2013.

12. Quoted in Allison Berg, *Mothering the Race: Women's Narratives of Reproduction, 1890–1930* (Urbana: University of Illinois Press, 2002), 1.

13. Anti-Defamation League, "Feminism Perverted: Extremist Women on the World Wide Web," www.adl.org/special_reports/extremist_women_on_web/feminism_intro.asp, accessed March 21, 2013; Jackie Litt and JoAnn Rogers, "Normalizing Racism: A Case Study of Motherhood in White Supremacy," in *Home-grown Hate: Gender and Organized Racism*, ed. Abby L. Ferber (New York: Routledge, 2003), 106.

14. Litt and Rogers, "Normalizing Racism," 106.

15. Helen Zia, "Women in Hate Groups: Who Are They? Why Are They There?" *Ms.*, March/April 1991, 20–27, 21.

16. www.stormfront.org/forum/showthread.php?t=222452&goto=next newest, accessed May 5, 2010.

17. www.crusader.net/resources/election.html, accessed May 5, 2010; Litt and Rogers, "Normalizing Racism," 108–109.

18. I discuss the connection of cleanliness and habits of white privilege in Sullivan, *Revealing Whiteness*, 72–75.

19. Miller, "Mind Wars," http://www.theoccidentalobserver.net/2011/02/mind-wars-raising-healthy-white-children-in-a-subversive-environment/, accessed March 21, 2013.

20. Ibid.

21. Charles Mills, "Liberalizing Illiberal Liberalism," Philosophy in an Inclusive Key Summer Institute (PIKSI) presentation at Penn State University, June 2012.

22. Mills, *The Racial Contract*, 18; Bonilla-Silva, *Racism without Racists*.

23. See, e.g., Amanda E. Lewis, *Race in the Schoolyard: Negotiating the Color Line in Classrooms and Communities* (New Brunswick: Rutgers University Press, 2003), 12–38; Vivian Gussin Paley, *White Teacher* (Cambridge: Harvard University Press, 2000).

24. Patricia Williams offers a poignant example of such confusion in *Seeing a Color-Blind Future: The Paradox of Race* (New York: Farrar, Straus and Giroux, 1997), 3. I discuss this incident more fully in *Revealing Whiteness*, 78.

25. Wright, *I'm Chocolate, You're Vanilla*. George Yancy also has noted white people's desire to believe that racial prejudice is a secondary layer applied on top of the racial innocence of white children, in *Look, a White!*, 21.

26. Henry C. Wright, quoted in Ronald G. Walters, *The Antislavery Appeal: Abolitionism after 1830* (Baltimore: Johns Hopkins University Press, 1976), 98.

27. Wright, *I'm Chocolate, You're Vanilla*, 7.

28. Williams, *Seeing a Color-Blind Future*, 3.

29. See, e.g., Paley, *White Teacher*; and Debra Van Ausdale and Joe R. Feagin, *The First R: How Children Learn Race and Racism* (Lanham, MD: Rowman and Littlefield, 2001).

30. York, *Roots and Wings*, 42; Po Bronson and Ashley Merryman, "See Baby Discriminate," *Newsweek*, Sept. 5, 2009, http://www.newsweek.com/id/214989/page/1, accessed March 21, 2013.

31. Van Ausdale and Feagin, *The First R*, 16.

32. Ibid., 20, 34.

33. Ibid., 13, 17.

34. Ibid., 17, 20.

35. Ibid., 57–58.

36. While an adult was close enough to the children to overhear and later record the following incident, that adult was researcher Debra Van Ausdale, with whom the children were familiar as a "nonsanctioning, playmate-adult" (ibid., 40). In the year of her observation of the daycare, unless the children were in immediate physical danger, Van Ausdale did not intervene in their activities. Because the children did not alter their race-baiting behavior in her presence—behavior that Van Ausdale observed them avoiding in front of their teachers—it is clear that they regarded her as a nonauthoritative "non-player" in their preschool world.

37. Ibid., 104.

38. Ibid.

39. Ibid., 105.

40. Ibid., 68–69. See also Paley, *White Teacher*, for an example of a child's realizing when she had stumbled onto an "unsafe" topic with her teacher, based on the teacher's facial expression (104).

41. Lewis, *Race in the Schoolyard*, 11.

42. Bronson and Merryman, "See Baby Discriminate."

43. Ibid.

44. Raffo, "White Noise."

45. Robert Huber captures well white people's uneasiness with explicit conversations about race in "Being White in Philly," *Philadelphia Magazine*, http://www.phillymag.com/articles/white-philly/, accessed March 21, 2013.

46. Bronson and Merryman, "See Baby Discriminate."

47. Ibid.

48. Barbara Mathias and Mary Ann French, *40 Ways to Raise a Nonracist Child* (New York: HarperResource, 1996), 73.

49. Lewis, *Race in the Schoolyard*, 18.

50. Ibid., 36.

51. Mathias and French, *40 Ways to Raise a Nonracist Child*, 75.

52. Jennifer E. Morales, "Unpacking the White Privilege Diaper Bag," in *Everyday Acts against Racism*, 41.

53. Ibid. 46.

54. Tim Wise, *White Like Me: Reflections on Race from a Privileged Son* (Brooklyn: Soft Skull Press, 2005), 74.

55. Hartigan, *Odd Tribes*, 150.

56. David Mura, "Explaining Racism to my Daughter," in Ben Jelloun, *Racism Explained to my Daughter*, 101–102.

57. Cf. Ben Jelloun, *Racism Explained to my Daughter*.

58. Staci Swenson, "'That Wouldn't Be Fair,'" in Reddy, ed., *Everyday Acts against Racism*, 51–52.

59. Raffo, "White Noise."

60. Reddy, ed., *Everyday Acts against Racism*, 244.

61. Arwyn, "Sula and sleep: on raising a white child and reading 'the n word,'" http://raisingmyboychick.blogspot.com/2009/07/sula-and-sleep-on-raising-white-child.html, accessed March 21, 2013.

62. Raffo, "White Noise."

63. Ibid.

64. Ibid.

65. Van Ausdale and Feagin, *The First R*, 204–205.

66. Michel Foucault, "Nietzsche, Genealogy, History," in *The Foucault Reader*, ed. Paul Rabinow (New York: Pantheon Books, 1984), 83.

67. http://www.weeville.com/redneck_collection.htm, accessed May 11, 2010. I will omit discussion of the number of things on which I have sprayed WD-40 or (my personal favorite because it has less odor) PAM cooking spray, which I now realize I wasn't "supposed" to do. See also http://afrogtokiss.net/2007/10/21/the-1000th-use-for-duct-tape/, accessed May 11, 2010, which made me recall my family's recent use of duct tape and red cellophane to temporarily replace a broken brakelight on our car. It hadn't hit me that this was a sign of being a redneck until I saw this Web site on "redneck antics."

68. Hartigan, *Racial Situations*, 106.

69. Thandeka, *Learning To Be White: Money, Race, and God in America* (New York: Continuum Press, 2007).

70. As was Sarah Patton Boyle, author of *The Desegregated Heart* (recounted in Fred Hobson, *But Now I See: The White Southern Racial Conversion Narrative* [Baton Rouge: Louisiana State University Press, 1999], 63–64).

71. On this point, see also Lara Trout, *The Politics of Survival: Peirce, Affectivity, and Social Criticism* (New York: Fordham University Press, 2010).

72. Yancy, *Look, a White!*, 22; emphasis added.

73. Thandeka, *Learning To Be White*, 1–2. See also white civil rights activist Lillian Smith's *Killers of a Dream*, where Smith recounts a similar experience with her parents and explains that she "felt compelled to believe they were right. It was the only way my world could be held together" (quoted in Hobson, *But Now I See*, 28); and the more contemporary admission of one young white woman that if she or her sister dated a black man, "my dad would pretty much disown us and stop talking to us" (quoted in Kim A. Case and Annette Hemmings, "Distancing Strategies: White Women Preservice Teachers and Antiracist Curriculum," *Urban Education* 40, no. 6 [November 2005]: 613).

74. Thandeka, *Learning To Be White*, 2.

75. Ibid.

76. Ibid., 1, 5, 9, 12.

77. Ibid., 2, 9.

78. Ibid., 13.

79. Ibid., 9, 16, 25, 20.

80. Ibid., 13, 21.

81. Ibid., 19, 20, 17.

82. Toni Morrison, "Home," in *The House that Race Built: Original Essays by Toni Morrison, Angela Y. Davis, Cornel West and Others on Black Americans and Politics in America Today*, ed. Wahneema Lubiano (New York: Vintage Books, 1998), 3–12.

83. Thandeka, *Learning to Be White*, 10, 20, 30, emphasis in original. Franz Fanon uses the term *peaceful violence* in Fanon, *The Wretched of the Earth*, trans. Constance Farrington (New York: Grove Press, 1963), 81.

84. Thandeka, *Learning to Be White*, 87.

85. Ibid., 86.

86. Ibid., 27.

87. Jennifer Ritterhouse, *Growing Up Jim Crow: How Black and White Southern Children Learned Race* (Durham: University of North Carolina Press, 2006), 9.

88. Ibid., 235.

89. Morrison, "Home," 5.

90. Ibid.

91. Thandeka, *Learning to Be White*, 19.

92. Van Ausdale and Feagin, *The First R*, 170.

93. Alison Bailey, "Despising an Identity They Taught Me to Claim," in *Whiteness: Feminist Philosophical Reflections*, ed. Chris J. Cuomo and Kim Q. Hall (Lanham, MD: Rowman and Littlefield, 1999), 85–104; Sullivan, *Revealing Whiteness*, 162.

94. Sundstrom, *The Browning of America*, 129.

95. George Yancy makes a similar point when he argues that white people "ought to be focused on how they raise *their own* biological white children" (Yancy, *Look, a White!*, 22; emphasis in original).

Chapter 4. The Dangers of White Guilt, Shame, and Betrayal

1. http://wiki.answers.com/Q/How_many_white_voters_voted_for_Obama_in_the_2008_presidential_election, accessed May 20, 2011.

2. Cartoon by Mike Lester of *The Rome News-Tribune* (GA), printed in the *Centre Daily Times*, State College, PA, April 15, 2008.

3. My preference for the term *affect* should not be read as an endorsement of geographies of affect over geographies of emotion. In the field of cultural geography, which recently has experienced an explosion of work on affect and emotion, a fight is brewing between these two approaches. A so-called posthumanist affective turn in the field has posited that affect is the more open,

theoretically rich term, marking transpersonal states or intensities of being that aren't (yet) pigeonholed into recognizable emotional categories or experienced by discrete persons. Emotions can be somewhat trite, on this view, as are the emotional geographers who allegedly want to merely talk to people about their feelings. Geographers of emotion have responded that the abstractions of affective geography have tended to replicate the well-worn binary of masculine reason versus feminine emotion, now in the guise of (masculine) affect versus (feminine) emotion (Deborah Thien, "After or Beyond Feeling? A Consideration of Affect and Emotion in Geography," *Area* 37, no. 4 [2005]: 450–56; Joanne Sharp, "Geography and Gender: What Belongs to Feminist Geography? Emotion, Power, and Change," *Progress in Human Geography* 33, no. 1 [2009]: 74–80). They also have charged that affective geography's emphasis on the virtual and transhuman, especially in the context of the social engineering of affect, wrongly ignores the relational emotional landscapes of people's everyday lives.

I agree with affective geography about the importance of examining how political formations generate affect, and I appreciate its insistence that affects are not sealed up inside atomistic individuals. I'm also not necessarily alarmed by the prospect of "engineering" affects since such "engineering"—think here of urban planning—already and inevitably occurs. The spatiality of different physical and social landscapes has a profound impact on human experience, much of which takes place through affective channels, such as the racialization of space. The questions that need to be asked regarding the "engineering" of affect are, Whose interests are being served by the production of particular affects, such as fear? and What affects might be cultivated that would encourage welcoming rather than oppressive ways of living with people different than oneself? At the same time, however, I don't find the emotional lives of people to be a trivial subject, nor do I think that the important political questions concerning white domination (or anything else) are located solely in impersonal or transpersonal domains. I am deeply interested in the personal effects of white racism, and with emotional geographers I disagree that speaking of the personal necessarily means operating with a notion of atomistic individualism. The domain of the personal can be profoundly political, as feminists have long argued, which means that emotions can be too.

In addition to geographies of emotion, I also am sympathetic with Steve Pile's description of psychoanalytic geography, which focuses on how emotion and affect unconsciously move between people (Pile, "Emotions and Affect in Recent Human geography").

4. Elizabeth Spelman, "Anger and Insubordination," in *Women, Knowledge, and Reality: Explorations in Feminist Philosophy*, ed. Ann Garry and Marilyn Pearsall (New York: Routledge, 1992) 263–73; Antonio Damasio, *The Feeling of What Happens: Body and Emotion in the Making of Consciousness* (New York: Harcourt, 1999). See also Martha Nussbaum, *Upheavals of Thought: The Intelligence of Emotions* (New York: Cambridge University Press, 2003).

5. For more on transaction and habit, see Sullivan, *Living Across and Through Skins* and *Revealing Whiteness*.

6. http://dictionary.reference.com/browse/emotion, accessed March 21, 2013.

7. This tradition is represented by Benedict de Spinoza, *The Ethics*, in *The Spinoza Reader: The Ethics and Other Works*, ed. and trans. Edwin Curley (Princeton: Princeton University Press, 1994) and extended by Friedrich Nietzsche, along with more contemporary scholars such as Gilles Deleuze and Teresa Brennan.

8. hooks, *Killing Rage*, 28.

9. Ibid., 18, 26.

10. Ibid., 30.

11. Ibid., 29.

12. Friedrich Nietzsche, *Thus Spake Zarathustra*, trans. R. J. Hollingdale (New York: Penguin Books, 1969), 46.

13. Baldwin, *The Fire Next Time*, 113.

14. http://www.ipoet.com/archive/beyond/King-Jr/Loving-Your-Enemies.html, accessed March 21, 2013.

15. And they follow in W. E. B. Du Bois's footsteps in doing so. See Du Bois, "The Souls of White Folk," in *Darkwater: Voices from within the Veil* (Mineola, NY: Dover, 1999).

16. Franz Fanon, *The Wretched of the Earth* (New York: Grove Press, 1965).

17. James Baldwin, "Unnameable Objects, Unspeakable Crimes," in *The White Problem in America*, ed. *Ebony* editors (Chicago: Johnson Publishing Company, 1966), 180. This essay was first printed with the title of "White Man's Guilt."

18. Theresa Brennan, *The Transmission of Affect* (Ithaca: Cornell University Press, 2004).

19. Ibid., 43–44, 67.

20. Martin Luther King Jr., "Loving Your Enemies," http://www.ipoet.com/archive/beyond/King-Jr/Loving-Your-Enemies.html, accessed March 21, 2013.

21. http://www.nytimes.com/2009/09/13/magazine/13contagion-t.html?_r=1&scp=1&sq=are%20your%20friends%20making%20you%20fat&st=cse, accessed March 21, 2013. See also Nicholas Christakis and James Fowler, *Connected: The Surprising Power of our Social Networks and How They Shape Our Lives* (New York: Little, Brown, 2009).

22. Dacher Keltner, Deborah Gruenfeld, Adam Galinsky, and Michael W. Kraus, "Paradoxes of Power: Dynamics of the Acquisition, Experience, and Social Regulation of Social Power," in *The Social Psychology of Power*, ed. A. Guinote and T. K. Vescio (New York: Guilford, 2009).

23. In this context, Martin Luther King's observations about psychology are interesting: "Modern psychology is calling on us now to love. But long before modern psychology came into being, the world's greatest psychologist who walked around the hills of Galilee called to us to love" (King, "Loving Your Enemies").

24. It's beyond the scope of my project to discuss the Freud's concept of "primary narcissism" (as distinct from "secondary narcissism") in connection

with healthy self-love. I avoid the term *primary narcissism* not only because of the everyday pejorative connotations of the word *narcissism,* but also because I don't think Freud's notion of healthy self-love is sufficiently transactional. See Freud, "On Narcissism: An Introduction" in *The Standard Edition of the Complete Psychological Works of Sigmund Freud,* volume XIV, ed. James Strachey (London: The Hogarth Press and the Institute of Psycho-analysis, 1957), 67–102.

25. Brennan, *Transmission of Affect,* 133.

26. Ibid., 126, 130–31.

27. Ibid., 121.

28. Ibid., 133–34; emphasis added. Compare with King's advice in "Loving Your Enemies:" "Just keep being friendly to that person [who is mistreating you]. Keep loving them. Don't do anything to embarrass them. Just keep loving them, and they can't stand it too long."

29. Ibid., 135.

30. Biko, *I Write What I Like,* 77. See also bell hooks's observation that white people "are convinced that their response to blackness must first and foremost be fear and dread" (hooks, *Killing Rage,* 14).

31. Margaret Blackburn White, *Becoming White: My Family's Experience as Slaveholders—and Why It Still Matters* (Bloomington: Author House, 2009), 90–97.

32. http://faculty.berea.edu/browners/chesnutt/classroom/lynchings_table_state.html, accessed March 21, 2013. The statistics provided by this Web site were gathered from the Archives at Tuskegee Institute. See also Trudier Harris, "White Men as Performers in the Lynching Ritual," in *Black on White: Black Writers on What It Means to Be White,* ed. David R. Roediger (New York: Schocken Books, 1998), 299–304.

33. Franz Fanon coins the phrase "peaceful violence" when describing the colonial situation in the Antilles in *The Wretched of the Earth,* 81. I say "generally" since as recently as 1998, a black man was dragged to his death behind a truck in Jasper, Texas, merely because he was black. See http://topics.nytimes.com/topics/reference/timestopics/people/b/james_jr_byrd/index.html, accessed March 21, 2013. Treyvon Martin's case is also relevant here even though his shooter was a multiracial Hispanic man. In February 2012, Martin, a seventeen-year-old African American, was shot to death while walking in his father's girlfriend's predominantly white gated neighborhood. http://en.wikipedia.org/wiki/Shooting_of_Trayvon_Martin, accessed March 21, 2013.

34. Brent Staples, "Just Walk on By: A Black Man Ponders His Power to Alter Public Space," *Ms.,* Sept. 1986, 54.

35. George Yancy, *Black Bodies, White Gazes: The Continuing Significance of Race* (Lanham, MD: Rowman and Littlefield, 2008), xix. Yancy also discusses this experience in *Look, a White! Philosophical Essays on Whiteness* (Philadelphia: Temple University Press, 2012), 31–33.

36. Yancy, *Black Bodies, White Gazes,* 5.

37. Brennan, *Transmission of Affect,* 15.

38. Hermann Herlinghaus, *Violence Without Guilt: Ethical Narratives from the Global South* (New York: Palgrave Macmillan, 2009), 8, 14.

39. Yancy, *Black Bodies, White Gazes*, xx.

40. Toni Morrison, *The Bluest Eye* (New York: Pocket Books, 1972).

41. James Baldwin, "White Man's Guilt," in *Black on White*, 322.

42. Mills, *The Racial Contract*, 89.

43. Jacobs, *Incidents in the Life of a Slave Girl*.

44. White, *Becoming White*, 113.

45. W. E. B. Du Bois, "The Souls of White Folk," in *Black on White*, 197.

46. Jeffrey T. Nealon, "Performing Resentment: White Male Anger; or, 'Lack' and Nietzschean Political Theory," in *Why Nietzsche Still: Reflections on Drama, Culture, and Politics*, ed. Alan D. Schrift (Berkeley: University of California Press, 2000), 274–92. As Ronald Sundstrom notes, resentful anger isn't restricted to white men; it also has fueled African American and Latino violence against Korean and other Asian Americans (Sundstrom, *The Browning of America*, 60).

47. Sandra Lee Bartky, "In Defense of Guilt," in *On Feminist Ethics and Politics*, ed. Claudia Card (Lawrence: University Press of Kansas, 1999), 29–51.

48. Amy Edgington, "Growing Up in Little Rock," in *Whiteness: Feminist Philosophical Reflections*, ed. Chris J. Cuomo and Kim Q. Hall (Lanham, MD: Rowman and Littlefield, 1999), 39.

49. Shelby Steele, *White Guilt: How Blacks and Whites Together Destroyed the Promise of the Civil Rights Era* (New York: HarperCollins Publishers, 2006), 24; emphasis in original.

50. Ibid., 24, 27.

51. Ibid., 34, emphasis in original.

52. Wilmot, *Taking Responsibility*, 93.

53. Ibid.

54. Edgington, "Growing Up in Little Rock," 43.

55. Thompson, "Tiffany," 15–16.

56. MacMullan, *Habits of Whiteness*, 179–80.

57. Naomi Zack, "White Ideas," in *Whiteness*, 81.

58. For a helpful overview of anti-racist criticisms of white guilt, see Alexis Shotwell, *Knowing Otherwise: Race, Gender, and Implicit Understanding* (University Park: Penn State University Press, 2010), 80–86.

59. Ibid., 73.

60. Ibid., 74.

61. Michael L. Morgan, *On Shame* (New York: Routledge, 2008), 15, 37, 45.

62. Shotwell, *Knowing Otherwise*, 93.

63. Ibid., 88.

64. Morgan, *On Shame*, 47.

65. Jean-Paul Sartre, *Being and Nothingness: A Phenomenological Essay on Ontology*, trans. Hazel E. Barnes (New York: Pocket Books, 1956), 347–50.

66. For an insightful account of how shame can be both ontological and social but not necessarily entail acceptance of another's criticism, see Cheshire Calhoun, "An Apology for Moral Shame," *The Journal of Political Philosophy* 12, no. 2 (2004): 127–46.

67. Morgan, *On Shame*, 35. See also Ursula Mahlendorf, *The Shame of Survival: Working Through a Nazi Childhood* (University Park: Penn State University Press, 2009).

68. Morgan, *On Shame*, 24, 40, 43.

69. MacMullan, *Habits of Whiteness*, 195.

70. Morgan, *On Shame*, 38.

71. Baldwin, "White Man's Guilt," in *Black on White*, 322.

72. June Price Tangney, "Recent Advances in the Empirical Study of Shame and Guilt," *American Behavioral Science* 38, no. 3 (1995): 1138, 1135.

73. Morgan, *On Shame*, 2.

74. MacMullan, *Habits of Whiteness*, 199.

75. Shotwell, *Knowing Otherwise*, 86.

76. Morgan, *On Shame*, 93–94.

77. Eve Kosofsky Sedgwick, *Touching Feeling: Affect, Pedagogy, Performativity* (Durham: Duke University Press, 2003), 64.

78. Ibid., 63.

79. Ibid., 64.

80. Ibid., 63.

81. I find unconvincing Sedgwick's (and others', such as Martha Nussbaum's) arguments that shame appears in infancy, when babies between three and seven months old begin to avert their gaze from that of adults. Such gaze aversion does occur, perhaps even universally, but calling it "the protoaffect of shame" (Sedgwick) or "primitive shame" (Nussbaum) and then attributing feelings of inadequacy and/or humiliation to the infant, expressed through his or her disrupted eye contact, begs the question (Sedgwick, *Touching Feeling*, 36, and Nussbaum, *Upheavals of Thought*, 196). Certainly, as Sedgwick claims, something having to do with communication and social relationships is at work in infant gaze aversion, but it's not at all clear that it concerns shame. Infant gaze aversion can be, for example, a way for infants to manage (over)stimulation by temporarily disengaging from the world around them; a manifestation of stranger anxiety; and/or an early sign of autism.

See also Judith Halberstam's scathing criticism of gay shame as an extension of white male privilege that, in practice, operates with a rigid identity politics that rejects feminism and queer of color critique (Halberstam, "Shame and White Gay Masculinity," *Social Text* 23, no. 3–4 [Fall-Winter 2005]: 219–33).

82. Tangney, "Recent Advances," 1135.

83. Ibid., 1137.

84. Ibid. See also J. P. Tangney, J. Stuewig, D. Mashek, and M. Hastings, "Assessing Jail Inmates' Proneness to Shame and Guilt: Feeling Bad about the Behavior or the Self?" *Criminal Justice and Behavior* 38 (2011): 710–34.

85. http://www.reuters.com/article/2011/04/18/us-gay-teen-suicide-idUS-TRE73H1GV20110418, accessed March 21, 2013.

86. http://www.nydailynews.com/archives/news/1995/03/11/1995-03-11_tv_fatal_attraction_jenny_.html, accessed June 2, 2011.

87. Morgan, *On Shame*, 44, 58.

88. Ibid., 85.

89. Tangney, "Recent Advances," 1140. See also June Price Tangney, Jeff Stuewig, and Debra J. Mashek, "Moral Emotions and Moral Behavior," *Annual Review of Psychology* 58 (2007): 345–72.

90. Tangney, "Recent Advances," 1139.

91. Ibid.

92. Ibid., 1140.

93. Ibid.

94. E. D. Sperberg, and S. D. Stabb, "Depression in Women as Related to Anger and Mutuality in Relationships," *Psychology of Women Quarterly* 22 (1998): 223–38.

95. Michael F. Mascolo, Kurt W. Fischer, and Jin Li, "Dynamic Development of Component Systems of Emotions: Pride, Shame, and Guilt in China and the United States," in *Handbook of Affective Sciences*, ed. Richard J. Davidson, Klaus R. Scherer, and H. Hill Goldsmith (New York: Oxford University Press, 2003), 375–408. See also Y. Wong and J.L. Tsai, "Cultural Models of Shame and Guilt," in *Handbook of Self-Conscious Emotions*, ed. J. Tracy, R. Robins, and J. Tangney (New York: Guilford Press), 210–23.

96. Mascolo, Fischer, and Li, "Dynamic Development of Component Systems of Emotions," 401.

97. They also can be located, for example, in terms of gender and geography. Women have been said to be more shame-prone than men, perhaps explaining why more white women than white men work in critical philosophy of race (Shotwell, *Knowing Otherwise*, 96). Historians claim that in nineteenth-century America, shame generally operated more in the South and guilt characterized the North when it came to social issues, including race. Scholars chalk up this difference to the high priority that the South placed on honor (versus conscience) and manners (versus morals). See Fred Hobson, *But Now I See: The White Southern Racial Conversion Narrative* (Baton Rouge: Louisiana State University Press, 1999), 11.

98. John Preston, *Whiteness and Class in Education* (Dordrecht: Springer, 2009), 169.

99. Preston, *Whiteness and Class in Education*, 183.

100. Ibid., 182.

101. Goad, *The Redneck Manifesto*, 52.

102. Ibid., 70, 103.

103. Ibid., 246.

104. Sandra Harding, *Whose Science? Whose Knowledge? Thinking from Women's Lives* (Ithaca: Cornell University Press, 1991). Other feminist

endorsements of the idea of white race traitors can be found in the work of Alison Bailey, Lisa Heldke, and Mag Segrest. I will address Segrest's *Memoir of a Race Traitor* (Boston: South End Press, 1994) in more detail below. See also Alison Bailey, "Locating Traitorous Identities: Toward a View of Privilege-Cognizant White Character," *Hypatia* 13, no. 3 (Summer 1998): 27–42; and Lisa Heldke, "On Being a Responsible Traitor," in *Daring to Be Good: Essays in Feminist Ethico-Politics*, ed. Bat-Ami Bar On and Ann Ferguson (New York: Routledge, 1998), 87–99.

105. Adrienne Rich, "Disloyal to Civilization: Feminism, Racism, and Gynephobia," in *On Lies, Secrets, and Silence: Selected Prose 1966–1978* (New York: W. W. Norton, 1979), 275–310.

106. Harding, *Whose Science? Whose Knowledge?*, 293, 292.

107. Ibid., 294.

108. Ibid.

109. I have been sympathetic to this idea, arguing that "key to being a white race traitor at this point in history is finding ways to use white racial privilege against itself" (Sullivan, *Revealing Whiteness*, 162). While I still believe that using white privilege against itself is important for white allies to do, I no longer think that characterizing this use as traitorous is wise or necessarily accurate.

110. http://www.postfun.com/racetraitor/features/abolish.html, accessed July 14, 2009.

111. Ibid. Naomi Zack also endorses defection from the white race in Zack, "White Ideas," in *Whiteness: Feminist Philosophical Reflections*, ed. Chris J. Cuomo and Kim Q. Hall (Lanham, MD: Rowman and Littlefield, 1999), 84.

112. http://www.postfun.com/racetraitor/features/abolish.html, accessed July 14, 2009.

113. Alcoff, *Visible Identities*, 216.

114. For more on this issue, see Sullivan, *Living Across and Through Skins*.

115. Michael J. Monahan, *The Creolizing Subject: Race, Reason, and the Politics of Purity* (New York: Fordham University Press, 2011), 134. For an insightful criticism of the voluntarist ideal at the heart of the race traitor model, see Shotwell, *Knowing Otherwise*, 111–16.

116. Preston, *Whiteness and Class in Education*, 175–76.

117. Ibid., 176.

118. Segrest, *Memoir of a Race Traitor*, ix.

119. Ibid., 80.

120. Ibid.

121. Ibid., 27.

122. Ibid, 4.

123. Zack, "White Ideas," 78.

124. Ibid., 79.

125. Rich, *On Lies, Secrets, and Silence*, 306.

126. Thompson, "Tiffany, Friend of People of Color," 18.

127. Ibid., 16.

128. Cris Mayo, "The Whiteness of Anti-Racist White Philosophical Address," in *The Center Must Not Hold: White Women Philosophers on the White-*

ness of Philosophy, ed. George Yancy (Lanham, MD: Rowman and Littlefield, 2010), 224.

129. Ibid.

130. Charles Scott, "In the Name of Goodness," in *Difficulties of Ethical Life*, ed. Shannon Sullivan and Dennis J. Schmidt (New York: Fordham University Press, 2008), 18.

131. I owe a big thanks to Sara Leland, whose dissertation on "Nietzschean Transformation Against the Grain of Race-Related Problems" (Penn State University, 2008) first helped me think about white anti-racist activity as something other than a heavy chore.

132. Cynthia Willett helped me consider my work on race as a development of different ethical habits for white people. See Willett, "Overcoming Habits of Whiteliness: Reading Shannon Sullivan's *Revealing Whiteness*," *Journal of Speculative Philosophy* 21, no. 3 (2007): 210–17.

133. Scott, "In the Name of Goodness," 23.

134. Ibid., 24.

135. Thanks to Robin James for her comments on her November 9, 2010, blog, which helped me think about this point. See "Contort Yourself: A follow-up to Shannon Sullivan's SPEP paper on experiencing white identity as a 'joyful passion'" (http://its-her-factory.blogspot.com/2010/11/contort-yourself-follow-up-to-shannon.html, accessed March 21, 2013).

136. Nietzsche, *Thus Spake Zarathustra*, 100.

137. Brennan, *The Transmission of Affect*, 124–25.

138. bell hooks, *Salvation: Black People and Love* (New York: HarperCollins, 2001), 16. While hooks speaks here of love between black people in particular, her point extends to all people, as her earlier *All About Love: New Visions* (New York: HarperCollins, 2001) demonstrates.

139. Baldwin, *The Fire Next Time*, 62.

140. Baldwin, "Unnameable Objects, Unspeakable Crimes," 321.

Conclusion

1. Quoted in Fred Hobson, *But Now I See: The White Southern Racial Conversion Narrative* (Baton Rouge: Louisiana State University Press, 1999), 17.

2. There is a long tradition of critical study of and commentary on whiteness in black communities, for example. See David R. Roediger, ed., *Black on White: Black Writers on What It Means to Be White* (New York: Schocken Books, 1999); *Ebony* ed., *The White Problem in America*; and George Yancy, ed., *What White Looks Like: African American Philosophers on the Whiteness Question* (New York: Routledge, 2004).

3. Sara Ahmed, *The Cultural Politics of Emotion* (New York: Routledge, 2004), 122.

4. Ibid.

5. Quoted in ibid., 42.

6. Ibid., 141.

7. bell hooks, *Salvation: Black People and Love* (New York: HarperCollins, 2001), 16, xxiv. See also bell hooks, *All About Love: New Visions* (New York: HarperCollins, 2000).

8. Ahmed, *The Cultural Politics of Emotion*, 122.

9. Ibid., 140–41.

10. See also Sheila Wilmot's insightful criticism of multiculturalism in *Taking Responsibility*, 71–73, 123–24.

11. Po Bronson and Ashley Merryman, "See Baby Discriminate," *Newsweek*, Sept. 5, 2009, http://www.newsweek.com/id/214989/page/1, accessed March 21, 2013.

12. Ibid.

13. Thomas H. Benton (pseudonym), "Love Me; I Celebrate Diversity," *The Chronicle of Higher Education*, Section C, Dec. 8, 2006, page C1. See also Iris Marion Young's thoughtful criticism of the ideal of integration and compelling argument that a desire for residential and civic "clustering" isn't necessarily problematic, even when acted on by white people (Young, *Inclusion and Democracy* [New York: Oxford University Press, 2000], 216–20); and Steve Biko's searing criticism of integration as a solution to apartheid in South Africa (Biko, *I Write What I Like*, 19–26).

14. W. E. B. Du Bois, "The Souls of White Folk," in *Darkwater: Voices from Within the Veil* (New York: Harcourt Brace, 1999), 18–19.

15. Ibid., 19.

16. Which is not to say that *Crash* doesn't suffer from other, related problems. The movie tends, for example, to downplay the existence and impact of white privilege by portraying tension between white and nonwhite people as merely one of many possible types of interracial conflict.

17. Benjamin DeMott, *The Trouble with Friendship: Why Americans Can't Think Straight about Race* (New York: The Atlantic Monthly Press, 1995).

18. Quoted in Ibid., 9.

19. Jennifer A. Richeson and Sophie Trawalter, "Why Do Interracial Interactions Impair Executive Function? A Resource Depletion Account," *Journal of Personality and Social Psychology* (2005): 945.

20. Jennifer Wexler, "The Concrete Work of Eliminating Your Racism," *Present Time* (Seattle), July 1992, 26. While this article was published in the 1990s, it is still being used by white anti-racism groups as of 2012.

21. Actually, the race of the man snuggled next to the white woman is ambiguous; he could be black, Latino, and/or Native American. I think it is no coincidence, however, that he is light skinned.

22. DeMott, *The Trouble with Friendship.*

23. In a related vein, see bell hooks's examination of the lack of friendship between black and white females (hooks, *Killing Rage*, 213–25). As hooks explains, "not much about patterns of bonding across race in American life suggests that black females and white females find it at all easy to socialize with one another or bond as friends. Most people seem to be in denial about how few bonds of affection and ties bind black and white women together" (217).

24. Lugones and Spelman, "Have We Got a Theory for You!," 581.

25. Alexis Shotwell also argues for distance as a crucial component of solidarity between white people and people of color, but she associates this distance with "the experience of bad feeling" that comes with guilt, shame, and other sad passions (Shotwell, *Knowing Otherwise: Race, Gender, and Implicit Understanding* [University Park: Penn State University Press, 2010], 124).

26. Donna-Dale Marcano, "In Defense of Ourselves: On Being Black Feminist Philosophers," presented at the Collegium of Black Women Philosophers Conference at Penn State University, April 16, 2010. Marcano's comment, in turn, reminds me of W. E. B. Du Bois's response to a young black girl's question of whether he trusts white people: "You do not and you know that you do not, much as you want to; yet you rise and lie and say you do; you must say it for her salvation and the world's; you repeat that she must trust them that most white folks are honest, and all the while you are lying and every level, silent eye there knows you are lying, and miserably you sit and lie on, to the greater glory of God" (Du Bois, "Of Work and Wealth," in *Darkwater*, 47).

27. Tim Wise, quoted in Thompson, Schaefer, and Brod, *White Men Challenging Racism*, 153.

28. Wise, *White Like Me*, 97.

29. Ibid., 98.

30. As this book was going to press, I discovered Mtali William Banda's description of his recent interaction with Wise after a public lecture, in which Wise was said to "righteously [go] about parading his whiteness . . . expecting [Black America] to give him a gold star" for speaking out against white privilege (http://soullatte.wordpress.com/2013/09/30/the-irony-behind-tim-wise-and-white-priviledge/, accessed December 14, 2013). If Wise indeed expects "some sort of moral medal" for his work, then as a good white person, rather than a white ally, he would be a big part of the very problem he's trying to solve.

31. Wendy Brown, *Edgework: Critical Essays on Knowledge and Politics* (Princeton: Princeton University Press, 2005), 21.

32. Ibid., 27.

33. Ibid., 23. See also Lisa Tessman's helpful discussion of the compatibility of loyalty and criticism in Tessman, *Burdened Virtues: Virtue Ethics for Liberatory Struggles* (New York: Oxford University Press, 2005), 144–49.

34. Brown, *Edgework*, 35.

35. Outlaw, "Rehabilitate Racial *Whiteness?*"

36. Ibid., 161.

37. See, for example, *Ebony* ed., *The White Problem in America*; Lugones, *Pilgrimages/Peregrinajes*; Roediger, ed., *Black on White*; and Yancy, ed., *What White Looks Like.*

Bibliography

Aanerud, Rebecca. "The Legacy of White Supremacy and the Challenge of White Antiracist Mothering." *Hypatia* 22, no. 2 (2007): 20–38.

Ahmed, Sara. *The Cultural Politics of Emotion.* New York: Routledge, 2004.

Alcoff, Linda Martín. *Visible Identities: Race, Gender, and The Self.* New York: Oxford University Press, 2006.

Anderson, Michelle. *The New Jim Crow.* New York: The New Press, 2010.

Andrieu, Pierre. "L'Assemblée nationale supprime le mot 'race' de la legislation." *Le Monde,* May 16, 2013; http://www.lemonde.fr/politique/article/2013/05/16/l-assemblee-nationale-supprime-le-mot-race-de-la-legislation_3272514_823448.html, accessed May 17, 2013.

Anti-Defamation League. Feminism Perverted: Extremist Women on the World Wide Web. 1998; www.adl.org/special_reports/extremist_women_on_web/feminism_intro.asp, accessed March 21, 2013.

Bailey, Alison. "Locating Traitorous Identities: Toward a View of Privilege-Cognizant White Character." *Hypatia* 13, no. 3 (1998): 27–42.

———. "Despising an Identity They Taught Me to Claim." In *Whiteness: Feminist Philosophical Reflections,* ed. Chris J. Cuomo and Kim Q. Hall. Lanham, MD: Rowman and Littlefield, 1999.

Baldwin, James. *The Fire Next Time.* New York: Dell, 1963.

———. "Unnameable Objects, Unspeakable Crimes." In *The White Problem in America,* ed. *Ebony* editors. Chicago: Johnson Publishing, 1966.

———. "Going to Meet the Man." In *Black on White: Black Writers on What It Means to Be White,* ed. David R. Roediger. New York: Schocken Books, 1998.

———. "White Man's Guilt." In *Black on White: Black Writers on What It Means to Be White,* ed. David R. Roediger. New York: Schocken Books, 1998.

Bartky, Sandra Lee. "In Defense of Guilt." In *On Feminist Ethics and Politics,* ed. Claudia Card. Lawrence: University Press of Kansas, 1999.

Bates, James Edward. "The Modern-Day Ku Klux Klan." *The Chronicle Review,* May 20, 2011, B18–B19.

Ben Jelloun, Tahar. *Racism Explained to my Daughter.* With responses from William Ayers, Lisa D. Delpit, David Mura, and Patricia Williams. New York: The New Press, 1999.

Bennett, Lerone Jr. "Tea and Sympathy: Liberals and Other White Hopes." In *The Negro Mood and Other Essays.* Chicago: Johnson Publishing, 1964.

Benton, Thomas H. (pseudonym). "Love Me; I Celebrate Diversity." *The Chronicle of Higher Education,* Section C (2006): C1, C4.

Berg, Allison. *Mothering the Race: Women's Narratives of Reproduction, 1890–1930.* Urbana: University of Illinois Press, 2002.

Berlet, Chip. "Taking Tea Partiers Seriously." *The Progressive* 74, no. 2 (2010): 24–27.

Biko, Steve. *I Write What I Like: Selected Writings.* Chicago: The University of Chicago Press, 1978.

Blassingame, John W., John R. McKivigan, and Peter P. Hinks, eds. *Narrative of the Life of Frederick Douglass, An American Slave Written by Himself.* New Haven: Yale University Press, 2001.

Bledsoe, Albert Taylor. *Liberty and Slavery: Or, Slavery in the Light of Moral and Political Philosophy.* In *Cotton is King, and Pro-Slavery Arguments Comprising the Writings of Hammond, Harper, Christy, Stringfellow, Hodge, Bledsoe, and Cartwright, on this Important Subject.* New York: Negro Universities Press, 1969.

Bonilla-Silva, Eduardo. *Racism without Racists: Color-blind Racism and the Persistence of Racial Inequality in the United States.* Lanham, MD: Rowman and Littlefield, 2003.

———, and Karen S. Glover. " 'We Are All Americans': The Latin Americanization of Race Relations in the United States." In *The Changing Terrain of Race and Ethnicity,* ed. Maria Krysan and Amanda E. Lewis. New York: Russell Sage Foundation, 2004.

Bordo, Susan. "Adoption." *Hypatia* 20, no. 1 (2005): 230–36.

Brennan, Teresa. *The Transmission of Affect.* Ithaca: Cornell University Press, 2004.

Bronson, Po, and Ashley Merryman. "See Baby Discriminate." *Newsweek.* 2009; http://www.newsweek.com/id/214989/page/1, accessed March 21, 2013.

Brown, Wendy. *States of Injury: Power and Freedom in Late Modernity.* Princeton: Princeton University Press, 1995.

———. *Edgework: Critical Essays on Knowledge and Politics.* Princeton: Princeton University Press, 2005.

Brown, William Garrott. *The Lower South in American History.* New York: Greenwood Press, 1969.

Butler, Judith. *Gender Trouble: Feminism and the Subversion of Identity.* New York: Routledge, 1990.

Calhoun, Cheshire. "Changing One's Heart." *Ethics* 103, no. 1 (1992): 76–96.

———. *Feminism, the Family, and the Politics of the Closet: Lesbian and Gay Displacement.* New York: Oxford University Press, 2000.

———. "An Apology for Moral Shame." *The Journal of Political Philosophy* 12, no. 2 (2004): 127–46.

Case, Kim A., and Annette Hemmings. "Distancing Strategies: White Women Preservice Teachers and Antiracist Curriculum." *Urban Education* 40, no. 6 (2005): 606–26.

Christakis, Nicholas, and James Fowler. *Connected: The Surprising Power of our Social Networks and How They Shape Our Lives.* New York: Little, Brown, 2009.

Colapietro, Vincent. "The Eclipse of Piety: Toward a Pragmatic Overcoming of a Theoretical Injustice." *Journal of Chinese Philosophy* 24 (1997): 457–82.

Damasio, Antonio. *The Feeling of What Happens: Body and Emotion in the Making of Consciousness.* New York: Harcourt, 1999.

Davis, Daryl. *Klan-Destine Relationships: A Black Man's Odyssey in the Ku Klux Klan.* Far Hills, NJ: New Horizon Press, 1998.

DeMott, Benjamin. *The Trouble with Friendship: Why Americans Can't Think Straight about Race.* New York: The Atlantic Monthly Press, 1995.

Doyle, Bertram Wilbur. *The Etiquette of Race Relations in the South: A Study in Social Control.* Chicago: University of Chicago Press, 1937.

Du Bois, W. E. B. *Black Reconstruction in America.* New York: The Free Press, 1962.

———. "The Souls of White Folk." In *Black on White: Black Writers on What It Means to Be White,* ed. David R. Roediger. New York: Schocken Books, 1998.

———. *Darkwater: Voices from Within the Veil.* New York: Harcourt Brace, 1999.

Ebony ed. *The White Problem in America.* Chicago: Johnson Publishing.

DuRocher, Kristina. *Raising Racists: The Socialization of White Children in the Jim Crow South.* Lexington: The University Press of Kentucky, 2011.

Edgington, Amy. "Growing Up in Little Rock." In *Whiteness: Feminist Philosophical Reflections,* ed. Chris J. Cuomo and Kim Q. Hall. Lanham, MD: Rowman and Littlefield, 1999.

Fallace, Thomas D. *Dewey and the Dilemma of Race: An Intellectual History, 1895–1922.* New York: Teachers College, 2011.

Fanon, Franz. *The Wretched of the Earth.* Trans. Constance Farrington. New York: Grove Press, 1963.

Faulkner, William. *Requiem for a Nun.* New York: Random House, 1951.

Faust, Drew Gilpin. *Southern Stories: Slaveholders in Peace and War.* Columbia: University of Missouri Press, 1992.

Fitzhugh, George. *Sociology for the South: Or the Failure of Free Society.* New York: Burt Franklin, 1965.

Fletcher, John, and Martin Stanton, eds. *John Laplanche: Seduction, Translation, and the Drives.* Trans. Martin Stanton. London: Institute of Contemporary Arts, 1992.

Foucault, Michel. *The History of Sexuality: Volume I.* Trans. Robert Hurley. New York: Random House, 1978.

————. "Nietzsche, Genealogy, History." In *The Foucault Reader*, ed. Paul Rabinow. New York: Pantheon Books, 1984.

————. "The Ethics of the Concern for Self as a Practice of Freedom." In *Ethics: Subjectivity and Truth*, volume 1 of *The Essential Works of Foucault, 1954–1984*, ed. Paul Rabinow. New York: New Press, 1997.

Fox-Genovese, Elizabeth, and Eugene D. Genovese. *The Mind of the Master Class: History and Faith in the Southern Slaveholders' Worldview*. New York: Cambridge University Press, 2005.

Foxworthy, Jeff. *You Might Be a Redneck If . . . This is the Biggest Book You've Ever Read*. Nashville: Thomas Nelson Publishers, 2004.

Freud, Sigmund. "On Narcissism: An Introduction." In volume XIV of *The Standard Edition of the Complete Psychological Works of Sigmund Freud*, ed. James Strachey. London: The Hogarth Press and the Institute of Psycho-analysis, 1957.

————. "Three Essays on Sexuality." In volume VII of *The Standard Edition of the Complete Psychological Works of Sigmund Freud*, ed. and trans. James Strachey. New York: W. W. Norton, 1960.

Frye, Marilyn. *The Politics of Reality: Essays in Feminist Theory*. Freedom, CA: Crossing Press, 1983.

Gallagher, Charles A. "Playing the White Ethnic Card: Using Ethnic Identity to Deny Contemporary Racism." In *White Out: The Continuing Significance of Racism*, ed. Ashley W. Doane and Eduardo Bonilla-Silva. New York: Routledge, 2003.

Genovese, Eugene D. *The World the Slaveholders Made: Two Essays in Interpretation*. Hanover, NH: Wesleyan University Press, 1988.

————. *The Slaveholders' Dilemma: Freedom and Progress in Southern Conservative Thought, 1820–1860*. Columbia: University of South Carolina Press, 1992.

Goad, Jim. *The Redneck Manifesto: How Hillbillies, Hicks, and White Trash Became America's Scapegoats*. New York: Simon and Schuster, 1997.

Hacker, Andrew. *Two Nations: Black and White, Separate, Hostile, Unequal*. New York: Scribner's, 2003.

Halberstam, Judith. "Shame and White Gay Masculinity." *Social Text* 23, no. 3–4 (2005): 219–33.

Hall, Kim Q. "My Father's Flag." In *Whiteness: Feminist Philosophical Reflections*, ed. Chris J. Cuomo and Kim Q. Hall. Lanham, MD: Rowman and Littlefield, 1999.

Harding, Sandra. *Whose Science? Whose Knowledge? Thinking from Women's Lives*. Ithaca: Cornell University Press, 1991.

Harris, Trudier. "White Men as Performers in the Lynching Ritual." In *Black on White: Black Writers on What It Means to Be White*, ed. David R. Roediger. New York: Schocken Books, 1998.

Hartigan, John Jr. *Racial Situations: Class Predicaments of Whiteness in Detroit*. Princeton: Princeton University Press, 1999.

————. *Odd Tribes: Toward a Cultural Analysis of White People*. Durham: Duke University Press, 2005.

Heldke, Lisa. "On Being a Responsible Traitor." In *Daring to Be Good: Essays in Feminist Ethico-Politics*, ed. Bat-Ami Bar On and Ann Ferguson. New York: Routledge, 1998.

———. "A Du Boisian Proposal for Persistently White Colleges." *Journal of Speculative Philosophy* 18, no. 3 (2004): 224–38.

Herlinghause, Hermann. *Violence without Guilt: Ethical Narratives from the Global South*. New York: Palgrave Macmillan, 2009.

Hill, Mike. "America's Biennial Gathering of Academic Racists: The 2002 American Renaissance Conference." *The Journal of Blacks in Higher Education* 35, no. 2 (2002): 94–99.

———. *After Whiteness: Unmaking an American Majority*. New York: New York University Press, 2004.

———, ed. *Whiteness: A Critical Reader*. New York: New York University Press, 1997.

Hobson, Fred. *But Now I See: The White Southern Racial Conversion Narrative*. Baton Rouge: Louisiana State University Press, 1999.

hooks, bell. *Feminist Theory: From Margin to Center*. Boston: South End Press, 1984.

———. *Killing Rage: Ending Racism*. New York: Henry Holt, 1995.

———. *All About Love: New Visions*. New York: HarperCollins, 2000.

———. *Salvation: Black People and Love*. New York: HarperCollins, 2001.

Huber, Robert. "Being White in Philly." *Philadelphia Magazine*. 2013; http://www.phillymag.com/articles/white-philly/, accessed March 21, 2013.

Hytten, Kathy, and John Warren. "Engaging Whiteness: How Racial Power Gets Reified In Education." *Qualitative Studies in Education* 16, no. 1 (2003): 65–89.

Ignatiev, Noel. "Abolitionism and the White Studies Racket." *Race Traitor* 10 (1999): 3–7.

Irigaray, Luce. *This Sex Which Is Not One*. Trans. Catherine Porter. Ithaca: Cornell University Press, 1985.

Jacobs, Harriet. *Incidents in the Life of a Slave Girl*. Cambridge: Harvard University Press, 1987.

———. "Muster." In *Black on White: Black Writers on What It Means to Be White*, ed. David R. Roediger. New York: Schocken Books, 1998.

Jones, Alison. "The Limits of Cross-Cultural Dialogue: Pedagogy, Desire, and Absolution in the Classroom." *Educational Theory* 49, no. 3 (1999): 299–316.

Keltner, Dacher, Deborah Gruenfeld, Adam Galinsky, and Michael W. Kraus. "Paradoxes of Power: Dynamics of the Acquisition, Experience, and Social Regulation of Social Power." In *The Social Psychology of Power*, ed. A. Guinote and T. K. Vescio. New York: Guilford, 2009.

King, Martin Luther Jr. "Loving Your Enemies." 1957; http://www.ipoet.com/archive/beyond/King-Jr/Loving-Your-Enemies.html, accessed March 21, 2013.

———. "Letter from a Birmingham Jail." 1963; www.africa.upenn.edu/Articles_Gen/Letter_Birmingham.html, accessed March 21, 2013.

Kristeva, Julia. *Powers of Horror: An Essay on Abjection.* New York: Columbia University Press, 1982.

Kruks, Sonia. "Simone de Beauvoir and the Politics of Privilege." *Hypatia* 20, no. 1 (2005): 178–205.

Lacy, Karyn R. *Blue-Chip Black: Race, Class, and Status in the New Black Middle Class.* Berkeley: University of California Press, 2007.

Laplanche, Jean. *Essays on Otherness.* New York: Routledge, 1999.

Lawlor, Steph. " 'Getting Out and Getting Away': Women's Narratives of Class Mobility." *Feminist Review* 63 (1999): 3–24.

Lazarre, Jane. *Beyond the Whiteness of Whiteness: Memoir of a White Mother of Black Sons.* Durham: Duke University Press, 1996.

Leland, Sara. "Nietzschean Transformation Against the Grain of Race-Related Problems" (dissertation). Pennsylvania State University, 2008.

Lewis, Amanda E. *Race in the Schoolyard: Negotiating the Color Line in Classrooms and Communities.* New Brunswick: Rutgers University Press, 2003.

———. "Some Are More Equal than Others: Lessons on Whiteness from School." In *White Out: The Continuing Significance of Racism.* New York: Routledge, 2003.

Lind, Michael. "The Beige and the Black." *New York Times Magazine,* Aug. 16, 1998, section 6, 38.

Litt, Jackie, and JoAnn Rogers. "Normalizing Racism: A Case Study of Motherhood in White Supremacy." In *Home-grown Hate: Gender and Organized Racism,* ed. Abby L. Ferber. New York: Routledge, 2003.

Litwack, Leon F. "Hellhounds." In *Without Sanctuary: Lynching Photography in America.* Santa Fe: Twin Palms Publishers, 2003.

Luft, Rachel E. "Intersectionality and the Risk of Flattening Difference." In *The Intersectional Approach: Transforming the Academy through Race, Class and Gender,* ed. Michele Tracy Berger and Kathlenne Guidroz. Chapel Hill: University of North Carolina Press, 2009.

Lugones, María C. "Playfulness, 'World'-Traveling, and Loving Perception." *Hypatia* 2, no. 2 (1987): 3–19.

———. *Pilgrimages/Peregrinajes: Theorizing Coalition Against Multiple Oppressions.* Lanham, MD: Rowman and Littlefield, 2003.

———, and Elizabeth Spelman. "Have We Got a Theory for You! Feminist Theory, Cultural Imperialism and the Demand for 'The Woman's Voice.' " *Hypatia* (WSIF) 1 (1983): 573–81.

MacMullan, Terrance A. *Habits of Whiteness: A Pragmatist Reconstruction.* Bloomington: Indiana University Press, 2009.

Mahlendorf, Ursula. *The Shame of Survival: Working Through a Nazi Childhood.* University Park: Penn State University Press, 2009.

Mamdani, Mahmood. *When Victims Become Killers: Colonialism, Nativism, and the Genocide in Rwanda.* Princeton: Princeton University Press, 2001.

Margolis, Joseph. "Personal Reflections on Racism in America." In *On Race and Racism in America: Confessions in Philosophy,* ed. Roy Martinez. University Park: Pennsylvania State University Press, 2010.

Mascolo, Michael F., Kurt W. Fischer, and Jin Li. "Dynamic Development of Component Systems of Emotions: Pride, Shame and Guilt in China and the United States." In *Handbook of Affective Sciences*, ed. Richard J. Davidson, Klaus R. Scherer, and H. Hill Goldsmith. New York: Oxford University Press, 2003.

Mathias, Barbara, and Mary Ann French. *40 Ways to Raise a Nonracist Child.* New York: Harper Resource, 1996.

Mayo, Cris. "The Whiteness of Anti-Racist White Philosophical Address." In *The Center Must Not Hold: White Women Philosophers on the Whiteness of Philosophy*, ed. George Yancy. Lanham, MD: Rowman and Littlefield, 2010.

Mazzocco, Philip J., Timothy C. Brock, Gregory J. Brock, Kristina R. Olsen, Mahzarin R. Banaji. "The Cost of Being Black: White Americans' Perceptions and the Question of Reparations." *Du Bois Review: Social Science Research on Race* 3, no. 2 (2006): 261–97.

McAfee, Noëlle. *Democracy and the Political Unconscious.* New York: Columbia University Press, 2008.

McKay, Claude. "The Lynching." In *Black on White: Black Writers on What It Means to Be White*, ed. David R. Roediger. New York: Schocken Books, 1998.

McWhorter, Ladelle. *Bodies and Pleasures: Foucault and the Politics of Sexual Normalization.* Bloomington: Indiana University Press, 1999.

———. *Racism and Sexual Oppression in Anglo-America: A Genealogy.* Bloomington: Indiana University Press, 2009.

Medina, José. *The Epistemology of Resistance: Gender and Racial Oppression, Epistemic Injustice, and Resistant Imaginations.* New York: Oxford University Press, 2012.

Miller, Christian. "Mind Wars: Raising Healthy White Children in a Subversive Environment." *The Occidental Observer: White Interests, Identity, and Culture*, 2011; http://www.theoccidentalobserver.net/2011/02/mind-wars-raising-healthy-white-children-in-a-subversive-environment/, accessed March 21, 2013.

Mills, Charles. *The Racial Contract.* Ithaca: Cornell University Press, 1997.

———. *Blackness Visible: Essays on Philosophy and Race.* Ithaca: Cornell University Press, 1998.

———. "Comments on Shannon Sullivan's *Revealing Whiteness.*" *Journal of Speculative Philosophy* 21, no. 3 (2007): 218–30.

Monahan, Michael J. *The Creolizing Subject: Race, Reason, and the Politics of Purity.* New York: Fordham University Press, 2011.

Morales, Jennifer E. "Unpacking the White Privilege Diaper Bag." In *Everyday Acts Against Racism: Raising Children in a Multicultural World*, ed. Maureen Reddy. Seattle: Seal Press, 1996.

Morgan, Michael L. *On Shame.* New York: Routledge, 2008.

Morrison, Toni. *The Bluest Eye.* New York: Pocket Books, 1972.

———. "Home." In *The House that Race Built: Original Essays by Toni Morrison, Angela Y. Davis, Cornel West, and Others on Black Americans and Politics in America Today*, ed. Wahneema Lubiano. New York: Vintage Books, 1998.

———. "The Talk of the Town: Comment." *The New Yorker*, Oct. 5, 1998; http://www.newyorker.com/archive/1998/10/05/1998_10_05_031_TNY_ LIBRY_000016504?currentPage=all, accessed March 21, 2013.

Moss, Kirby. *The Color of Class: Poor Whites and the Paradox of Privilege*. Philadelphia: University of Pennsylvania Press, 2003.

Mura, David. "Explaining Racism to my Daughter." In Tahar Ben Jelloun, *Racism Explained to My Daughter*. New York: The New Press, 1999.

Nealon, Jeffrey T. "Performing Resentment: White Male Anger; or, 'Lack' and Nietzschean Political Theory." In *Why Nietzsche Still: Reflections on Drama, Culture, and Politics*, ed. Alan D. Schrift. Berkeley: University of California Press, 2000.

Nietzsche, Friedrich. *Thus Spake Zarathustra*. Trans. R. J. Hollingdale. New York: Penguin Books, 1969.

Nussbaum, Martha. *Upheavals of Thought: The Intelligence of Emotions*. New York: Cambridge University Press, 2003.

Ollivier, Enora. "Le mot 'race' indésirable." *20 Minutes*, May 16, 2013, 6.

Osborne, Peter. *Philosophy in Cultural Theory*. New York: Routledge, 2000.

Outlaw, Lucius. "Rehabilitate Racial *Whiteness*?" In *What White Looks Like: African-American Philosophers on the Whiteness Question*, ed. George Yancy. New York: Routledge, 2004.

Painter, Nell Irvin. "Slavery and Soul Murder." In *Black on White: Black Writers on What It Means to Be White*, ed. David R. Roediger. New York: Schocken Books, 1998.

Paley, Vivian Gussin. *White Teacher*. Cambridge: Harvard University Press, 2000.

Park, Shelley. "Mothering across Racial and Cultural Boundaries." In *Everyday Acts Against Racism: Raising Children in a Multicultural World*, ed. Maureen Reddy. Seattle: Seal Press, 1996.

Pattillo-McCoy, Mary. *Black Picket Fences: Privilege and Peril among the Black Middle Class*. Chicago: University of Chicago Press, 1999.

Perry, Twila L. "Transracial Aadoption: Mothers, Hierarchy, Race, and Feminist Legal Theory." In *Critical Race Feminism: A Reader*, ed. Adrien Katherine Wing. New York: New York University Press, 2003.

Pile, Steve. "Emotions and Affect in Recent Human Geography." *Transactions of the Institute of British Geography* 35 (2009): 5–20.

Preston, John. *Whiteness and Class in Education*. Dordrecht: Springer, 2009.

Proudfoot, Merrill. *Diary of a Sit-In*. Chicago: University of Illinois Press, 1990.

Read, Warren. *The Lyncher in Me: A Search for Redemption in the Face of History*. St. Paul: Borealis Books, 2008.

Reddy, Maureen T. "Working on Redemption." In *Everyday Acts Against Racism: Raising Children in a Multicultural World*, ed. Maureen Reddy. Seattle: Seal Press, 1996.

Rich, Adrienne. *On Lies, Secrets, and Silence: Selected Prose, 1966–1978*. New York: Norton, 1979.

Richeson, Jennifer A., and Sophie Trawalter. "Why Do Interracial Interactions Impair Executive Function? A Resource Depletion Account." *Journal of Personality and Social Psychology* 88, no. 6 (2005): 934–47.

Ritterhouse, Jennifer. *Growing Up Jim Crow: How Black and White Southern Children Learned Race.* Durham: University of North Carolina Press, 2006.

Roediger, David R., ed. *Black on White: Black Writers on What It Means to Be White.* New York: Schocken Books, 1999.

Sachs, Andrea. "10 Questions for Toni Morrison." *Time.com*, May 7, 2008; http://www.time.com/time/arts/article/0,8599,1738303,00.html, accessed March 21, 2013.

Sartre, Jean-Paul. *Being and Nothingness: A Phenomenological Essay on Ontology.* Trans. Hazel E. Barnes. New York: Pocket Books, 1956.

———. *Anti-Semite and Jew: An Exploration of the Etiology of Hate.* Trans. George J. Becker. New York: Schocken Books, 1976.

Sartwell, Crispin. *Act Like You Know: African-American Autobiography and White Identity.* Chicago: University of Chicago Press, 1998.

Scott, Charles. "In the Name of Goodness." In *Difficulties of Ethical Life*, eds Shannon Sullivan and Dennis J. Schmidt. New York: Fordham University Press, 2008.

Sedgwick, Eve Kosofsky. *Touching Feeling: Affect, Pedagogy, Performativity.* Durham: Duke University Press, 2003.

Segrest, Mab. *Memoir of a Race Traitor.* Boston: South End Press, 1994.

———. " 'The Souls of White Folks.' " In *The Making and Unmaking of Whiteness*, ed. Birgit Brander Rasmussen, Eric Klinenberg, Irene J. Nexica, and Matt Wray. Durham: Duke University Press, 2001.

Sennett, Richard, and Jonathan Cobb. *The Hidden Injuries of Class.* New York: Vintage Books, 1973.

Sharp, Joanne. "Geography and Gender: What Belongs to Feminist Geography? Emotion, Power, and Change." *Progress in Human Geography* 33, no. 1 (2009): 74–80.

Shotwell, Alexis. *Knowing Otherwise: Race, Gender, and Implicit Understanding.* University Park: Pennsylvania State University Press, 2010.

Skeggs, Beverley. *Formations of Class and Gender: Becoming Respectable.* London: Sage, 1997.

Spelman, Elizabeth. "Anger and Insubordination." In *Women, Knowledge, and Reality: Explorations in Feminist Philosophy*, ed. Ann Garry and Marilyn Pearsall. New York: Routledge, 1992.

Sperberg, E. D., and S. D. Stabb. "Depression in Women as Related to Anger and Mutuality in Relationships." *Psychology of Women Quarterly* 22 (1998): 223–38.

Spinoza, Benedict de. *A Spinoza Reader: The Ethics and Other Works.* Ed. and trans. Edwin Curley. Princeton: Princeton University Press, 1994.

Srivastava, Sarita. " 'You're Calling Me a Racist?' The Moral and Emotional Regulation of Antiracism and Feminism." *Signs: Journal of Women in Culture and Society* 31, no. 1 (2005): 29–62.

Staples, Brent. "Just Walk on By: A Black Man Ponders His Power to Alter Public Space." *Ms.* Sept. 1986, 54, 88.

Steele, Shelby. *White Guilt: How Blacks and Whites Together Destroyed the Promise of the Civil Rights Era.* New York: HarperCollins, 2006.

Stubblefield, Anna. *Ethics Along the Color Line.* Ithaca: Cornell University Press, 2005.

Sullivan, Shannon. *Revealing Whiteness: The Unconscious Habits of Racial Privilege.* Bloomington: Indiana University Press, 2006.

———. "White World Traveling." *The Journal of Speculative Philosophy* 18, no. 4 (2004): 300–304.

———. *Living Across and Through Skins: Transactional Bodies, Pragmatism, and Feminism.* Bloomington: Indiana University Press, 2001.

Sundstrom, Ronald R. *The Browning of America and the Evasion of Social Justice.* Albany: State University of New York Press, 2008.

Szalavitz, Maia. "The Trouble with Tough Love." *The Washington Post*, Jan. 29, 2006, B01; www.washingtonpost.com/wp-dyn/content/article/2006/01/28/AR2006012800062.html, accessed March 21, 2013.

Tangney, June Price. "Recent Advances in the Empirical Study of Shame and Guilt." *American Behavioral Science* 38, no. 3 (1995): 1132–45.

———, Jeff Stuewig, and Debra J. Mashek. "Moral Emotions and Moral Behavior." *Annual Review of Psychology* 58 (2007): 345–72.

Tangney, J. P., J. Stuewig, D. Mashek, and M. Hastings. "Assessing Jail Inmates' Proneness to Shame and Guilt: Feeling Bad about the Behavior or the Self?" *Criminal Justice and Behavior* 38 (2011): 710–34.

Tate, Greg. *Everything but the Burden: What White People are Taking from Black Culture.* New York: Harlem Moon, 2003.

Taylor, Paul. "Race, Ethics, Seduction, Politics: On Shannon Sullivan's *Revealing Whiteness.*" *Journal of Speculative Philosophy* 21, no. 3 (2007): 201–209.

Tessman, Lisa. *Burdened Virtues: Virtue Ethics for Liberatory Struggles.* New York: Oxford University Press, 2005.

Thandeka. *Learning to Be White: Money, Race, and God in America.* New York: Continuum, 2007.

Thien, Deborah. "After or Beyond Feeling? A Consideration of Affect and Emotion in Geography." *Area* 37, no. 4 (2005): 450–56.

Thompson, Audrey. "Tiffany, Friend of People of Color: White Investments in Antiracism." *Qualitative Studies in Education* 16, no. 1 (2003): 7–29.

Thompson, Cooper, Emmett Schaefer, and Harry Brod, eds. *White Men Challenging Racism: 35 Personal Stories.* Durham: Duke University Press, 2003.

Thompson, Becky. *Mothering without a Compass: White Mother's Love, Black Son's Courage.* Minneapolis: University of Minnesota Press, 2000.

Thrift, Nigel. *Non-representational Theory: Space Politics Affect.* New York: Routledge, 2008.

Trout, Lara. *The Politics of Survival: Peirce, Affectivity, and Social Criticism.* New York: Fordham University Press, 2010.

Van Ausdale, Debra, and Joe R. Feagin. *The First R: How Children Learn Race and Racism.* Lanham, MD: Rowman and Littlefield, 2001.

Vice, Samantha. "How Do I Live in This Strange Place?" *The Journal of Social Philosophy* 41, no. 3 (2010): 323–43.

Walters, Ronald G. *The Antislavery Appeal: Abolitionism after 1830.* Baltimore: The Johns Hopkins University Press, 1976.

Wexler, Jennifer. "The Concrete Work of Eliminating Your Racism." *Present Time* (Seattle), July 1992, 26–28.

White, Margaret Blackburn. *Becoming White: My Family's Experience as Slaveholders—and Why It Still Matters.* Bloomington, IN: Author House, 2009.

Willett, Cynthia. "Overcoming Habits of Whiteliness: Reading Shannon Sullivan's *Revealing Whiteness.*" *Journal of Speculative Philosophy* 21, no. 3 (2007): 210–17.

Williams, Patricia J. *Seeing a Color-blind Future: The Paradox of Race.* New York: Farrar, Straus, and Giroux, 1997.

Wilmot, Sheila. *Taking Responsibility, Taking Direction: White Anti-Racism in Canada.* Winnipeg: Arbeiter Ring, 2005.

Wilson, Elizabeth A. *Psychosomatic: Feminism and the Neurological Body.* Durham: Duke University Press, 2004.

Wise, Tim. *White Like Me: Reflections on Race from a Privileged Son.* Brooklyn: Soft Skull Press, 2005.

Wong, Y., and J. L. Tsai. "Cultural Models of Shame and Guilt." In *Handbook of Self-Conscious Emotions,* ed. J. Tracy, R. Robins, and J. Tangney. New York: Guilford Press, 2007.

Wray, Matt. *Not Quite White: White Trash and the Boundaries of Whiteness.* Durham: Duke University Press, 2006.

Wright, Marguerite A. *I'm Chocolate, You're Vanilla: Raising Healthy Black and Biracial Children in a Race-Conscious World.* San Francisco: Jossey-Bass, 1998.

X, Malcolm. *The Autobiography of Malcolm X.* New York: Ballantine Books, 1964.

Yancy, George. *Look, a White! Philosophical Essays on Whiteness.* Philadelphia: Temple University Press, 2012.

———. *Black Bodies, White Gazes: The Continuing Significance of Race.* Lanham, MD: Rowman and Littlefield, 2008.

———, ed. *What White Looks Like: African-American Philosophers on the Whiteness Question.* New York: Routledge, 2004.

York, Stacey. *Roots and Wings: Affirming Culture in Early Childhood Programs.* St. Paul: Redleaf Press, 2003.

Young, Iris Marion. *Inclusion and Democracy.* New York: Oxford University Press, 2000.

Zack, Naomi. "White Ideas." In *Whiteness: Feminist Philosophical Reflections,* ed. Chris J. Cuomo and Kim Q. Hall. Lanham, MD: Rowman and Littlefield, 1999.

Zia, Helen. "Women in Hate Groups: Who Are They? Why Are They There?" *Ms.* March/April 1991, 20–27.

Zizek, Slavoj. "Love Thy Neighbor? No, Thanks!" In *The Psychoanalysis of Race,* ed. Christopher Lane. New York: Columbia University Press, 1998.

Index